Faust Adaptations from Marlowe to Aboudoma and Markland

Comparative Cultural Studies
Steven Tötösy de Zepetnek, Series Editor

The Purdue University Press monograph series of Books in Comparative Cultural Studies publishes single-authored and thematic collected volumes of new scholarship. Manuscripts are invited for publication in the series in fields of the study of culture, literature, the arts, media studies, communication studies, the history of ideas, etc., and related disciplines of the humanities and social sciences to the series editor via e-mail at <clcweb@purdue.edu>. Comparative cultural studies is a contextual approach in the study of culture in a global and intercultural context and work with a plurality of methods and approaches; the theoretical and methodological framework of comparative cultural studies is built on tenets borrowed from the disciplines of cultural studies and comparative literature and from a range of thought including literary and culture theory, (radical) constructivism, communication theories, and systems theories; in comparative cultural studies focus is on theory and method as well as application. For a detailed description of the aims and scope of the series including the style guide of the series link to <http://docs.lib.purdue.edu/clcweblibrary/seriespurduecs>. Manuscripts submitted to the series are peer reviewed followed by the usual standards of editing, copy editing, marketing, and distribution. The series is affiliated with *CLCWeb: Comparative Literature and Culture* (ISSN 1481-4374), the peer-reviewed, full-text, and open-access quarterly published by Purdue University Press at <http://docs.lib.purdue.edu/clcweb>.

Volumes in the Purdue series of Books in Comparative Cultural Studies include <http://www.thepress.purdue.edu/series/comparative-cultural-studies>

Lorna Fitzsimmons, ed. *Faust Adaptations from Marlowe to Aboudoma and Markland*
Regina R. Félix and Scott D. Juall, eds., *Cultural Exchanges between Brazil and France*
James Patrick Wilper, *Reconsidering the Emergence of the Gay Novel in English and German*
Li Guo, *Women's* Tanci *Fiction in Late Imperial and Early Twentieth-Century China*
Arianna Dagnino, *Transcultural Writers and Novels in the Age of Global Mobility*
Elke Sturm-Trigonakis, *Comparative Cultural Studies and the New* Weltliteratur
Lauren Rule Maxwell, *Romantic Revisions in Novels from the Americas*
Liisa Steinby, *Kundera and Modernity*
Text and Image in Modern European Culture, ed. Natasha Grigorian, Thomas Baldwin, and Margaret Rigaud-Drayton
Sheng-mei Ma, *Asian Diaspora and East-West Modernity*
Irene Marques, *Transnational Discourses on Class, Gender, and Cultural Identity*
Comparative Hungarian Cultural Studies, ed. Steven Tötösy de Zepetnek and Louise O. Vasvári
Hui Zou, *A Jesuit Garden in Beijing and Early Modern Chinese Culture*
Yi Zheng, *From Burke and Wordsworth to the Modern Sublime in Chinese Literature*
Agata Anna Lisiak, *Urban Cultures in (Post)Colonial Central Europe*
Representing Humanity in an Age of Terror, ed. Sophia A. McClennen and Henry James Morello
Michael Goddard, *Gombrowicz, Polish Modernism, and the Subversion of Form*
Shakespeare in Hollywood, Asia, and Cyberspace, ed. Alexander C.Y. Huang and Charles S. Ross
Gustav Shpet's Contribution to Philosophy and Cultural Theory, ed. Galin Tihanov
Comparative Central European Holocaust Studies, ed. Louise O. Vasvári and Steven Tötösy de Zepetnek
Marko Juvan, *History and Poetics of Intertextuality*
Thomas O. Beebee, *Nation and Region in Modern American and European Fiction*

Faust Adaptations from Marlowe to Aboudoma and Markland

Edited by
Lorna Fitzsimmons

Purdue University Press
West Lafayette, Indiana

Library of Congress Cataloging-in-Publication Data

Names: Fitzsimmons, Lorna, 1957- editor.
Title: Faust Adaptations from Marlowe to Aboudoma and Markland / edited by
  Lorna Fitzsimmons.
Description: West Lafayette, Indiana: Purdue University Press, 2017. |
  Series: Comparative Cultural Studies | Includes bibliographical references
  and index.
Identifiers: LCCN 2016014560| ISBN 9781557537584 (pbk.: alk. paper) |
  ISBN 9781612494722 (epdf) | ISBN 9781612494739 (epub)
Subjects: LCSH: Faust,—approximately 1540—Adaptations. | Faust,
  —approximately 1540—Appreciation.
Classification: LCC PN6071.F33 F25 2017 | DDC 809/.93351—dc23
LC record available at https://lccn.loc.gov/2016014560

Cover image: Homunculus in the phial. From Goethe's *Faust*. Illustrated by Franz
Xaver Simm. Stuttgart: German Publishing House, 1899. Via Wikimedia Commons.

Contents

Introduction to *Faust Adaptations from Marlowe to Aboudoma and Markland*

Lorna Fitzsimmons

Faust Adaptations from Marlowe to Aboudoma and Markland takes a comparative cultural studies approach to the Faust legend. Comparative cultural studies is a contextual, globally oriented approach, drawing on the methods of cultural studies and comparative literature. The book provides an interdisciplinary and intercultural vantage point on the Faust theme as it has been adapted in some key texts from the early modern period to the present. Examining English, German, Dutch, and Egyptian adaptations of the Faust theme analytically and contextually, it consists of articles on the Faust works of Christopher Marlowe, Johann Wolfgang von Goethe, Adelbert von Chamisso, Byron, Heinrich Heine, Thomas Mann, D. J. Enright, Konrad Boehmer, Mahmoud Aboudoma, Bridge Markland, Andreas Gössling, and Uschi Flacke. These studies demonstrate not only the enduring meaningfulness of the Faust concept, but also its adaptability to different genres, eras, and cultures.

The legend of the early modern scholar, Faustus, who compacts his soul to the devil, arose in the context of the Reformation in Germany. Since then, a broad range of adaptations of the legend have been rendered in literature, drama, music, and visual and mixed media. As a result, the Faust theme has become one of the most important in Western history and is more and more global in its audiences and adaptation. As David C. John observes in this book, in his article on Egyptian playwright and director Mahmoud Aboudoma's recent Faustian adaptation, "although the Faust figure himself is correctly understood to be first and foremost quintessentially German, through centuries of reception and adaptation he has come to represent the struggling human in many lands and cultures" (see ch. 8, "*Faust's Dreams* and Egyptian Identity").

The Egypt of Aboudoma is necessarily far removed from that of the Reformation circumstances in which the Faust theme first emerged in the sixteenth century. The anonymous Faust Book, the *Historia von D. Johann Fausten* (*The Historie of the Damnable Life and Deserved Death of Doctor John Faustus*), is a product of

1

religious conflict between Protestants and Catholics in Western Europe. Its satire of Catholicism is pointed. The protagonist Faustus is a learned scholar who turns to illicit arts and is eventually damned. Faustus is an object of derision and amusement as he undertakes travels and indulges in pranks, usually forgetful of the ultimate, hell-bound fate of his soul. The book engages with abstract concepts and questions of universal import: human relations to divinity, the afterlife, freedom, social mobility, love, repentance, and professional integrity. It was widely read and translated, and its popularity invited its adaptation. The English playwright Christopher Marlowe's tragic adaptation, *Doctor Faustus*, stimulated a wave of other theatrical adaptations when it was performed in Europe, and the theme was increasingly adapted into music and other forms.

Like most of the adaptations discussed in this book, Aboudoma's أحلام فاوست (Faust's Dreams), a play written in Arabic in 2002, claims as its primary source the most well-known version of the Faust theme, Goethe's *Faust* (1808, 1832). An outstanding work of the Romantic period in German culture, Goethe's drama was influenced by another popular form into which the theme had been adapted, the puppet play, yet far exceeds the limits of that genre in the aesthetic heights it attains. The renowned Goethean adaptation inspires and entertains through its rescripting of the iconoclastic hero and the inclusion of a broad range of new characters, situations, and themes that reflect the literary and cultural concerns of the turbulent beginnings of the modern period. The heterogeneity of the sources on which Goethe drew in adapting the Faust theme renders his poetic drama highly appealing to a broad range of audiences.

One of the most creative recent adapters of the Goethean *Faust* and the Faustian puppet play, Berlin-based performance artist Bridge Markland, has renovated the terms in which *Faust* is understood with her daring dramaturgy. Intensifying the carnivalesque appeal of the puppet play through her frenetic aesthetic, Markland unbinds the Faustian conventions in her one-woman show *Faust in the Box* (2006), an innovative visual and aural experience that brings new meaning to the concept of the "Eternal Feminine" ("das Ewig-Weibliche") (Goethe line 12110). Working with both German and English versions of the show, Markland is indicative of the new transnationalism in Faust performance, as well as the increasing importance of women's contributions to this traditionally male-dominated tradition.

As Aboudoma's title, *Faust's Dreams,* suggests, the Faust theme represents imaginative frames of mind, which are, of course, conducive to stimulating the adaptive impulse. Although Aboudoma's sombre interpretation of the theme contrasts deeply with that of Markland's ebullient adaptation, these imaginative revisionings revitalize the multisidedness of the Faustian tradition, which has tragic and comic streams. The traditional Faust character is a male questioner who is at odds with his life. He imagines a different experience and seeks to realize it. The tragic, comic, or tragicomic outcomes of the Faust character's imaginings vary from culture to culture, and take on different meanings within different historical contexts. We are concerned here with the "unbound Faust," a selection of adaptations inspired by the Faust theme that do not exact a literalist replication of the principal sources but rather extend the latter in new directions.

As Linda Hutcheon notes, the motives for adaptation are numerous, and fidelity is rarely a primary concern (xiii). The history of adaptation reaches almost to the beginnings of cultural records. Departing from the traditional binarization and subordination of adaptations, contemporary adaptation studies emphasize the importance of both the sources and the adaptation and their intertextual relationships (McCabe 8). The field's growing interest in the relations between the processes of translation and adaptation lends itself to comparative cultural studies frameworks (Krebs). As scholarship grows, we discover that intertexual connections between works are much more extensive than immediately obvious. Unbinding these connections enables valuable critical insights. While more literalist productions of Faust works, such as Peter Stein's *Faust* (John, "Complete *Faust* on Stage"), are important in their own right, the dominant trend is recent years has been creative adaptations, and much work remains to be done with respect to this vast corpus.

Since the post-World War II period, the adaptation of the Faust theme has become increasingly mediated and global, with the effect that studies of the Faust concept are more often falling beyond the domain of solely German studies (a categorization complicated, even during the early modern period, by the wide influence of Marlowe's *Doctor Faustus*) and the disciplines of literature and theater arts. The field of Faust studies has greatly expanded in the range of its subject matter, methodologies, and languages. Recent Faust research includes work in Russian, Spanish, and French (see, e.g., Jakuševa; Hernández; Peslier; Girard; Gervais), in addition to important contributions in German (see, e.g., Müller; Anderegg; Scholz; Hajduk; Schoenberg; Nasched; Behzadi) and English (see, e.g., Carter; Bartels and Smith; Stevenson; Laan; Krimmer; Greenberg; John; Boyle; Schulte; Drábek; Oergel; Colvin; Kraus), including work on intercultural adaptations such as Ninagawa Yukio's production of Marlowe's *Doctor Faustus* in Tokyo (Borlik). Often interdisciplinary and cross-cultural, contemporary Faust studies participates in scholarly debate on a broad range of concerns, from postcolonialism to religion and gender (see, e.g, Keim; Krimmer; Oergel). The continued relevance of the Faust theme is widely evident, not only in European productions such as Romanian director Silviu Purcărete's staging of Goethe's *Faust* at the Edinburgh International Festival in 2009, or the revival of French composer Henri Pousseur's *Votre Faust* (Your Faust) in Berlin in 2013, but also in the Seoul library and theater where a multiplayer *Faust* game is intriguing people in Korea, or the growing market for Faustian concepts in products for children in many places today.

The studies in this book have been selected because they are of value in expanding knowledge not only of the canonic Faust works in cultural context but also of creative voices and cultural moments articulated through the Faustian prism that are important despite being lesser known. The popularity and familiarity of the Faust theme enables peoples from very different circumstances to communicate with others locally, regionally, or transnationally by adapting the well-known characters and scenes for their own purposes, whether to express topical issues or timeless dilemmas.

The fascination in reading or attending a performance of a creative adaptation such as Aboudama's *Faust's Dreams* lies in its complex enmeshment of several versions of the Faust theme with other, often non-Western sources, producing a rich tapestry of intercultural expression which is meaningful not only for local audiences but also those further afield. The vast number of Faust adaptations that have been produced in the last two hundred years are evidence of the pleasure taken in revisiting the theme, and also its malleability as a vehicle of social commentary. Hutcheon astutely identifies the pleasure of adaptations as one of "repetition with variation, comfort with surprise" (5). We often take pleasure in observing, reading, or hearing the echoes and divergences in the treatment of the Faust theme, with the known anchoring or instigating our interest in the broader circumference of the theme's circulation. And when the intent is to displease, to provoke, or outrage, as is not unusual in the world of Faust, it is rarely just the novelty that holds our attention, but rather the play of variations of the theme.

The variation can be on a gross or miniscule scale, from a complete updating of the plot to subtle shifts in the dialogue of cardinal scenes from the sources. The unbound Faust may not be contracted to the devil, as in Byron's *Manfred* or Gössling's *Faust, der Magier* (The Magician Faust), or Mephistopheles may be feminized as Mephistophela, as in Heine's "*Tanzpoem*" ("dance-poem") *Der Doktor Faust* (*Doctor Faust, a Ballet Poem*). In turn, the adaptation of the satiric thrust of the Faust theme varies significantly in different periods and cultures. An outstanding exemplum is Thomas Mann's novel *Doktor Faustus: Das Leben des deutschen Tonsetzers Adrian Leverkühn, erzählt von einem Freunde* (*Doctor Faustus: The Life of the German Composer Adrian Leverkühn as Told by a Friend*) (1947), an unparalleled literary exploration of aesthetics that is also unforgettable in its sociopolitical acuity. A number of the works examined in this book, such as Marlowe's *Doctor Faustus*, Goethe's *Faust*, and Mann's *Doctor Faustus*, remain strong grounds on which to question the assumption that an adaptation must be in some sense lesser than its sources. As Hutcheon suggests, adaptations are aesthetic entities in their own right (6, 9). We undertake this book, therefore, not necessarily to apply judgments of fidelity but rather to explore the play of variations inherent in any adaptation. In a work such as Aboudoma's *Faust's Dreams,* the range of variation is demonstrative, and this makes the piece all the more engaging in its creative reinterpretation of the theme. But Aboudoma is not alone in this regard. Creativity characterizes the adaptive approach exhibited in the works discussed here. Faust is unbound, in this book, through adaptive transformations that are often highly original.

The first article in this collection is Ehrhard Bahr's history of the Faust legend. Bahr provides an overview of key Faust works from the anonymous chapbook of 1587 to Marlowe's tragedy *Doctor Faustus*, Bonneschky's puppet play, Goethe's *Faust*, and Mann's *Doctor Faustus*. The author discusses how these texts' engagement with the question of religious grace shapes their representation of the eponymous protagonist. Articulating a forceful Lutheran lesson, the chapbook was highly popular in Protestant countries. Its account of the sorcerer's adventures and affair amuse while instructing. Before Faustus dies, he warns his students not to follow in his footsteps. His lack of faith is his downfall. In Christopher Marlowe's hands, he becomes a tragic hero. Bahr argues that this changes the Christian framework of the story. Marlowe's Faust is an overreacher rather than a "miserable sinner." The tragic Faust had a wide influence, as evident in the puppet play of Guido Bonneschky (1850). On the puppet stage, though, the Faustian hero was joined by Kasperele, whose comic antics modified the form and lightened the tone. The Faust puppet theater would have a deeply felt impact on Goethe, who never forgot his experience of it. Among signs of its influence on Goethe's *Faust* is the depiction of Helena in Act III. While the Goethean Faust is infused with Romantic differences from the chapbook's Faustus, Thomas Mann returns to the Faust book for his portrait of the modern artist in his acclaimed novel *Doctor Faustus*. A commentary on the decline of German culture, Mann's work remains the most profound adaptation of the Faust legend since Goethe's *Faust*.

Returning to a popular Faust adaptation of the Romantic era, Christa Knellwolf King discusses questions of identity in her article on Adelbert von Chamisso's story *Peter Schlemihl* (1814). Knellwolf King conceives of Faustian adaptations as "new constellations" of the familiar narrative, and Chamisso's is certainly a luminous one. Knellwolf King's focus is on the contrast Chamisso develops between the "soul" and the "shadow" in this famous story of the man who exchanges his shadow for wealth, but not his soul. The scholarship of this Faustian narrative has had difficulty in explaining the meanings of the protagonist's shadow. A biographical reading suggests that the shadow represents the author's identity problems, as a Catholic Frenchman in Germany. However, Knellwolf King finds that the shadow cannot be reduced to one meaning. The sale of the shadow does not incur damnation, unlike the deal the early modern Faustus makes to become a spirit. Schlemihl is reduced to being an outcast, because he clings to his soul. Alone, he learns about himself. His experiences as a botanical traveler adapt the theme of the "wandering Jew." They are also of contemporary interest from an ecocritical standpoint. Knellwolf King contextualizes Chamisso's departures from the concept of the soul as found in the Faust legend by discussing their relation to post-Enlightenment understanding of consciousness. She concludes that this adaptation of the Faust theme lends support to Jung's theory that the experience of evil can help a person become complete.

Furthering scholarship of Faust adaptations in the Romantic period, Frederick Burwick's analysis of Byron's Faustian dramas *Manfred* (1817), *Cain* (1821), and *The Deformed Transformed* (1822) includes an interesting discussion of Goethe's responses to the Byronic Faust and Byron himself. The Byronic Faust tends to be autobiographical and rather image conscious, Burwick suggests. The concept of *kalon*, the Greek ideal of beauty, physical and moral, appears disrupted in all three plays. The incest-ridden *Manfred*, although clearly Faustian, departs from Faust tradition in its lack of a demonic pact. Burwick shows that, in addition to Goethe's *Faust*, other sources of the play include *Paradise Lost*, the legend of Tannhäuser, and the myth of Prometheus. In *Cain*, Byron foregrounds defiance, a distinguishing feature of the "Byronic hero." Like Goethe's *Faust*, Byron's Cain thirsts for knowledge. In his murderous impulse, he illustrates the effects of pursuing knowledge rather than love. Goethe applauded the depth of feeling and thought Byron gave to the character. It seemed, to the Weimar poet, that Byron's creativity was nourished by his "hypochondriacal" nature. Although Goethe wrote that he was "disturbed" by Byron's "self-torment," he admired the British poet's work. Detecting the influence of his Mephistopheles in *The Deformed Transformed*, Goethe commented that Byron's devil was comparable yet "thoroughly original and new." In his opinion, though, Byron held to "too much empiria," which Eckermann interpreted as an excessive "empiricism." In a word, Byron and the Byronic Faust were "clever," in Goethe's view, and the Byronic devil at times a peer of Mephistopheles in the "great and free" language expressed.

Although Heinrich Heine openly admired elements of Goethe's *Faust*, he turned to earlier versions of the Faust theme as principal sources of his adaptation of the Faust theme, *Doctor Faust, a Ballet Poem*, discussed here by Beate I. Allert. Heine's *Faust* is a libretto for a ballet, one of the most distinctive features of which is the reshaping of Mephistopheles as the female Mephistophela. In creating his adaptation, Heine drew on a number of sources, including the Spies imprint of the Faust Book, Marlowe's *Doctor Faustus*, and Faust puppet plays. Allert provides a discussion of the contexts of Heine's libretto and a commentary on its plot. She finds that the ballet represents "the horror of recurrent images that actually are timeless and defy their specific meaning in the context in which they were initially used." Although Heine seems to want to innovate, the old figures keep surfacing, just as Faust seems ensnarled in a cycle of familiar events.

The conflicts of the twentieth century thrust the Faust theme into the foreground, forthrightly politicized. In his article on Mann's *Doctor Faustus*, Ehrhard Bahr examines the novel as a political document. Composed while the author was in exile in Los Angeles during World War II, the novel is an analysis of elements of the German mentality perceived to be related to National Socialism. In recasting Faustus as a composer, Mann reflects upon German cultural history and his own life. Bahr explains that Mann's fascination with music began at an early age, with his interest in Wagner, which had a long-lasting influence on the literature he created. When the National Socialists coopted Wagner, Mann objected strongly. Although Wagner was important in the development of Mann's understanding of German identity, however, the writer did not center *Doctor Faustus* around Wagner. Instead, Mann turned to the 1587 chapbook *Historia von D. Johann Fausten* as a key source for the novel. Its protagonist, Adrian Leverkühn, is a composer who contracts syphilis. Nietzsche's biography is an important source of Mann's depiction of the Faustian Leverkühn's life. It was Mann's familiarity with the work of Theodor Adorno that led him to characterize Leverkühn's music as twelve-tone. Bahr suggests that the representation of music in *Doctor Faustus* parallels Germany's pursuit of international political hegemony. The ambitious composer is equated with the decline of Germany. Mann is also self-critical of his own belligerent writings during World War I. The epilogue of the novel reflects on Mann's political pronouncements after the German surrender.

Among the poets who have adapted Faust thematics, British poet D. J. Enright is less well-known than many. In his article, Arnd Bohm examines Enright's writings on the Faust theme. Enright wrote an interesting critical commentary on Goethe's *Faust*, published in 1945. His poetic *Faust Book*, upon which Bohm's discussion centers, appeared in 1979. It consists of seventy-three poems principally indebted to Goethe's and Marlowe's Faust adaptations. Bohm detects a "shimmer of mockery over the entire set of poems." The sequence of events is mainly that of Goethe, with some admixtures from Marlowe. Enright tends to foreground political themes from the twentieth century. Hence, Mephistopheles is a "man of the people," while still "a Prince's man." Enright suggests that democracy may not live up to its promises. So, too, literacy may appear a great boon, yet the quality of life is not necessarily improved by it. Through his reworking of the Faust story, Enright repeatedly suggests that in the world where profiteering prevails, appearances may be deceptive and expectations unfulfilled. Enright also updates the feminine in the Faust story, supplying Gretchen with a sewing machine instead of a spinning wheel, and adding a new character, Meretrix, a "go-go dancer" to whom Faust is attracted. Although sometimes obscene, Enright's language is often witty, making ample use of puns. Bohm concludes that this Faust is "more of a human being than his prototypes," whose end is closer to that of Goethe's *Faust* than Marlowe's tragedy.

The musical legacy of the Faust theme is extensive. In his article, Dutch composer Konrad Boehmer discusses the genesis of his opera *Doktor Faustus* (Doctor Faustus) (1985). Boehmer recalls his childhood memory of being "horrified" by Goethe's depiction of the loss of Philemon and Baucis in *Faust*. It was not until the late sixties that he returned to the theme, having read Hanns Eisler's libretto for a Faust opera. However, the rise of serialism had devalued operatic composition. A reconceptualization was necessary. Boehmer explains that he decided to synthesize "evolutionary" and serial techniques. He developed his dramatis personae from documents about the historical Faust. One of these, a letter by Johannes von Heidenberg, abbot Trithemius, led the composer to conceive of the abbot as a Mephistophelean opponent of Faust. The visionary Hans Böhm became the basis of a third character. Boehmer set out to "deconstruct" Faust, treating the mythic material ironically. Accounting for the canonization of the Faust theme in terms of the rising middle class, the composer chose the operatic form as most typical of that class. Yet his intent is not merely to continue the operatic tradition, but to reinterpret it.

Egyptian playwright Mahmoud Aboudoma's play *Faust's Dreams* (2002) is a thought-provoking reinterpretation of the Faust theme. Intercultural theater scholar David G. John considers the play to be a "surrealistic" response to globalization and contemporary Egyptian sociopolitical conflicts. John begins his article on the play with an overview of the reception of Goethe's *Faust* in Egypt, which grew in the early twentieth century. He then provides a descriptive analysis of *Faust's Dreams*.

The play consists of seven dreams, set between heaven and earth. Funereal in tone, it includes a number of biblical themes, such as the tree of knowledge and Christ's resurrection, synthesized with adaptations of Goethean scenes such as the "Prologue in Heaven" ("Prolog im Himmel") and "Walpurgis Night" ("Walpurgisnacht"). Among the characters are three Mephistos and two females redolent of Margarete and Helena. A dialogue outline, provided by Aboudoma, is included. John concludes that the play expresses deep concerns about Egyptian identity.

Contemporary German performance artist Bridge Markland's *Faust in the Box* stands out as an innovative contribution to Faust performances. Markland stages her adaptation of Goethe's *Faust I* using puppets, Barbie dolls, pop music, and a large box. Lynn Marie Kutch has recently interviewed Markland about her work and draws on this interview in her analysis of *Faust in the Box*. Markland's integration of aural and visual materials in this adaptation shows ingenuity. The German version of the performance contains over one hundred musical segments, with excerpts from a broad range of music, such as the Rolling Stones' "Sympathy for the Devil" and Shirley Bassey's "Where Do I Begin?" In her interview with Kutch, Markland explained that she creates "collages from people's lives, enhancing facts from their life with music." Kutch argues that Markland's musical montage enacts a subversive, ironic aesthetic by which the performer disrupts expectations. In her analysis, Kutch focuses on Markland's adaptation of the "Dungeon" scene of *Faust*. In this scene, Markland performs to a montage of musical pieces by groups such as Led Zeppelin and Seeed, a German reggae band. Exploring the impact of the music montage, Kutch suggests that Markland's aesthetic influences the audience's emotional engagement. Visually, Markland's performance makes effective use of compression. It is also economical, in that Markland takes on all roles, from Mephistopheles to Margarete, using one moveable set.

Interested, like Kutch, in contemporary German Faust adaptations, Waltraud Maierhofer looks at two recent Faustian novels, Andreas Gössling's *Faust, der Magier* (2007) and Uschi Flacke's *Hannah und der Schwarzkünstler Faust* (Hannah and Faust, the Necromancer) (2004). These novels, both of which are historical fiction, are evidence of the thriving German market for witchcraft fantasy. Maierhofer approaches the books not from the perspective of fidelity criticism but rather in order to explore how these stories "re-mediate" the famous legend for modern audiences. Both novels adapt the Faust theme by omitting the famous pact. The supernatural elements of the Faust narrative are, in general, reduced, but both authors attempt to evoke the atmosphere of the period. The award-winning *Hannah und der Schwarzkünstler Faust* targets teenage girls as its audience. The heroine is around ten years old at the novel's start. The Faust of this story finds young Hannah and takes her under his wing. This unlikely pair undertake travels, and the heroine seeks to learn from the necromancer. Eventually leaving him, she writes an account of Faust's death. Gössling's *Faust, der Magier* differs from Flacke's in being intended for adult readers. Its representation of Faust reflects the author's attention to historical detail, although the book contains romance and adventure elements. This Faust's life is narrated from his childhood, as an abused foster child, to adulthood. Avoiding summoning the devil, he goes on the run, is imprisoned, and eventually becomes a fortune-teller. Maierhofer finds that both of these narratives involve some degree of updating. In *Hannah und der Schwarzkünstler*, the heroine's modern outlook is likely to appeal to young readers. In *Faust, der Magier*, the Faustian character has some modern ideas which make the narrative more accessible for contemporary readers. Maierhofer concludes that both of these novels are likely to engage audiences who have some familiarity with the Faust theme.

This book thus traverses over four hundred years of Faust adaptations, ranging from the early modern tragedy by Marlowe, which exerted a significant influence in the adaptation history of the Faust legend in Europe and many other cultures around the world, to the present. Each adaptation is a distinctive expression of key facets of the period and culture in which it was created. In each, the figure of the unbound, adapted, Faust enables insights into cultural differences but also binding commonalities.

Works Cited

Anderegg, Johannes. *Transformationen: Über Himmlisches und Teuflisches in Goethes* Faust. Bielefeld: Aisthesis, 2011.

Bartels, Emily C., and Emma Smith, eds. *Marlowe in Context*. Cambridge: Cambridge UP, 2013.

Behzadi, Lale. "Ausblick und Spiegelung: Goethes *Faust* in der arabischen Literatur." *Orient und Okzident. Zur Faustrezeption in nicht-christlichen Kulturen*. Ed. Jochen Golz and Adrian Hsia. Köln: Böhlau, 2008. 67–76.

Borlik, Todd A. "A Season in Intercultural Limbo: Ninagawa Yukio's *Doctor Faustus*, Theatre Cocoon, Tokyo." *Shakespeare Quarterly* 62.3 (2011): 444–56.

Boyle, Nicholas. "The Cryptoclassicism of Goethe's *Faust*." *Publications of the English Goethe Society* 80.2–3 (2011): 78–89.

Carter, William. H. "Faust's *Begehren*: Revisiting the History of Political Economy in *Faust II*." *Goethe Yearbook* 21 (2014): 103–28.

Colvin, Sarah. "Mephistopheles, Metaphors, and the Problem of Meaning in *Faust*." *Publications of the English Goethe Society* 79.3 (2010): 159–71.

Drábek, Pavel, and Dan North. "What Governs Life: Svankmajer's *Faust* in Prague." *Shakespeare Bulletin* 29.4 (2011): 525–42.

Gervais, Pauline. "De Goethe à Gounod: le livret de Faust ou la canonisation d'un écart textuel." *Cahiers d'études germaniques* 59 (2010): 79–89.

Girard, Marie-Hélène. "La Résurrection du passé ou le *Second Faust* revisité." *Études littéraires* 42.3 (2011): 15–32.

Goethe, Johann Wolfgang von. *Faust. Sämtliche Werke*. Vol. 7.1. Ed. Albrecht Schöne. Frankfurt: Deutscher Klassiker Verlag, 1994.

Greenberg, Martin. "Goethe and Evil: *Faust, Part One*." *Yale Review* 100.3 (2012): 91–117.

Hajduk, Stefan."Goethes Gnostiker: Fausts vergessener Nihilismus und sein Streben nach Erlösungswissen." *Goethe Yearbook* 17 (2010): 89–116.

Hernández, Isabel. "'Para gozar a esta mujer diera el alma': El mito fáustico y sus rescrituras en la literatura española." *Revista de Literatura* 73.146 (2011): 427–47.

Hutcheon, Linda. *A Theory of Adaptation*. New York: Routledge, 2006.

Jakuševa, Galina Viktorovna [Якусева, Галина Викторовна]. *Faust v iskusenijach XX veka: Gëtevskij obraz v russkoj i zarubeznoj Literature* [Фауст в искусенияч XX века. Гётевский образ в русской и зарубезной Литературе] [Faustian Temptation in the Twentieth Century. Goethean Images in Russian and Foreign Literature]. Moscow: Nauka, 2005.

John, David G. *Bennewitz, Goethe,* Faust: *German and Intercultural Stagings*. Toronto: U of Toronto P, 2012.

John, David G. "The Complete *Faust* on Stage: Peter Stein and the Goetheanum." *Goethe's* Faust *and Cultural Memory: Comparatist Interfaces*. Ed. Lorna Fitzsimmons. Lanham: Lehigh UP, 2012. 107–28.

Keim, Katharina. "Contemporary African and Brazilian Adaptations of Goethe's *Faust* in Postcolonial Context." *International Faust Studies: Adaptation, Reception, Translation*. Ed. Lorna Fitzsimmons. London: Continuum, 2008. 244–58.

Kraus, Justice. "Expression and Adorno's Avant-Garde: The Composer in *Doktor Faustus*." *The German Quarterly* 81.2 (2008): 170–84.

Krebs, Katja, ed. *Translation and Adaptation in Theatre and Film*. Abingdon: Routledge, 2014.

Krimmer, Elizabeth. "'Then Say What Your Religion Is': Goethe, Religion, and Faust." *Religion, Reason, and Culture in the Age of Goethe*. Ed. Elisabeth Krimmer and Patricia Anne Simpson. New York: Camden House, 2013. 99–119.

Laan, James M. van der, and Andrew Weeks, eds. *The Faustian Century: German Literature and Culture in the Age of Luther and Faustus*. Rochester: Camden House, 2013.

MacCabe, Colin. Introduction. *True to the Spirit*. Ed. Colin MacCabe, Kathleen Murray, and Rick Warner. Oxford: Oxford UP, 2011. 3–25.

Müller, Jan-Dirk. *Das Faustbuch in den konfessionellen Konflikten des 16. Jahrhunderts*. München: Bayerische Akademie der Wissenschaften, 2014.

Nasched, Shahir. "Faust—erstmals 1929 in arabischer Sprache." *Goethe-Spuren in Literatur, Kunst, Philosophie, Politik, Pädagogik*. Ed. Detlef Ignasiak and Frank Lindner. Bucha bei Jena: Quantus, 2009. 40–42.

Oergel, Maike. "The Faustian 'Gretchen': Overlooked Aspects of a Famous Male Fantasy." *German Life and Letters* 64.1 (2011): 49–53.

Peslier, Julia, ed. *Reviviscences de Faust: au théâtre, à l'opéra et sur la scène littéraire. Coulisses* 43 (2011).

Schoenberg, E. Randol, ed. *Apropos* Doktor Faustus: *Briefwechsel Arnold Schönberg—Thomas Mann, Tagebücher und Aufsätze 1930–1951*. Vienna: Czernin, 2009.

Scholz, Rüdiger. *Die Geschichte der Faust-Forschung: Weltanschauung, Wissenschaft und Goethes Drama*. Würzburg: Königshausen & Neumann, 2011.

Schulte, Hans, John K. Noyes, and Pia Kleber, eds. *Goethe's* Faust: *Theater of Modernity*. Cambridge: Cambridge UP, 2011.

Schwartz, Peter J. "'I'll burn my books!': Faust(s), Magic, Media." *Goethe's Ghosts: Reading and the Persistence of Literature*. Ed. Simon Richter and Richard A. Block. Rochester: Camden House, 2013. 186–215.

Stevenson, Ruth. "The Comic Core of Both A- and B-Editions of *Doctor Faustus*." *Studies in English Literature 1500–1900* 53.2 (2013): 401–19.

Author's Profile

Lorna Fitzsimmons teaches in the Humanities Program at the California State University. She specializes in interdisciplinary humanities. She is the editor of *Goethe's Faust and Cultural Memory: Comparatist Interfaces*; *International Faust Studies: Adaptation, Reception, Translation*; and *Lives of Faust: The Faust Theme in Literature and Music. A Reader*; and coeditor of *The Oxford Handbook of Faust in Music* (forthcoming).

Chapter 1

The Chapbook of Doctor Faustus as Source and Model

Ehrhard Bahr

Abstract

In his article, "The Chapbook of Doctor Faustus as Source and Model," Ehrhard Bahr traces the history of the Faust legend as documented by the anonymous Faust Book (1587) and its English translation of 1592, Christopher Marlowe's tragedy *Doctor Faustus*, the Faust puppet play tradition of the eighteenth century, Gotthold Ephraim Lessing's Faust fragment of 1759, Goethe's *Faust* drama of 1808 and 1832, and Thomas Mann's novel of 1947. The discussion concentrates on the question of grace that is raised in the Faust Book of 1587 and determines the characterization of the protagonist as miserable sinner (chapbook), tragic "overreacher" (Marlowe), striving individual (Goethe), or modern artist (Thomas Mann).

The chapbook of Doctor Faustus is an outstanding example of influence in the history of world literature. As soon as the book appeared in print in Germany in 1587, it was reprinted sixteen times within five years to meet the demands of German readers. It was translated into Danish (1588), English (1588 or 1589, second edition, 1592), Dutch (1592), French (1598), and Czech (1611). The second edition in English appeared under the title *The Historie of the damnable life, and deserued death of Doctor Iohn Faustus, Newly imprinted and in conuenient places imperfect matter amended: according to the true Copie printed at Franckfort, and translated into English by P.F. Gent. . . . Imprinted at London by Thomas Orwin . . . 1592*. The *Historie* served as source and model for Christopher Marlowe's *Tragicall History of D. Faustus*, which was first published in 1604, Marlowe having died in 1593.

The German text, entitled *Historia / Von D. Johann / Fausten / dem weit-beschreyten / Zauberer und Schwartzkünstler / Wie er sich gegen dem Teuffel auff eine benandte Zeit verschriebe / Was er hierzwischen für seltzame Abentheuwer gesehen / selbs angerichtet vnd getrieben / biß er endtlich seinen wol verdienten Lohn empfangen* (History of D. Johann Faustus / the Infamous Sorcerer and Black Magician / How He Did Oblige Himself for a Certain Time to the Devil / What Strange Adventures Happened to Him / Which He Saw and Pursued / Until He at Last Got His Well-Deserved Reward), was printed in Frankfurt in 1587 by Johann Spies, a well-known Protestant publisher. The first print of the Faust Book was based on a manuscript in the Duke-August Library in Wolfenbüttel, Germany. The author was anonymous. This Wolfenbüttel text and the Spies text were largely identical, but according to H. G. Haile, who edited the Wolfenbüttel manuscript and translated it into English, some chapters were deleted and Christian admonitions were added to the printed version of the text (130).

The English term "chapbook" fits the Faust Book better than the German designation as *Volksbuch*, which was introduced by the German Romanticists who believed that there was a late medieval-early modern prose literature written "of the people, by the people, and for the people." But this was not the case, since the lower classes were illiterate. Chapbooks were "cheap books," written and printed for the entertainment and moral edification of the middle class and the urban nobility. They are now classified as prime examples of the popular literature of the sixteenth century.

There is no doubt that the fascination with the protagonist of the Faust Book originated from popular legends about the historical Faustus. There was indeed an historical Faust figure, or possibly several (Durrani 19–21), referred to in some primary sources, and there are numerous secondary-source references. One of the primary sources is an entry into the account book of the bishop of Bamberg in 1520, referring to a sum of money paid to Doctor Faustus for a horoscope. Another is a statement in the records of the city of Ingolstadt of 1528, registering the expulsion of Dr. Jörg (George) Faustus of Heidelberg from the city limits. An entry in the records of the city of Nuremberg of 1532 notes that Dr. Faustus, "the great sodomite and necromancer," was refused safe conduct at Fürth. Two of these primary sources express doubt about the identity or moral character of the defendant. One describes him as "a certain man who called himself Dr. George Faustus," while the other does not hesitate to call him by foul names ("Documents" 24–25).

The secondary sources consist of statements by contemporary authorities who have heard about Dr. Faustus, such as Martin Luther, Philipp Melanchthon, and various other sources, such as local chronicles. Without exception they express their moral and religious repugnance and suspect him of dealings with the devil. According to the *Tischreden*, Luther stated that Faust, "who called the devil his brother-in-law," would have destroyed him, if he "had given him even a hand." Conrad Mutianus Rufus, a canon of the church, reports from Erfurt in 1513 that "a certain soothsayer by the name of George Faust, the demigod of Heidelberg," had come to town, but "his claims, like those of all diviners, [were] idle." In 1540 Philipp von

Hutten reports that the predictions concerning the Welser expedition to Venezuela had been correct: "the philosopher Faust hit the nail on the head, for we struck a very bad year." In his *Locorum Communium Collectanea* of 1563 Johannes Manlius quotes from the lectures of Philipp Melanchthon who said that he "knew a certain man by the name of Faust from [Knittlingen]," which was a small town near his birthplace. Melanchthon writes about the exploits of this Faust figure, among them his attempt to fly to heaven, which ended with his crash to the ground, almost killing him ("Documents" 23–31).

Most informative about the nature of the secondary sources is a letter by an abbot named Johannes Trithemius of August 1507 who claims to have happened upon Dr. Faustus on his travels. He reports that the sorcerer fled from the inn as soon as he heard of Trithemius's arrival. There was nothing left to the abbot but to comment on the rumors that he heard about Dr. Faustus:

> The man . . . who has presumed to call himself the prince of necromancers, is a vagabond, a babbler and a rogue, who deserves to be thrashed so that he may not henceforth rashly venture to profess in public things so execrable and so hostile to the holy church. . . . Certain priests in the same town told me that he had said, in the presence of many people, that he had acquired such knowledge of all wisdom and such a memory, that if all the books of Plato and Aristotle . . . had totally passed from the memory of man, he himself, through his own genius . . . would be able to restore them all with increased beauty. ("Documents" 22–23)

Other rumors that Trithemius reports from the city of Würzburg concern Faust's blasphemous statements that Christ's miracles "were not so wonderful, that he himself could do all the things which Christ had done, as often and whenever he wished." From another town the abbot heard that Dr. Faustus had been appointed as schoolmaster, but was accused of lewd conduct with his students and had avoided punishment by flight ("Documents" 23). Trithemius had good reason to make exaggerated accusations, because he himself was suspected of practicing magic and wanted to assert his moral superiority. Most of his charges were based on second-hand information. It is obvious from his letter that the facts about Dr. Faustus had become the subject of legends already during his life time.

Scholars dealing with these primary and secondary sources have reconstructed the life of the historical Dr. Faustus, beginning with his birth ca. 1480 in either Knittlingen (Württemberg) or Helmstadt near Heidelberg (Mahal, *Die Spuren*; Baron). He is supposed to have studied at either Heidelberg or Wittenberg or even Cracow. Most of his alleged appearances were in southwestern Germany: Bamberg, Ingolstadt, and Nuremberg. The *Chronica von Thüringen* (ca. 1550) placed Dr. Faustus in eastern Germany and Bohemia. The fact that the various sources record either George or Johann as his first name seems to indicate that there were at least two different men involved to claim his name and reputation. Some scholars have even speculated about a father-and-son team (Durrani 19–21). It is thought that Faust suffered a violent death ca. 1540–41 in Staufen near Freiburg in the Breisgau region.

The Spies Faust Book of 1587, based on the Wolfenbüttel manuscript, is a compilation of material related to the protagonist available toward the end of the sixteenth century. Its anonymous author added tales about the exploits and adventures of other magicians as well as extensive quotations from learned sources, such as Hartmann Schedel's *Buch der Croniken*, also known as *Weltchronik*, of 1493. What made the Spies Faust Book noticeable was the strong Lutheran message that it conveyed. Although written in simple language as a "Warning to All Ambitious, Curious, and Godless Men," as the subtitle states, it was able to convey and explicate some of the fine points of Luther's doctrine of justification. Modern editors of the chapbook have considered its author a well-educated man. The book was a popular success not only in Germany, but also in many other Protestant countries. In Germany the Faust Book of 1587 was succeeded by a series of new versions by identified authors: Georg Rudolff Widman in 1599, Johann Nikolaus Pfitzer in 1674, and an anonymous author who called himself "a man who loves Christianity" in 1725 (Schöne 1084–86). Goethe probably read Pfitzer's version of 1674 and was acquainted with the 1725 version, but received his original inspiration from the puppet play of Doctor Faust, as it was presented at fairs.

The Spies Faust Book consists of 227 pages, not including an eight-page index of the chapter headings, and is divided into three parts of sixty-eight chapters in total. The first part deals with the protagonist's birth as son of a peasant in Roda near Weimar. His uncle in Wittenberg raised him as his own child and sends him to the university to study theology. He received a master's degree and became a Doctor Theologiae, as indicated by the capital *D* before his name in the title of the chapbook: *Historia von D. Johann Fausten*. But he soon called himself a Doctor Medicinae and became an astrologer and mathematician. After acquiring knowledge of sorcery, he goes to a great dense forest which is called the Spesser Forest near Wittenberg. There he conjures the devil who tries to intimidate him by a great storm in the forest, by a griffon or dragon, and by a fiery star that transforms into a glowing ball. When D. Faustus persists, the devil finally appears in the figure of a grey friar and agrees to visit him at his house the next morning (pt. 1, 2). Afterwards there are three disputations between D. Faustus and the Spirit, who reveals himself as Mephostophiles during the third meeting. During the first disputation, D. Faustus demands that the Spirit should be subservient and obedient to him, withhold no information which he might require, and tell him nothing untruthful in response to any of his questions. But the Spirit answers that he is not able to do so, unless he has permission from his "government and sovereignty" (pt. 1, 3). There is a hierarchy in hell that he is obliged to obey as a devil of low rank. During the second disputation, D. Faustus agrees to comply with the following demands: that he will agree to be the Spirit's property, surrender himself with a document, defy all Christian believers, and renounce the Christian faith and resist any reconversion. During the final disputation, D. Faustus agrees to sign a contract stipulating that he chose the Spirit named Mephostophiles for his

instruction and service and promises in return that after twenty-four years the Spirit
might do with his "body, soul, flesh, blood and property" whatever pleases him (pt. 1,
6). The Faust Book presents the full wording of the contract or pact, written in blood
in his own hand. It includes his explanation that he summoned the devil because he
wanted "to speculate upon the *Elementa*" (pt. 1, 6), and did not have such skills nor
did he expect to acquire them from his fellowmen.

As soon as the pact is signed, Mephostophiles begins to live in the form of
a monk with D. Faustus, providing his master with food and drink and twenty-
five crowns per week. Faustus has an assistant by the name of Christoph Wagner,
described as "a reckless lout," who is aware of the arrangement and eager to profit
from it (pt. 1, 9). The assistant later becomes the protagonist of a spin-off, entitled
the *Wagnerbuch* of 1593, which deals with the assistant's separate pact with the
devil (*Wagnerbuch*).

The first conflict with Mephostophiles occurs when D. Faustus wants to get
married. Since matrimony is an institution of God, the devil opposes it. When D.
Faustus does not listen, Satan himself appears and frightens him to death, reminding
him of his pact. If he stays committed to Satan, Mephostophiles will provide him
with all the women he desires. Evidently D. Faustus avails himself of this offer, as
the text indicates (pt. 1, 10). There is even a Leporello list of the women recruited for
him during the last years of his contract (pt. 3, 57).

But this "swinish and Epicurish life" (pt. 3, 57) does not distract D. Faustus from his inquisitiveness. He asks Mephostophiles about the fall of Lucifer, the
place and regions of hell, and specifically about the torments of hell. The final question directed at his servant concerns his salvation: what would he do, if he were in
his place? Mephostophiles answers that he would lean toward God and do everything not to cause God's wrath. He thinks that God would even forgive him. But
D. Faustus has denied God, and it is too late for him to be redeemed by the grace
of God. Both D. Faustus and Mephostophiles agree not to touch upon this painful
question again (pt. 1, 17).

The second part deals with D. Faustus's travels through space (pt. 2, 25), his
descent into hell (pt. 2, 24) and his travels in Europe, Africa, and Asia (pt. 2, 26–27).
America is not mentioned due to the author's reliance on Schedel's *Buch der Croniken*. On his visit to Rome, the Lutheran bias of the Spies Faust Book is revealed. As
D. Faustus observes the sinful life at the Pope's palace, he asks: "Why did not the
devil make a Pope of me?" He expresses the thought that he believed that he alone
was "the devil's swine or sow, but [the devil] will let me fatten for a while yet. These
swine in Rome are already fattened and ready to roast and boil" (pt. 2, 26). As an
invisible guest at the Pope's dinner table, he plays pranks on him, absconding with
his food and wine for a meal of his own on the Capitoline mountain.

The reports of his visits to the other European cities, including Paris, Vienna,
and Prague, show evidence of the author's liberal borrowings from Schedel's *Buch
der Croniken*. The story of his visit to Constantinople is informed by anti-Islamic
prejudice. He appears before Sultan Suleiman II (r. 1520–66) in the disguise of

the Pope and enters the Sultan's harem to demonstrate his sexual prowess in the disguise of the prophet Mohammed. In Africa he travels to Cairo. India, Armenia, and Persia are mentioned among the Asian countries on his itinerary. From a high mountain, D. Faustus even means to see Paradise, guarded by "the angel Cherubin with his flaming sword" at the source of the four rivers Ganges, Nile, Tigris, and Euphrates (pt. 2, 27).

The third and last part of the Faust Book deals with the adventures of D. Faustus at the court of the Emperor Charles V (r. 1519–56) and with merry pranks he plays upon other people. At the Emperor's request, he makes the spirits of Alexander the Great and his wife appear (pt. 3, 33). This feat is later followed by showing Helen of Troy to his students (pt. 3, 49). During the last year of his life, he has Helen of Troy as his concubine and bedfellow. They even have a child, whom Faustus calls Justus Faustus. Both mother and child vanish after D. Faustus dies (pt. 3, 59). The rest of the stories deal with people whom Faustus deceives or ridicules, such as the knight on whom he conjures a pair of stag's horns, or the horse dealer whom he cheats by selling him a phantom horse. These folktales constitute the major portion of part 3 and may have been added for the purpose of entertainment, but originally had nothing to do with the fate of D. Faustus.

Essential to the religious argument about the infamous sorcerer and black magician is the story of the Old Man and Neighbor who wants to convert D. Faustus from his sinful life. He invites Faustus for dinner and cites examples from the Bible in order to persuade him to seek for grace and pardon. This chapter raises the issue of grace that will become the crucial test of his damnation or salvation. Faustus follows the Old Man's advice and wants to revoke his promise to the devil, but his spirit threatens to kill him and forces him to sign a second pact with his own blood (pt. 3, 52–53).

The final eight chapters are devoted to the last year of the life of D. Faustus. He makes his will, adopting Christoph Wagner as his son and heir and leaving him his worldly possessions and books. Faustus even provides Wagner with a spirit in the form of an ape, named Auerhahn, who will serve him (pt. 3, 60–61). Auerhahn is a euphemism for the devil's name Urian in German and is also used in the puppet plays. The other chapters deal with the laments of D. Faustus that he has to die and suffer the torments of hell. In chapter sixty-six, expressly entitled "The Lamentation of Doctor Faustus," he bewails the fact that the devil is not only taking away his body, but also his soul, and will plunge him into an "unspeakable place of darkness and torture." As the souls of others have "beauty and rest," he must "suffer all manner of horror, stench, privation, disgrace, trembling, fear, pain, misery, howling, weeping and gnashing" (pt. 3, 66). When D. Faustus exclaims that "there [i]s no mighty fortress to protect him," it is a special allusion to the best known of Luther's hymns, written between 1527 and 1529.

When Mephostophiles announces the day of Faustus's demise, the scholar goes to see his students and invites them for a meal in an inn in the village of Rimlich near Wittenberg. There he addresses his students and tells them about his pact with the devil, warning them not to defy baptism, the sacrament of Christ, and God himself. He asks his students to bury him, for he died, as he says,

> both a bad and a good Christian, a good Christian, because I heartily re-pented and in my heart always prayed for mercy that my soul may be de-livered. A bad Christian, because I know, that the devil will have my body and that I would willingly give him so that he would leave my soul in quiet.
> (pt. 3, 68)

When his students express their sympathy, D. Faustus tells them that his neighbor had advised him to repent, but he was afraid that the devil would kill him. He adds that "like Cain who also said that his sins were greater than God was able to forgive, he thought that he had made it too filthy in writing the pact in his own blood" (pt. 3, 68). This statement touches upon the central concept of Luther's doctrine of justifica-tion, based on Romans 3.28: "Therefore we conclude that a man is justified by faith [alone] without the deeds of the law." The doctrine teaches that God is able to forgive a great sinner such as Cain, as long as he believes in God's grace. But neither Cain nor D. Faustus have this faith. They cannot be redeemed by good works, but by faith alone. In the absence of such faith, they are condemned.

After this speech, his students go to bed, but during midnight they hear a lot of noise from the room of D. Faustus and his cry for help, yet they are afraid to rescue him. Next morning they find "no Faustus, but the walls of his room were covered with blood, his brains were splattered against the wall, for the devil had beaten him from one wall against another. There were also his eyes and teeth on the floor. It was a gruesome and horrifying spectacle to behold." His body is finally found in the yard on a pile of manure, "most gruesome to look at, because his head and limbs were torn into pieces." The students bury D. Faustus in the village and return to Wittenberg to tell Wagner about his master's final hours. There they find the History of D. Faustus written by himself without the ending, which the students add (pt. 3, 68).

The Spies Faust Book ends with an address to the Christian reader, warning to avoid sorcery and to fear God. The special reference to those with inquisitive minds is a Lutheran warning against the dangers of Renaissance science and discoveries. To speculate upon the Elementa, as Faustus attempts to do (pt. 1, 6), was an abomi-nation to orthodox Lutherans. The life of D. Faustus was designed to serve as a fear-ful example "to love God alone, take him always before our eyes and pray to him, to serve and love him, with our whole heart and soul" (pt. 3, 68).

The protagonist of the German chapbook of 1587 was conceived as an anti-hero of Martin Luther. The numerous references to Wittenberg, where Luther used to teach, make this place name an obvious signal to the reader. But in addition there was a central experience in Luther's life that is presented in the chapbook as a nega-tive parody. Luther's conversion of 1505 had the same setting as the conjuring of the devil by D. Faustus. Both events took place in a great dense forest during "a ferocious storm that bent the trees to the ground" (pt. 1, 2). While the sorcerer was not intimidated by the storm, Luther, who was on his way to Erfurt to study law, was filled with deadly fear and promised to become a monk, if he would survive. The parallels are profound: as Luther dedicates his future life to the service of God, D. Faustus commits himself to the devil. By comparison, the story of D. Faustus and his reactions to life at the Vatican is a commonplace appeal to Protestant expectations about Rome. The most subtle point of the reception is the reference to Luther's doctrine of justification. It is the lack of *sola fide* ("by faith alone") that is the final reason for the damnation of Faustus.

The English Faust Book follows the plot of the German original. The translation is fairly close, but the division of chapters is different: sixty-three chapters instead of sixty-eight. The geographic locations are the same: Rhode or Roda, Wittenberg, and Rimlich. The references to Luther are missing, such as, for example, the allusion to his most famous hymn, but otherwise there are no critical omissions. Even though the impression of 1592, printed by Thomas Orwin in London, was the second revised edition, it is still a remarkable example of the rapid transfer of the story from the European continent to England.

The English chapbook in its first or second edition served as source for most of the narrative material and the personnel of Christopher Marlowe's *Tragicall History of D. Faustus*, first printed in 1604 (the so-called A-text). A different text, entitled *The Tragicall History of the Life and Death of Doctor Faustus* and published in 1616, is called the B-text. Both texts include, in addition to Mephostophilis, the traditional characters of Wagner, the German Emperor Charles V, the Old Man, and persons from the folktales. But a number of characters were added to dramatize the story, such as the Good Angel and Bad Angel, the Seven Deadly Sins, Pope Adrian, Bruno as the rival Pope, appointed by the Emperor, and a few others, among them two German magicians, three scholars, and Robin, a Clown. But the most important change was that Marlowe made Doctor Faustus the hero of an Elizabethan tragedy. He is no longer the miserable sinner and horrifying example of the chapbook, but a scholar with Renaissance ambitions. The Prologue prepares the audience that the protagonist is not a victorious general as Hannibal or a great lover like Marc Anthony:

> Not marching in the fields of Trasimene
> Where Mars did mate the warlike Carthagens,
> Nor sporting in the dalliance of love
> In courts of kings where state is overturned,
> Nor in the pomp of proud audacious deeds
> Intends our muse to vaunt his heavenly verse. (lines 1–6)

The chorus provides the background of the protagonist's life story, relating the familiar facts from the chapbook about his childhood and education:

> Now is he born of parents base of stock
> In Germany within a town called Rhode;
> At riper years to Wittenberg he went
> Whereas his kinsmen chiefly brought him up.
> So much he profits in divinity

That shortly he was graced with doctor's name,

Excelling all, and sweetly can dispute

In th' heavenly matters of theology. (lines 11–18)

There is a shift from the narrative of the chapbook to the tragedy of Faustus when the protagonist is compared to the Icarus of Greek mythology: "His waxen wings did mount above his reach /And melting, heavens conspired his overthrow!" (lines 20–21). The Christian substance of the story is in conflict with a drama that claims a conspiracy by the heavenly powers against the protagonist.

The tragedy begins with "Faustus in his study," a scene that became iconic in the transmission of the plot from the Elizabethan drama, performed by English actors in Germany, via the puppet plays of the eighteenth century to Goethe's fragment of 1790. Even the libretto of Charles Gounod's Faust opera of 1859 retained this scene, as did Paul Valéry's *Mon Faust* (*My Faust*) of 1940 and Václav Havel's *Pokušení* (*Temptation*) of 1986. Marlowe's Faustus is intent on studying the fields of knowledge offered by the medieval university:

Settle thy studies Faustus, and begin

To sound the depth of that thou wilt profess.

Having commenced, be a divine in show—

Yet level at the end of every art

And live and die in Aristotle's works. (1.1.1–5)

He discusses the medieval fields of logic, medicine, law, and even theology, but dismisses them as unsatisfactory. He finds black magic more attractive, because "a sound magician is a demi-god! / Here tire my brains to get a deity" (1.1.59–60). In the following scene, reminding the audience of a morality play, the Good and Bad Angel fight over Faustus's decision to read or not read Scriptures. Scenes like this are repeated again and again at crucial points. Two German magicians support his decision in favor of black magic. As soon as night arrives, Faustus conjures Lucifer and four devils and requests the services of Mephostophilis, who appears and introduces himself as a servant of Lucifer. The plot follows the chapbook, except for the comical scenes, typical of Elizabethan drama, that show Wagner and Robin the Clown and their dealing with two devils throughout the drama. Faustus signs the traditional pact with blood and gives his body and soul to Lucifer and his servant Mephostophilis in exchange for twenty-four years of service. The pact is spelled out in detail in act 2 (lines 96–116).

Here is becomes obvious that Marlowe's Faustus does not only want to speculate the elements, but also has a political agenda. With the help of Mephostophilis he expects to be a

great emperor of the world

And make a bridge through the moving air

To pass the ocean with a band of men;

[And] join the hills that bind the Afric shore

> And make that country continent to Spain,
> And both contributory to my crown;
> The Emperor shall not live but by my leave,
> Nor any potentate of Germany. (1.3.103–10)

But these wishes are never brought to fruition. The action follows the plot of the chapbook with the same questions about Lucifer and hell as well as about marriage (1.3–2.1). Faustus is exposed to the Good and the Bad Angel and tries to repent, but Lucifer and Beelzebub intervene with a show of the Seven Deadly Sins that captivates the sinner (2.2.116–77).

Act 3 deals with Faustus's travel to Rome, but in addition to the chapbook story there is a political plot added about Bruno, a rival Pope, appointed by the Emperor. The plot, which reflects the conflict between the Vatican and the German Emperors, is decided by Faustus in favor of the Emperor. Welcomed at the court of Emperor Charles V, Faustus conjures the images of Alexander the Great and his paramour. At the same time Faustus plays his tricks on an envious courtier and a horse-courser and serves a dish of ripe grapes in the middle of winter, as related in the chapbook (act 4).

The action in act 5 deals with the deadline of the pact and the impending catastrophe of Faustus's damnation. The Old Man of the chapbook appears and advises Faustus to "call for mercy and avoid despair." Although he is reminded by the scholars, whom he invited for a farewell dinner, that divine "mercy is infinite," Faustus is convinced that his "offense can ne'er be pardoned" (5.2.41–42). When the Good Angel leaves him, the Bad Angel takes over the action. As soon as the clock strikes twelve, the devils enter and drag Faustus to hell (5.2). The following day the assembled scholars only find "Faustus' limbs / All torn asunder" by the devils (5.3).

The major exception of act 5 to the chapbook is the symbolic value attributed to Helen of Troy. In the chapbook she is a succubus, a devil in female form, and a pagan spirit. Intercourse with her is a sin. However, her appearance before the scholars in act 5 reveals the difference between her attraction in the chapbook and in Marlowe's tragedy, where she evokes in Faustus an appreciation of classical beauty inspired by the Renaissance. The most beautiful lines of the drama are devoted to Faustus's address of Helen of Troy:

> Was this the face that launched a thousand ships
> And burnt the topless towers of Ilium?
> Sweet Helen, make me immortal with a kiss.
> Her lips suck forth my soul. See where it flies!
> Come Helen, come, give me my soul again.
> Here will I dwell, for heaven is in these lips
> And dross is all that is not Helena.
> I will be Paris, and for love of thee
> Instead of Troy shall Wittenberg be sacked;
> And I will combat with weak Menelaus

And wear thy colors on my plumed crest.
Yea, I will wound Achilles in the heel
And then return to Helen for a kiss.
O, thou art fairer than the evening's air
Clad in the beauty of a thousand stars,
Brighter art thou than flaming Jupiter
When he appeared to hapless Semele,
More lovely than the monarch of the sky
In wanton Arethusa's azure arms,
And none but thou shalt be my paramour. (5.1.96–115)

In Marlowe's tragedy Helen of Troy incorporates the idea of beauty as divine and one could speculate about salvation through beauty. However, Marlowe did not take this step. Erich Heller analyzes the dilemma Marlowe faced due to the clash between orthodox Christianity and Renaissance appreciation of classical beauty: "Who speaks of Faust's sin [in Marlowe's *Faust*]? The plot, but not the poetry" (11). The beauty of the lines addressing Helen of Troy is supposed to absolve Faustus from damnation. R. M. Dawkins refers to the same dilemma, when he summarizes the plot of the drama: "the play tells 'the story of a Renaissance man who had to pay the medieval price for being one'" (qtd. in Barnet viii). But the Chorus returns to the traditional message of the Faust story at the end of the drama:

Cut is the branch that might have grown full straight
And burnèd is Apollo's laurel bough
That sometime grew within this learnèd man.
Faustus is gone: regard his hellish fall,
Whose fiendful fortune may exhort the wise
Only to wonder at unlawful things,
Whose deepness doth entice such forward wits
To practice more than heavenly power permits. (5.3.1–8)

While the first three lines bemoan Faustus's fate with an image from classical mythology, the final lines pronounce his fall as a legitimate warning in terms of the traditional theology of the chapbook, which does not allow experimentation beyond the borders of established knowledge. In spite of this verdict, Marlowe's achievement is the elevation of Faustus from miserable sinner to tragic protagonist. Both the chapbook and Marlowe's drama are informed by traditional Christianity, but Faustus's fall is that of a tragic character who tries to overreach his adversary. As Mephostophilis says, he "Begets a world of idle fantasies / To overreach the devil; but all in vain" (5.2.14–15).

During the sixteenth and seventeenth centuries, companies of English actors traveled the continent and performed plays from the corpus of Elizabethan drama without referring to the names of Shakespeare or Marlowe. The plays were probably adapted to appeal to the level of the German-speaking audience and depended largely on pantomime, but none of these texts survived. The local announcements document the performances of plays about Doctor Faust in Strasbourg in 1597 and in Graz in 1608. The announcements of the German companies sometimes advertised the dialect of the actors, as for example, "Saxon High German" or "High German" ("Documents" 170). When Gotthold Ephraim Lessing recommends the old Faust plays in his *Literaturbriefe* of 1759 as a kind of Shakespearean model for contemporary German dramatists to follow, he refers to the German versions of Marlowe's tragedy, but the name of the English playwright is not mentioned (*Werke* 5: 72–73).

The German puppet plays of Doctor Faust that were performed during the seventeenth and eighteenth centuries at country and city fairs followed the model of the traveling theater companies. The texts of the puppet plays were not influenced by the chapbook directly, but by the texts of the theater companies, as the ubiquitous scene of Faust in his study suggests. Hardly any texts survive because they constituted the capital of the companies and it was not in their interest to make the texts available to their competitors. In 1846 Karl Simrock published the reconstruction of a puppet play that is probably much older. The manuscript of the puppet-showman Guido Bonneschky, first published in 1850, is considered more authentic because its plot is rudimentary and leaves plenty of opportunity for improvisation and ad-libbing by the puppet player, while Simrock's text is adapted to the conventions of nineteenth-century comedy, with rhymed verse for many of the scenes with Faust and the nobility (Mahal *Johann Faust*). The plot of both texts is very similar and employs the German comic stock figure Kasperle, or Casper (also known as Hanswurst or Pickelhäring), who provides comic relief from Faust's dealings with the devil. Both plays are divided into four acts and begin with the iconic scene of Faust in his study from Marlowe's tragedy. The following outline and quotes are from the Bonneschky text. The protagonist is bored with academic studies, especially theology, and resolves to apply himself to black magic:

> I have attained by my own efforts to the rank of doctor, and I have carried on this profession honourably for eighteen years. But what is all this to me? Doctor I am, doctor I remain, and beyond that I cannot go in the field of theology. Ha! That is too little for my spirit, which aims at being revered by posterity. I have resolved to apply myself to necromancy, and through that to reach my heart's desire—to make my name immortal. (1.1)

Voices to the Right and Left, reminiscent of the Good and Bad Angel in Marlowe's tragedy, fight over his soul. The Voice to the Right tells him to pursue the study of theology, but Faust decides to follow the Voice to the Left and takes up the study of necromancy (1.1). He selects Mephistopheles as servant from an assembly of devils and offers him a pact with a deadline of twenty-four years (1.5). Meanwhile, Wagner, Faust's famulus, has hired Casper as a servant, who quickly learns to conjure spirits like his master. Faust does not travel to Rome, and nor does he appear at the Emperor's court. Instead, he shows up at the court of the Duke of Parma. Casper arrives as his advance party in Parma and makes fun of the duke and his counsellor. Faust entertains the duke with conjuring the images of biblical figures such as David and Goliath, Samson and Delilah, Judith and Holofernes, and Lucretia as a paragon of Roman virtue (3.3). Mephistopheles traps Faust with the image of Helen of Troy. Her sinful attraction marks the return to traditional Christian values, as she is used by Mephistopheles to regain his power over Faust (4.5). The scholar is cheated by the devil, who reduces the time of the pact to twelve years. Faust receives his punishment for his sinful life and the Furies carry him off into the sky (4.8). Meanwhile, Casper, now a night watchman, encounters Auerhahn, also known as Urian, a devil of lower rank. When the devil demands his soul, Casper denies that he has a soul. Moreover, Auerhahn cannot get him, because he is indispensable as night watchman in Wittenberg. The puppet play ends with Casper deciding to "make right merry with a can of schnaps and laugh at the silly devils" (4.9). Casper represents the common man who exposes the affectations of academics and noblemen with his coarse humor. Not even the devils are able to intimidate him with their threats and in the end he appears beyond their reach. The intellectual Faustus becomes the fool, while Casper survives.

Johann Wolfgang von Goethe became acquainted with the story of D. Faust through the puppet theater in his hometown Frankfurt and in Strasbourg, where he studied in the early 1770s, as confirmed by his autobiography *Dichtung und Wahrheit* (*Poetry and Truth*): "The significant puppet play about [Faust] resounded and hummed within me in many tonal variations" (306). Textual evidence of the influence of the puppet play on Goethe's *Urfaust* of 1775 is the first scene of the protagonist in his study:

> I've studied now, to my regret,
> Philosophy, Law, Medicine,
> And—what is worst—Theology
> From end to end with diligence.
> Yet here I am, a wretched fool
> And still no wiser than before.
>
> Hab nun, ach, die Philosophei,
> Medizin und Juristerei,
> Und leider auch die Theologie
> Durchaus studiert mit heißer Müh.
> Da steh ich nun, ich armer Tor
> Und bin so klug, als wie zuvor. (lines 1–6)

Goethe may not have borrowed the so-called "Knittel verse," a late medieval doggerel, from the puppet play, because many of them were in prose. But there were other models available to him to imitate sixteenth-century discourse. The Knittel verse is not used exclusively for the *Urfaust*, not even for the opening monologue that switches meter after thirty-five lines. The main influence of the puppet play consists of the formulation of the Faustian situation. Goethe transferred this scene without any changes to the fragment of 1790 and the final version of *Faust I* of 1808.

Working for more than sixty years on his Faust drama, Goethe never abandoned the chapbook model, as he encountered it in the puppet play tradition. The earliest version, the *Urfaust*, a manuscript copied by a lady-in-waiting at the court of Saxe-Weimar where Goethe had moved in 1775, was not discovered until 1887. The next text, *Faust. Ein Fragment (Faust: A Fragment)* of 1790, is the first printed version—although incomplete—that was available to Goethe's contemporary readers. In 1808, *Faust. Der Tragödie erster Teil (Faust. A Tragedy, Part I)* was published and in 1832, *Faust. Der Tragödie zweiter Teil in fünf Akten (Faust. Part II of the Tragedy in Five Acts)* was completed and printed posthumously. Before that, the third act of part 2 had been published in 1827 under the title *Helena, klassisch-romantische Phantasmagorie. Zwischenspiel zu Faust (Helen: Classico-Romantic Phantasmagoria: A Faust Intermezzo)*. Goethe made a lot of changes, but as late as 1826 he called the appearance of Helen of Troy in the third act of *Faust II* his "oldest concept" of the Faust story in a letter to Wilhelm von Humboldt on October 22 of the same year.

Goethe's reading of later versions of the German chapbook cannot be dated exactly, but it appears that he became familiar with the Faust Book by Johann Nikolaus Pfitzer of 1674 and the anonymous version by Christlich Meynenden ("one who loves Christianity") of 1725 at a later date. Some critics have argued that Pfitzer's version containing the story of Faust's love for "a beautiful, but poor maid" provided the central motif for the tragedy of Margarete or Gretchen, but that is doubtful, because there were other more important influences, such as a trial for infanticide in Frankfurt in 1772 and the author's guilt feelings about his desertion of a minister's daughter from Alsace while he was studying law in Strasbourg in the early 1770s. Goethe did not read Marlowe's *Tragicall History of D. Faustus* until 1818.

A scene from a Faust drama published anonymously by Lessing in 1759 and described in greater detail in 1784 by one of his friends documents that the Enlightenment dramatist was not willing to condemn Faust for seeking knowledge, which he considered "the noblest drive" given by God to mankind (*Werke* 2: 780). It is doubtful that Goethe took his cue for a happy ending of his Faust tragedy from Lessing, because he employed Catholic imagery for the salvation of the protagonist to convey his own idea of redemption integrated into the natural process of creation. Human striving is met by cosmic "love from above" ("die Liebe gar / Von oben") (*Faust* line 11938–39, my translation). Goethe's setting of the scene is a mountain gorge populated by famous saints and sinners. The immortal part of Faust is carried by angels into the higher atmosphere and introduced to a Penitent alias Gretchen and the Mater Gloriosa. They rise "to higher spheres" ("zu höhern Sphären") with Faust in pursuit (line 12094). The erotic nature of the event is revealed in the last two lines of the drama: "Woman, eternally / shows us the way" ("Das Ewig-Weibliche / Zieht uns hinan") (lines 12110–11).

The salvation of Faust is Goethe's most profound deviation from the chapbook. The other is the substitution of the traditional pact between Faust and the devil by a wager that the scholar will stop striving and "lie contented on a bed of sloth" ("beruhigt je mich auf ein Faulbett legen") (line 1692). Both Mephistopheles and Faust win and lose the wager. The tragedy of Margarete that dominates *Urfaust* and *Faust I* is Goethe's ultimate contribution to the Faust tradition. While she is sentenced to die for infanticide in *Urfaust*, she is saved by divine intervention in part 1. Modern Faust dramas and novels owe their success to the Margarete character, as examples by Mikhail Bulgakov, Václav Havel, and Thomas Mann show.

Most of the chapbook motifs that Goethe preserved are to be found in *Faust II*. Like his chapbook namesake, Goethe's Faust appears before the Emperor and is ordered to conjure images from Greek history or mythology: in the chapbook they are Alexander the Great and his wife, in Goethe's *Faust* Paris and Helen of Troy. As Goethe's protagonist fails to understand that the images are not for real, he travels back in time to classical Greece to witness the development of culture with Helen of Troy as its culmination. She is no longer a devilish succuba, as in chapters 49 and 59 of the chapbook, but the representation of classical beauty. As a medieval ruler, Faust invites Helen to his throne and has a son with her. When the child dies in an accident due to his willfulness, Helen of Troy disappears together with him, as she does in the chapbook.

There are no obvious parallels in the chapbook for Faust's career as the Emperor's vassal in acts 4 and 5. As a modern entrepreneur he plans to reclaim a swamp as fertile land for future generations. It is a utopia that Mephisto cannot provide. Faust pronounces the words of the wager—although in the subjunctive—that seal his fate on earth:

> to the moment I could say:
> tarry a while, you are so fair—
> …
> Envisioning those heights of happiness,
> I enjoy my highest moment.
>
> Zum Augenblicke dürft' ich sagen:
> Verweile doch, du bist so schön!
> …
> Im Vorgefühl von solchem hohen Glück
> Genieß' ich jetzt den höchsten Augenblick. (lines 11581–86)

Faust dies. His body is buried by Mephisto's slaves, but the devil cannot hold on to the immortal part of Faust. According to Goethe's concept of grace, Faust has nothing else to do but strive. His efforts are met with "love from above." Angels intervene and avert tragedy, depriving Mephisto of his prize.

The last impressive example of the influence of the chapbook is Thomas Mann's *Doktor Faustus: Das Leben des deutschen Tonsetzers Adrian Leverkühn, erzählt von einem Freunde* (*Doctor Faustus: The Life of the German Composer Adrian Leverkühn as Told by a Friend*), begun in Los Angeles in 1943 and published in

1947 (see ch. 5, "Thomas Mann's *Doctor Faustus* as Political Document"). Since the novel was to interpret and explain the German catastrophe of the twentieth century, it made sense to return to the original version of the Faust legend, which ends with the condemnation of the protagonist. Goethe's *Faust,* with the salvation of its protagonist, was too optimistic as a model for such a project. For the biography of his Faust figure, as told by his friend Serenus Zeitblom, Mann followed the plot of the chapbook, dealing with the protagonist's childhood, his youth, and his study of theology at the university. For the middle period of his life, Mann superimposes the life story of Friedrich Nietzsche on the biography of his Faust figure, calling him Adrian Leverkühn ("live boldly") and making him a modern composer.

His fatal confrontation with evil was derived from an anecdote from Nietzsche's biography, dealing with the philosopher's encounter with a prostitute. For the novel, this encounter serves as the devil's pact of the Faust legend. But it is not the prostitute, named Esmeralda, who represents evil, but Leverkühn's challenge of fate in their sexual union. He disregards her altruistic warning of a syphilitic infection. This arrogance is the evil that seals the pact and is comparable to the pride exhibited by the Faust figure of the chapbook. Esmeralda reappears in the Leverkühn plot as Madame de Tolna, an aristocratic Hungarian woman and patron of the composer's music, who fulfills the function of Goethe's Eternal Feminine in disguise (Vaget 185).

There is no Mephistopheles in the novel, but only Leverkühn's report of a meeting with the devil to reconfirm the pact, including the stipulation of a twenty-four-year period of service and the prohibition against love. This devil may be a figment of his imagination, or a strategy to convey the Faustian agenda of his career to his friend Serenus Zeitblom, who serves as narrator of his biography. In the end Mann combined both the Faust legend and Nietzsche's biography in Leverkühn's last meeting with his friends, which is based on Faustus's last conversation with his students and the philosopher's paralytic collapse in 1889. Leverkühn's last composition is entitled *The Lamentation of Doctor Faustus* and uses the twelve-syllable line from the chapbook "For I die as both a wicked and good Christian." These syllables form the theme of the twelve-tone composition that exemplifies Leverkühn's success or "breakthrough" as a composer. While Doctor Faustus dies at the hands of the devil, Leverkühn is affected, like Nietzsche, by dementia for the next ten years of his life until he dies in the care of his mother. The chapbook pronounces that Faustus died a "deserved death" and earned his eternal condemnation. Thomas Mann's novel, however, does not end with Leverkühn's death, but with Zeitblom's prayer for the soul of his friend and his fatherland.

The most difficult aspect of the novel is its linkage to the German catastrophe. While it is easy to identify music with Germany (Potter), it is far more complicated to associate it with German imperialism. This requires the inclusion of Thomas Mann's involvement with Richard Wagner's music and with conservative nationalism during World War I, when he defended German culture as superior to Western civilization in his *Reflections of a Nonpolitical Man* of 1918. The novel of 1947 was to serve as his personal and national confession, as he proposed a parallel between the German quest for musical hegemony and German ambitions of world domination. When Leverkühn's friends rushed to join the army in 1914 in order to conquer Paris, the composer declared twice: "I cannot go to Paris. You all are going in my place" (325, 327). This statement is not a reflection of German chauvinism, but an expression of German contempt of politics that led to the seizure of power by the Nazis. As Zeitblom has to admit that the Germans never got to Paris during World War I, he becomes a witness to Germany's final defeat in World War II and the crimes committed in its name, including the ignominy of the concentration camps.

As this survey of representative texts shows, Mann's novel maintained the religious substance of the chapbook of 1587 and is perhaps the prime example to show its influence over the centuries. Marlowe was too close to the English chapbook to avoid the religious question. His *Tragicall History of D. Faustus* offered the prospect of salvation through beauty, but Marlowe stuck to the chapbook ending. Lessing's draft of a Faust drama was the first to make a break with the damnation of Faust. In Goethe's version, Faust follows Gretchen and the Mater Gloriosa and rises above. Under the impact of the carnage of World War II, Thomas Mann revoked the positive ending of Goethe's *Faust* and reintroduced the question of grace. The chapbook served not only as model for the plot of his novel, but also for the issue of the salvation of the sinner and his fatherland. The novel does not provide an answer, but leaves the question of grace at the end to the prayer of a lone survivor who hopes beyond hopelessness.

Works Cited

Barnet, Sylvan. Introduction. Christopher Marlowe. *Doctor Faustus*. Ed. Sylvan Barnet. New York: Signet Classic, 1969. vii–xix.

Barnet, Sylvan. "The Source of *Doctor Faustus*." Christopher Marlowe. *Doctor Faustus*. Ed. Sylvan Barnet. New York: Signet Classic, 1969. 110–59.

Baron, Frank. *Doctor Faustus: From History to Legend*. Munich: Fink, 1978.

Berghahn, Klaus L. "Transformations of the Faust Theme." *Lives of Faust: The Faust Theme in Literature and Music. A Reader*. Ed. Lorna Fitzsimmons. Berlin: De Gruyter, 2008. 160–69.

Bonneschky, Guido. *The Puppet-Play of Doctor Faust. Lives of Faust: The Faust Theme in Literature and Music. A Reader*. Ed. Lorna Fitzsimmons. Berlin: De Gruyter, 2008. 175–203.

Curran, Jane. "Hanswurst, Kasperle, Pickelhäring and Faust." *International Faust Studies: Adaptation, Reception, Translation*. Ed. Lorna Fitzsimmons. New York: Continuum, 2008. 36–51.

"Documents." *Lives of Faust: The Faust Theme in Literature and Music. A Reader*. Ed. Lorna Fitzsimmons. Berlin: De Gruyter, 2008. 170–74.

Durrani, Osman. "The Historical Faust." *Lives of Faust: The Faust Theme in Literature and Music. A Reader*. Ed. Lorna Fitzsimmons. Berlin: De Gruyter, 2008. 19–21.

Goethe, Johann Wolfgang von. *Faust I & II*. Ed. and trans. Stuart Atkins. New York: Suhrkamp, 1984.

Goethe, Johann Wolfgang von. *From My Life: Poetry and Truth, Parts One to Three*. Trans. Robert R. Heitner. Ed. Thomas P. Saine and Jeffrey L. Sammons. Princeton: Princeton UP, 1994.

Goethe, Johann Wolfgang von. *Werke*. Vol. 3.1. Ed. Erich Trunz. München: C. H. Beck, 1981.

Haile, G. H., ed. *The History of Doctor Johann Faustus: Recovered from The German*. Urbana: U of Illinois P, 1965.

Havel, Vaclav. *Temptation*. Trans. Marie Winn. New York: Grove, 1989.

Heller, Erich. *The Artist's Journey into the Interior, and Other Essays*. New York: Vintage Book, 1968.

Historia von D. Johann Fausten: *Text des Druckes von 1587: Kritische Ausgabe mit den Zusatztexten der Wolfenbütteler Handschrift und der zeitgenössischen Drucke*. Ed. Stephan Füssel and Hans Joachim Kreutzer. Stuttgart: Reclam, 1988.

Lessing, Gotthold Ephraim. "Dramatische Fragmente." *Werke*. Vol. 2. Ed. Karl Eibl, Herbert Georg Göpfert, Karl S. Guthke, Gerd Hillen, Albert von Schirnding, and Jörg Schönert. München: C. Hanser, 1970. 487–89, 774–83.

Lessing, Gotthold Ephraim. "Literaturbriefe I." *Werke*. Vol. 5. Ed. Karl Eibl, Herbert Georg Göpfert, Karl S. Guthke, Gerd Hillen, Albert von Schirnding, and Jörg Schönert. München: C. Hanser, 1970. 72–73.

Mahal, Günther. *Faust: Die Spuren eines geheimnisvollen Lebens*. Berne: Scherz, 1980.

Mahal, Günther, ed. *Doktor Johannes Faust: Puppenspiel in vier Aufzügen hergestellt von Karl Simrock*. Stuttgart: Reclam, 1991.

Mann, Thomas. *Doctor Faustus: The Life of the German Composer Adrian Leverkühn as Told by a Friend*. Trans. John E. Woods. New York: Vintage Books, 1997.

Marlowe, Christopher. *Doctor Faustus*. Ed. Sylvan Barnet. New York: Signet Classic, 1969. 21–109.

Palmer, Philip Mason, and Robert Pattison More. *The Sources of the Faust Tradition from Simon Magus to Lessing*. New York: Haskell House, 1965.

Potter, Pamela. *Most German of the Arts: Musicology and Society from the Weimar Republic to the End of Hitler's Reich*. New Haven: Yale UP, 1998.

Schöne, Albrecht, ed. *Faust*. By Johann Wolfgang von Goethe. Vol. 2. Darmstadt: Wissenschaftliche Buchgesellschaft, 1999.

Vaget, Hans R. "Mann, Joyce, and the Question of Modernism in Doctor Faustus." *Thomas Mann's Doctor Faustus: A Novel at the Margin of Modernism*. Ed. Herbert Lehnert and Peter C. Pfeiffer. Columbia: Camden House, 1991. 167–91.

Das Wagnerbuch von 1593. Ed. Günther Mahal. Tübingen: Francke, 2005.

Author's Profile

Ehrhard Bahr is a member of the Germanic Languages faculty at the University of California, Los Angeles. He is a former President of the Goethe Society of North America. His publications include *Weimar on the Pacific: German Exile Culture in Los Angeles and the Crisis of Modernism*; *The Novel as Archive: The Genesis, Reception, and Criticism of Goethe's Wilhelm Meisters Wanderjahre*; and *Georg Lukács*.

Chapter 2

Adelbert von Chamisso's *Peter Schlemihl* and the Quest for the Self

Christa Knellwolf King

Abstract

In this article, "Adelbert von Chamisso's *Peter Schlemihl* and the Quest for the Self," Christa Knellwolf King discusses the well-known novella, *Peter Schlemihl* (1814), by Adelbert von Chamisso as an interpretation of the Faust typology. Concentrating on Chamisso's transformation of the Faustian pact with the devil, it analyzes the story's reasons for subdividing the negotiations between Schlemihl and the devil into two stages: an initial exchange of Schlemihl's shadow for Fortunatus's purse of inexhaustible wealth, and the devil's subsequent effort to make Schlemihl part with his soul in exchange for regaining his shadow. The most important emphasis of Chamisso's Faustus narrative, this article argues, is that it goes beyond analyzing the craving and limits of human knowledge and certainty that characterized the early modern versions of the Faust typology in order to examine a contemporary character's quest for self-understanding. The article concludes that the irresolvable ambiguities of the story are occasioned by Chamisso's own inability to reconcile his ideals about moral and scientific integrity with the principles of a society lusting for wealth and power.

When the hero of the sixteenth-century Faust Book sells his soul to the devil in exchange for power, pleasure, and knowledge, there is a certain consensus about the meanings of "soul." In spite of long-standing controversies about who "owned" the soul (God or an individual human being) (Knellwolf King 79), there was a shared notion that the soul was a nonmaterial but absolutely real entity that resided in the human body. However, after the secularizing endeavors of the age of Enlightenment,

31

the traditional view of the soul as the immortal core of embodied existence was challenged (Hoffmann).

Despite these changes, the Faust story continued to attract emulators who imagined ever new constellations of the narrative pattern. In my earlier study of the transformations of the Faust story between 1580 and 1730, I argued that the main emphasis of the English and German Faust Books of the late sixteenth century was to explore the boundaries of legitimate curiosity, but at the same time they already interrogated the meanings of "soul." When curiosity established itself as a valorized quality in the context of Enlightenment secularization of scientific research, the skepticism of the age also questioned the existence of a soul. While this development made it viable to shrug off metaphysical components of identity as empty figments of the imagination, it remained nevertheless impossible to shed deeply engrained fears of the devil as the personified force of evil who was believed to gain control over the sacred core of a human being.

The resulting conflict between intellectual rejections of traditional personifications of evil and visceral terror about the devil is dramatized in Adelbert von Chamisso's (1781–1838) world-famous novella *Peter Schlemihl* (1814). When Chamisso describes the eponymous hero of this tale as entering into a contract with the devil, he describes two different bargaining processes between the tempter and the innocent victim. Appearing in the guise of an inconspicuous member of contemporary society, the devil enters into a relationship with Schlemihl by offering him a seemingly harmless bargain. Failing to understand what he is doing, Schlemihl readily exchanges his shadow for Fortunatus's legendary purse of inexhaustible riches. Schlemihl agrees to the bargain concerning a part of himself that is considered to be secular—his shadow—but he stolidly clings to the immaterial entity which is described by the traditional term soul, even though the devil offers to return his shadow in exchange for his soul in a second round of bargaining. Schlemihl remains adamant in spite of experiencing great suffering as a result of having to live without a shadow.

When Chamisso subdivides the negotiation with the devil into two stages, he complicates our attempt to interpret the meanings of that which Schlemihl sacrifices. Both "objects" of exchange are seminal parts of himself whose loss amounts to a disintegration of identity. Furthermore, both are nonmaterial qualities or properties which are charged with symbolic significance in spite of being connoted differently. The parallelism in the plot structure between "shadow" and "soul" reinforces the semantic overlaps in the metaphorical meanings of these terms. Their semantic contiguity brings about a doubling of the idea of soul while the reader is also challenged to accept an unambiguous differentiation between two very similar concepts (Webber 48; Reber; Fröhler).

The reader's commonsensical knowledge of the world reduces the shadow to a purely physical property belonging to bodies exposed to a source of light. But the narrator insists that almost everyone encountered by Schlemihl interprets his missing shadow as a mark that he has lost his soul. The breach of a basic law of nature, which characterizes the story world of *Peter Schlemihl*, hence forces us to think through the similarities and differences between "soul" and "shadow." This chapter explores the implications of Chamisso's decision to contrast two quasi-synonymous but differently connoted qualities. It draws on philosophical and neuroscientific theories of self and embodied experience in order to explain in what ways Chamisso's interrogation of the parallel meanings of "shadow" and "soul" challenges our understanding of individual and social identity.

The Differentiation between "Shadow" and "Soul"

It is not surprising that Chamisso scholarship has struggled with the meanings of Schlemihl's shadow (Lehmann 21–23). Following a biographical line of interpretation, it has been suggested that the missing shadow should be read as a metaphorical description of Chamisso's own lack of a recognizable cultural identity, which he famously encapsulates in the formulation that he counts as a Frenchman in Germany and a German in France, a Catholic among Protestants and a Protestant among Catholics, a philosopher among believers and a bigoted Christian among freethinkers (Lahnstsein 7; Schwann; Schmid 19–21, 31–32; Chamisso, *Korrespondenzen*). However, the horror expressed by those who see Schlemihl without his shadow goes beyond this character's failure to be acknowledged as a member of a cultural community. It is impossible to say what exactly he does not have. Yet, the horrified responses which he encounters from other people demonstrate that the loss of his shadow is interpreted as a mark of insurmountable otherness: the responses to Schlemihl's shadowless existence suggests that he is believed to have lost his soul.

The attempt to obtain a reliable understanding of "shadow" and "soul" is rendered more difficult because Chamisso frequently moves between playful and deeply serious modes, describing Schlemihl's tearful misery about his shadowless existence, as well as mocking the figure of an unprincipled merchant who "enjoyed the general esteem; he was accompanied by a broad, palish shadow" (*Peter Schlemihl* 59). The idea that lack of moral integrity causes the shadow to fade is an expression of Chamisso's mockery of petty bourgeois pretenses, while his description of the devil's ability to separate the body from its shadow interrogates the nature and significance of nonmaterial components of human identity. Annemarie Wambach suggests that Chamisso presents us with two narratives which draw on diverging meanings of the shadow. On the one hand, the story's internal logic suggests that Schlemihl is excluded from social intercourse as a punishment for a moment of transgression while, on the other hand, society is described as morally corrupt (Wambach 178). These diverging interpretations are tightly enmeshed, causing Schlemihl a great deal of suffering.

There are moments when Schlemihl is horrified by his guilty imposture as Count Peter, while the story argues that he never lost the purity of his heart (Freund 60). In spite of his endearing qualities, Schlemihl can never quite extricate himself from the contaminating influence of money. Even after he has discarded Fortunatus's fateful purse, the consequences of having—just once—succumbed to his desire for wealth and influence continue to harm him. The novella is full of ambiguities, one of which revolves around whether Schlemihl's craving for money (or rather for financial security) is indicted as a moral shortcoming or whether it is treated as an understandable, and hence forgivable, sin. In any event, it is impossible to tell whether *Peter Schlemihl* is a story about a repentant sinner who finds inner peace, although failing to be reintegrated into a social community, or whether it is an indictment of a society which is based on empty pretenses and ruthless struggles for power.

Concerning Chamisso's ambiguous use of "shadow" and "soul," Marko Pavlyshyn argues that Chamisso eclectically blends Christian associations of "soul" with concepts borrowed from Platonic and idealist philosophy (132). Although the narrative logic insists that there is a radical difference between "shadow" and "soul," Pavlyshyn is right to draw attention to their synonymous function: "Schlemihl is indifferent to the consequences of his first bargain with the devil until he realizes that an existence without shadow has marred his chances of gaining his beloved Mina" (134).

In spite of the semantic contiguity between "shadow" and "soul," the novella dramatizes its hero's refusal to part with his soul and hence explicitly differentiates between Schlemihl and the traditional Faustus figure. Schlemihl is named after a stock figure from Jewish folklore, a character who is proverbially unfortunate but whose simplicity is also an expression of his innocence and purity of heart (Haarmann 43–54, 46–47). Chamisso's own loving description of a character who may be clumsy but of childlike innocence has trivialized the fact that Schlemihl "fails to resist the corrupt materialism which accompanies wealth and dehumanizes all values" (Pavlyshyn 138).

Still, Schlemihl ends up neither in hell nor in irredeemable misery. He experiences great suffering, but at the end of the story, he can counter the concern that is voiced by his faithful servant Bendel and his inaccessible but nevertheless devoted Mina: "Your old friend too is better provided for than formerly, and if he does penance it is penance of reconciliation" (*Peter Schlemihl* 120). Chamisso's phrase "Busse der Versöhnung" (562) seems ambiguous. While the core meaning of "Busse" is that of an act of penance or contrition performed by a sinner desiring to atone for his transgressions, the combination of "Busse" and "Versöhnung" establishes a relationship between penance and reconciliation. However, the grammatical structure makes it impossible to tell whether Schlemihl is doing penance in order to obtain reconciliation or whether the kind of reconciliation experienced by him might itself be a punishment. The latter interpretation of "Busse der Versöhung" might come across as an improbable parallel meaning excluded by the context. It nevertheless underlines an important detail in Chamisso's adaptation of the typical Faust narrative: Schlemihl experiences great suffering, but he can escape from the verdict of damnation which concludes early modern versions of the Faust legend and he can be saved without divine or female intercession.

By describing a character who transgresses the high moral code with which he identifies, Chamisso shifts the emphasis from a study of the limits of acceptable behavior to an investigation of what constitutes human completeness. In the course of his life as a botanical traveler, Schlemihl makes every effort to cultivate his integrity. Most importantly, he learns to liberate himself from the defining gaze of fellow beings who judge him incapable of meeting the standards and values of their culture. Engaging with the difficulties of a sensitive character struggling to experience himself as a member of a society, the novella explores the development of consciousness as something that is inseparable from the ability to act with honesty and integrity.

Before discussing further the interconnections between Chamisso's understanding of identity and his idea of honesty and responsibility, I would like to comment on recent developments in the neurosciences which similarly argue for the inseparability between the self's ability to cause and sense its experience of itself.

Antonio Damasio's neuroscientific approach to consciousness concentrates on the processes involved in the emergence of consciousness to explain the parallelism between the active and the receiving functions of consciousness. Damasio outlines "two stages of evolutionary development of the self, the self-as-knower having had its origin in the self-as-object" (8). He argues that the deeply engrained, popular understanding of the self as a character who oversees the control of a mental switchboard is completely wrong. A more correct view, he says, is that the self emerges as a result of an interplay between embodied experience and awareness of the capacity for physical sensation. Damasio employs the metaphor of a "symphony of Wagnerian proportions" to describe the complexity of the events that lead to the emergence of consciousness. He concludes that the capacity for creating a sense of self, along with the experiences collected in the course of a life, comes into being "only as life unfolds" (18).

Reading *Peter Schlemihl* via Damasio helps us understand the beneficial consequences of the moral transgression and subsequent suffering of Chamisso's hero. Schlemihl's goal, accordingly, is not merely that of coming to sense (physical and intellectual) stimuli but also of being jolted out of his state of narcissistic detachment into a conscious and responsible recognition of himself and his place in the world.

A similar account of the emergence of consciousness (as a sensory-intellectual experience of embodied existence) has been offered by Daniel Heller-Roazen. His fascinating history of the self's quest for self-consciousness proposes the existence of a sense of sensing: the "inner touch." Heller-Roazen's arguments can be used to explain why Schlemihl's quest for self-experience progresses most effectively at the moment when the self is threatened. Heller-Roazen discusses Rousseau's account of an unpleasant encounter with a large dog which ran towards him at full speed and he concludes that "it is no accident that the philosopher comes to himself in being thrown to the ground. This was an event of the destruction and survival of the self: 'In this instant,' the philosopher wrote, in deliberate terms, 'I was being born again'" (217).

Without extraneous stimuli there is no response, and without extraneous intrusions into the self's eudaemonic cocoon, there is no consciousness. At the beginning of his strange story, Schlemihl has little awareness of himself. When the devil appears in the guise of an elderly gentleman, dressed in inconspicuous grey, he recoils but he does so as a cowed creature who protests that he has nothing to offer, rather than as a confident and conscious owner of a unique self. The devil's flattering draws him out of his apathy when he accosts Schlemihl as follows:

> During the short time when I enjoyed the happiness of being near you, I observed, Sir,—will you allow me to say so—I observed, with unutterable admiration, the beautiful, beautiful shadow in the sun, which with a certain noble contempt, and perhaps without being aware of it, you threw off from your feet. (31)

The reader shares Schlemihl's surprise and incredulity about his interlocutor's assertion that a shadow is something special, wondering at anyone who might believe that skill is required for the body to cast a shadow. It is the grey fellow's admiration of the shadow's beauty which draws attention to it as something special. While the novella strictly concentrates on the physical shadow, cast by the material body, its metaphorical dimension comments on the devil's attempt to gain control over Schlemihl's image-making capacity, that is, his imagination but also his capacity for projecting, or asserting, himself (Braun). Herdman speculates about the nature of the loss symbolized by the Schlemihl story: "probably it is the psychic wholeness on which he depends to function in the world" (42). Schlemihl is certainly incomplete without his shadow. While he loses the capacity to make his presence felt as a prerequisite to being accepted by his society, we might say that he also gains something. At the end of the story, he may still lack certain qualities (such as the ability to make himself generally accepted) but he has asserted his integrity in the eye of the reader.

The Shadow of the Author: Schlemihl and Chamisso

In the second edition of *Peter Schlemihl* (1834) (see Hoffmann 49), Chamisso added a prefatory poem which directly addresses the hero of his novella and which compares his own fortunes to those of his imaginary creation. Chamisso also insists that Schlemihl is an historical personage. It is in the same spirit of make-believe that Schlemihl recounts the moment of his worst weakness in the form of a confession to his author, stating that the first experience of owning mountains of gold unleashed a filthy lust which led him to throw himself physically onto the gold and wallow in it until he fell asleep. The dream following on from this experience is about his dear Chamisso, his author, no longer alive.

The moment when Schlemihl surrenders to his fateful lust for gold gives rise to an encounter with his author. By contrast with Roland Barthes's argument that the imaginative freedom of the reader is obtained by the death of the author, Chamisso's story dramatizes the death of himself as author as a means of asserting himself as author. The fuzzy boundaries between being and imagination are challenged because the death of the author enables his imaginary character to gain a deeper level of consciousness than he had ever possessed. On one level, Schlemihl's act of succumbing to the greedy pleasure of fingering the coins is so detrimental to the sensitive spirit of the author that it occasions a fantasy of his death. But the created character's transgressive disregard for higher values also makes him realize the threat of death, and renders him conscious of the finite nature of existence. Paradoxically, it is the appearance of evil which both challenges and affirms the validity of the author's creative energy. It releases him from a state of vacuum into "a region in which the solitary thinker is never by himself" (Heller-Roazen 218). On the level of narrative, the imaginary character's dream about the death of his author threatens the termination of the story and by doing so causes the narrative to gather new momentum.

Schlemihl's nightmare about the death of his author is contrasted with a happy dream which he experiences after he throws away the fateful purse: he sees Bendel and Mina wearing festive garlands. He says that it appeared that Chamisso was ahead of him, in the crowd, and everyone seemed happy, with no shadows despite the light. When Schlemihl gets rid of the devil's gold, he is rewarded with a happy dream. While taking pleasure in the joyful experience, he also presents himself as an author who makes every effort to retain the receding images of his "soul" ("Seele"). His "soul" hence becomes equated with his imaginative faculty, or "his cognitive organ" (Pavlyshyn 133).

Schlemihl recounts his dream about a shadowless existence with a great deal of pleasure. As Wambach emphasizes, the dream is not marked by escapism (181). While the passage gives vent to wistful regret about the illusory quality of his dream, it also shows his egalitarian disregard for materialist shadows which play such an important role in everyday life. Schlemihl's dream hence describes a vision according to which human relationships can be formed on the basis of inner qualities rather than external factors.

"What Sort of a Thing is Your Soul?"

When the man in grey allows Schlemihl to see his shadow once again, he is appalled by its subservience to the will of another person. Looking at the two shadows at the feet of his grey interlocutor, he comments that "mine seemed to belong to him as much as his own; it accommodated itself to all his movements and all his necessities" (*Peter Schlemihl* 75). The recognition that it is the devil whose physical movements his shadow has mimicked enhances Schlemihl's sense of loss.

This painful experience destroys his last bit of self-control: "When I saw my poor shadow again, after so long a separation, and found it applied to such base uses, at a moment when for its sake I was suffering nameless anguish, my heart broke within me, and I began to weep most bitterly" (75). The devil enjoys Schlemihl's misery and further taunts him by comparing the relationship between body and shadow with that between the human being and his worldly possessions: "Excellent purse! and even if the moths had devoured your shadow, there would be a strong bond of union between us" (101). The devil's power, though, is challenged when Schlemihl shows himself capable of severing the bond to his worldly possessions. He remains disconnected from his physical shadow but he has asserted his willpower and, what is more, he has acted according to the dictates of the moral core of his being: his soul.

I have already argued that discussion of the meanings of the "shadow" is throughout the story coupled with a study of the meanings of "soul." To this end, the story scrutinizes the agents (or personified forces) which dictate the moral framework of human behavior: God and the devil. Schlemihl's tempter comments in a conciliatory tone that "the devil is not so black as he is represented" (98). It is in the spirit of wishing to conform to the norms of polite society that he appears in the guise of an unobtrusive gentleman in grey who confronts Schlemihl with the philosophical arguments of the period:

> May I then be allowed to ask, what sort of a thing is your soul? Have you
> ever seen it? Do you know what will become of it when you are once de-
> parted? Rejoice that you have found somebody to take notice of it; to buy,
> even during your lifetime, the reversion of this X, this galvanic power, this
> polarising influence, or whatever the silly trifle may turn out to be; to pay
> for it with your bodily shadow, with something really substantial; the hand
> of your mistress, the fulfilment of your prayers. Or will you rather deliver
> over the sweet maiden to that contemptible scoundrel, Mr. Rascal? (73)

The devil has distanced himself from the paraphernalia of the traditional fantasies of a horned creature with a cloven hoof. He has further updated his self-presentation by familiarizing himself with scientific attempts to explain the nature of the soul (Goodall 117–32; Priestley 121–23). Employing the scientific jargon of his age, he refers to the soul as the variable "X," a ploy that draws attention to its status as an object of investigation, rather than as a known entity. The terms used to describe the soul relegate it to the demesnes of the infinitesimally small or otherwise evanescent that escape the measuring and observing powers of scientific instruments.

The devil presents himself as one of the cognoscenti of early nineteenth-century science when he refers to the hypothesis that the soul might be the seat of the electrical currents which had recently been identified as a vital component of the muscles: he talks about the idea of its being a galvanic force, a part of animal magnetism or a magnetic principle that causes the polarization which might generate not only physical but also metaphysical processes. This eloquent overview of scientific theories touches on contemporary attempts to account for metaphysical principles. When he reduces what was traditionally described as the sacred core of being to a material entity, Schlemihl's tempter behaves like Mephistopheles in Goethe's *Faust* when he corrupts a young student with his description of the insidious power afforded by the study of metaphysics, rather than inculcating respectful admiration for the soul (line 1949).

In a rhetorical gesture that illustrates the subtlety of the devil, Chamisso's devil claims that the whole spectrum of scientific speculations is less substantive than humankind's "leibhaftiger Schatten" (532). The translation of this phrase as "bodily shadow" (73) loses the associations of the German formulation. The adjective "leibhaftig" emphasizes the shadow's indivisible bond with a body and it also alludes to a euphemistic method of referring to the devil without naming him: "der

Leibhaftige." The resulting pun focuses on the body as an embodiment of evil which connects the idea of the shadow (as a both insubstantial and physical quality) to the culturally defined personification of evil. Thence a web of associations suggests that there is something devilish about the body's physicality, which, of course, is an idea that has pervaded the history of Christian culture (Nuttall 9).

Presenting himself as a man of the world, the grey tempter is familiar with the most recent arguments in natural science: "He unfolded his views of life and the world, and soon introduced metaphysics, from whence the word was to emanate which should solve all mysteries" (94). Chamisso here discusses the quest for the one "word" which is presumed capable of answering all questions while also affirming the meaning of life: the "Wort" invoked by the grey philosopher alludes to the first verse of St. John's Gospel, where the word is described as the original creative agency or force: "In the beginning was the Word, and the Word was with God, and the Word was God." The passage also alludes to a seminal moment in Goethe's *Faust* when his hero is trying to find a German equivalent that can capture the full import of the word which has the power to call into existence that which it enunciates. Marveling about this phenomenon, Goethe's Faust believes that the extraordinary capacity of the creating force needs to be described by a term that encapsulates activity or agency and hence substitutes the alternative formulation "in the beginning was the act" ("im Anfang war die Tat!") (lines 1224–37).

By contrast, Schlemihl's grey interlocutor makes no attempt to relate the understanding of the "word" to any larger concept or phenomenon in the real or imagined past of humankind. Nor does he try to relate his abstract arguments to the feelings of his listener. Schlemihl acknowledges that he is impressed by his grey companion's intellectual skills: "This rhetorician appeared to me to build his firmly cemented edifice with great ability. It seemed to bear itself on its firm and solid foundation, and stood, as it were, on its own absolute necessity" (95). But Schlemihl also says that the argument failed to move him: "I should have cheerfully surrendered myself to him, if he would have taken possession of my soul as well as of my understanding" (95).

When Schlemihl comments that the grey philosopher failed to take "possession of my soul," he plays with another meaning of the term, foregrounding the idea of the soul as the "cognitive organ" which enables a person to be moved (Pavlyshyn 133). Chamisso is playfully reminding us that the devil's tireless scheming to get hold of Schlemihl's soul could have been achieved easily, if he had tried to touch it with inspiring sentiments. The context makes it clear, however, that "taking possession" of the soul does not mean the same as having control over it. If the devil had attempted to stir the soul with sublime sentiments, he would not be the embodiment of evil. It is in this vein that Schlemihl prefaces the description of the rhetorician's empty philosophical construct with the observation that he feels uncomfortable about speculation. Addressing Chamisso as his mentor and friend, he says, "From that time I have let many things be settled as they could, renounced much which I might have understood or learnt, and, following your counsels by trusting to my innate senses, that voice of the heart, I have gone forward in my own road as far as I was able" (95). In his own attempt to sense the core of his being, Schlemihl talks about the existence of a moral sense, which he seeks to define more closely when he says that it is the "voice of the heart" ("Stimme in mir"). The English translation refers to "innate senses" in the plural and, moreover, locates the source of the voice of intuition in the heart (Heller-Roazen 145). Rather than violate Chamisso's ideas, the translation here draws attention to the metaphorical quality of all concepts which are embraced by the term "soul."

An important feature of the novella is that it playfully enmeshes different meanings which are grounded in their own narrative traditions and philosophical-medical schools of thought. Most importantly, it places the established Christian understanding of the soul, which informs the traditional Faust plot, side by side with alternative explanations of the nonmaterial qualities of human existence. Just before the grey tormentor leaves Schlemihl for the last time, he gives him a glimpse of the fortune of the rich Thomas John, who had so haughtily treated the poor traveler at the beginning of the tale. Reaching one last time into his endlessly resourceful pockets, the grey fellow draws out the pale and dehumanized figure of Thomas John. Acting like a character in a morality play or one of the damned in Dante's *Divina Commedia*, John grants the narrator's request that he should summarize his condition: "I have been judged by the just judgment of the Lord. I have been condemned by the just judgment of the Lord" ("Justo judicio Dei judicatus sum. Justo judicio Dei condemnatus sum") (551). Schlemihl is horrified so dreadfully that he hurls the fateful purse into the deepest abyss and addresses his tormentor with the words familiar from popular legends about the devil: "I conjure thee, in the name of God, monster, begone, and never again appear before these eyes" (102). The theatricality of the episode, however, is not only at odds with the rest of the narrative but the stylistic divergence also interrogates the implications of this scene. For example, it makes us ask whether there is any reason to accept the Latin phrase as reliable evidence.

In my book on early versions of the Faust typology, I argued that most literary versions of the Faust narrative challenge the idea that the Faustian character should end up in hell. I interpreted Faust, or Faustus, as a personification of the independent and courageous scientist and explorer. When Enlightenment philosophy rendered the Faustian craving for knowledge legitimate, later treatments, such as Goethe's version of the typology, came to revolve around the morality of power and wealth.

Schlemihl's spontaneous horror in the presence of the grey tempter gives voice to the fear with which the cautionary tale traditionally frames the bold investigations of metaphysical assumptions. But *Peter Schlemihl* also contrasts the chapbooks' visceral fear of the devil as the one who gets the sinner's soul with a post-Enlightenment portrayal of the soul as a metaphor for consciousness. It is in the vein of Schlemihl's religiously inspired, philosophical reflections that he summarizes his reasons for refusing to sell his "soul." He simply states, "I knew not how it would end" (99). While Schlemihl asserts that he does not "know" what will happen when he dies, he does not simply succumb to skeptical nihilism. Instead he gives voice to a deeply engrained trust in the existence of something inside himself, an inner voice or inner sense, which prevents him from selling, or betraying, himself.

At this point it is worth remembering that the impossibility of knowing was at the heart of Chamisso's explicitly named Faust story. In his youthful experimental work, "Faust" (1803), he portrays a hero who is prepared to commit suicide in order to gain certainty (Haarmann 46). When he realizes that no objective knowledge can be gained as long as he is alive, he decides to conclude his quest by pushing a sword into his own heart while he states, "Eternal damnation, into your lap!—Perhaps only destruction, perhaps recognition, but certainty in spite of everything" ("Verdammnis, ewige, in deinen Schoss!—Vielleicht Vernichtung nur, vielleicht Erkenntnis, Gewißheit doch" ["Faust" 471–82]).

Chamisso's Faust is an angry young man who courageously lays the blame for the human craving for knowledge at the door of his maker because he created him with a mind that desires to plumb the mysteries of existence (476). The piece is ambiguously poised between confirming the need for the blind faith demanded of the simple Christian and a Promethean challenge to a tyrannical godhead. It nevertheless also outlines the theory of self (or consciousness) which he was to develop in *Peter Schlemihl* a decade later. In his opening monologue, Chamisso's Faust says:

> the inner light casts the images out there
> into the suspended night,
> an empty reflection of our own ego,
> and this is how the world which we recognize comes into being.

> Es wirft das Licht, das innre, dort hinaus
> Auf ausgespannte Nacht die Bilder hin,
> Ein leerer Widerschein des eignen Ichs,
> Und so entsteht die Welt, die ich erkenne. (472)

The metaphor of the "ausgespannte Nacht" describes darkness as a substance that can be stretched out like a canvas so that it renders visible the images projected onto it. This image may have been inspired by historical fascination with the magic lantern. In this passage, though, Chamisso talks of a light that has its source inside the self. By contrast with the Platonic theory of understanding, there is neither an external source of light nor are there material objects outside the self. Chamisso's imagery shows that he is following F. W. J. Schelling, who posited an "absolute identity" between the object and the subject of investigation, so that the entire world comes to be described as a projection of inner realities: "Nature is to be visible mind [*Geist*], mind invisible nature. *Here*, therefore, in the absolute identity of the mind *in* us and the nature *outside* us, the problem of how a nature outside ourselves is possible must dissolve" (Schelling, qtd. in Bowie 39; Knellwolf, "Geographic" 50–55).

In contrast with his earlier "Faust," Chamisso's *Peter Schlemihl* notably refrains from the speculative reasoning that is associated with the quest for absolutes.

Although he takes for granted Schelling's argument that there is a bond ("Band") which links all parts of a pantheistically connected universe, he insists that this bond can only be recognized through lived experience rather than abstract reasoning (Schelling 458; Pavlyshyn 137).

Conclusion

My interpretation of Chamisso's mature version of the Faust narrative has argued that his *Peter Schlemihl* draws on a long tradition of characters who are described as having entered into a pact with the devil. Chamisso's most important transformation of the narrative pattern is that he sketches a Faust character who can atone for his sins and escape damnation through his own initiative.

Schlemihl's deeply human cravings for wealth, power, and belonging get him into trouble, but it is also his ability to face the consequences of his materialism that outlines him as a responsible character. Schlemihl is saved, but he is saved from rabid materialism, rather than from the fire and brimstone of the traditional hell. For all his flaws, he is also saved because he is capable of inspiring love and loyalty: in his servant Bendel, in his beloved Mina, who treasures his memory despite her obedience to her parents, and in his dog. (That his companion is a poodle seems a playful allusion to Goethe's *Faust*.) Finally, Schlemihl is also loved by Chamisso himself, who says in his letter to Julius Eduard Hitzig of September 27, 1813, which came to be included in most later editions of the novella, "I loved him" ("Ich hatte ihn lieb") (494).

The description of Schlemihl's encounter with evil, moreover, teaches us that evil can sometimes be the cause of good. The devil's influence is not thoroughly evil, for example, insofar as the money left over from Schlemihl's period of wealth is used for the foundation of a hospital. In this sense Chamisso illustrates a seminal tenet of Carl Jung's psychology: the encounter with evil is a necessary step in the human quest for completeness. The experiences triggered by Schlemihl's encounter with evil enabled him to grow and develop.

However, I would like to go further and conclude with the observation that *Peter Schlemihl* suggests that the experience of evil, instanced by a moral transgression, does not in itself lead the hero to completeness. Something else is required before the self can experience and assert itself as a sentient being. Schlemihl can atone for his thoughtless greed by serving the interests of science as a botanical traveler and by cultivating his higher self. It is his devoted study of flora and fauna, and his loving dealings with his authors (Chamisso and the creator of the universe), which enable him to feel fully alive. In other words, he reaches the state of consciousness which Heller-Roazen, quoting Thomas Aquinas, describes as the supreme moment when "we sense and we think that we are" (299). *Peter Schlemihl* might be read as an illustration of the claim that it is at the moment when we have learnt to experience ourselves as feeling and thinking beings, that is, when we have come to sense ourselves as sensing, that we attain moral integrity.

Chamisso remained aware that such high ideals could not be realized in daily life. It seems that his realistic assessment of the immoral principles on which social success is based prevented him from sketching a proper happy end for his quasi-autobiographical novella. While Schlemihl escapes the hell of the early modern Faust figures, he has to be satisfied with a compromise that leaves him as a social outsider for the rest of his life. Schlemihl dreams of an ideal society, where people are accepted for what they are, instead of depending on the shadows cast by their social recognition. But he also accepts the discrepancy between the ideal and the real world. The end of the story accordingly shows Peter Schlemihl to have found a niche for himself, although he can never be part of the establishment.

Acknowledgments

Christa Knellwolf King acknowledges the assistance of Peter King. The research for her article was conducted during a Lise-Meitner fellowship awarded by the Austrian Science Fund (FWF), project M 1290-G20.

Works Cited

Bowie, Andrew. *Schelling and Modern European Philosophy*. London: Routledge, 1993.

Braun, Peter. *Mediale Mimesis: Licht- und Schattenspiele bei Adelbert von Chamisso und Justinus Kerner*. München: Fink, 2007.

Chamisso, Adelbert von. "Faust, Ein Versuch." *Adelbert v. Chamissos sämtliche Werke*. Vol. 1. Leipzig: Bibliographische Anstalt, 1917. 471–82.

Chamisso, Adelbert von. *Fortunati Glückseckel und Wunschhütlein: Ein Spiel (1806)*. Ed. E. F. Kossmann. Nendeln, Liechtenstein: Kraus, 1968.

Chamisso, Adelbert von. *Korrespondenzen und Transformationen: neue Perspektiven auf Adelbert von Chamisso*. Ed. Maria-Theres Federhofer and Jutta Weber. Göttingen: V&R Unipress, 2012.

Chamisso, Adelbert von. *Peter Schlemihl*. Trans. John Bowring. London: Robert Hardwicke, 1861. <http://www.gutenberg.org/files/21943/21943-h/21943-h.htm>.

Chamisso, Adelbert von. *Peter Schlemihl. Adelbert v. Chamissos sämtliche Werke*. Vol. 1. Leipzig: Bibliographische Anstalt, 1917. 493–564.

Damasio, Antonio. *Self Comes to Mind: Constructing the Conscious Brain*. London: William Heinemann, 2010.

Flores, Ralph. "The Lost Shadow of Peter Schlemihl." *The German Quarterly* 47.4 (1974): 567–84.

Freund, Winfried. *Literarische Phantastik: die phantastische Novelle von Tieck bis Storm*. Stuttgart: Verlag W. Kohlhammer, 1990.

Fröhler, Birgit. *Seelenspiegel und Schatten-Ich: Doppelgängermotiv und Anthropologie in der Literatur der deutschen Romantik*. Marburg: Tectum-Verlag, 2004.

Goethe, Johann Wolfgang von. *Faust. Eine Tragödie, Erster Teil*. Stuttgart: Philipp Reclam, 1986.

Goodall, Jane. "Electrical Romanticism." *Frankenstein's Science: Experimentation and Discovery in Romantic Culture*. Ed. Christa Knellwolf and Jane R. Goodall. Aldershot: Ashgate, 2008. 117–32.

Haarmann, Herrmann. "Fremd in der Welt, zu Hause in der Sprache: Adelbert von Chamisso und die Berliner Romantik." *Internationales Archiv für Sozialgeschichte der deutschen Literatur (IASL)* 15.2 (1976): 43–54.

Haldane, Michael. "Two Nineteenth-Century English Translators of Chamisso's *Peter Schlemihl*: Sir John Bowring and Emilie de Rouillon. A Comparative Analysis." *English Studies* 89.6 (2008): 662–78.

Heller-Roazen, Daniel. *The Inner Touch: Archaeology of a Sensation*. New York: Zone Books, 2009.

Herdman, John. *The Double in Nineteenth-Century Fiction: The Shadow Life*. New York: St. Martin's, 1991.

Hoffmann, Volker. "Peter Schlemihl und der Graue: Fremdverführung als teuflische Selbsverführung." *Der gefundene Schatten: Chamisso-Reden 1985 bis 1993*. Ed. Dietrich Krusche and Hilde Domin. Munich: A-1-Verlag, 1993. 46–64.

Jung, Carl Gustav. *Jung on Evil*. Ed. Murray Stein. London: Routledge, 1995.

Knellwolf King, Christa. *Faustus and the Promises of the New Science: From the Chapbooks to Harlequin Faustus, c. 1580–1730*. Aldershot: Ashgate, 2009.

Lahnstein, Peter. *Adelbert von Chamisso: Der Preuße aus Frankreich*. München: List Verlag, 1984.

Lehmann, Ruth. *Der Mann ohne Schatten in Wort und Bild: Illustrationen zu Chamissos "Peter Schlemihl" im 19. und 20. Jahrhundert*. Frankfurt: Peter Lang, 1995.

Nuttall, A.D. *The Alternative Trinity: Gnostic Heresy in Marlowe, Milton, and Blake*. Oxford: Clarendon, 1998.

Pavlyshyn, Marko. "Gold, Guilt and Scholarship: Adelbert von Chamisso's *Peter Schlemihl*." *Passagen: 50 Jahre Germanistik an der Monash Universität / Passages: 50 Years of German Studies at Monash University*. Ed. Franz-Josef Deiters, Axel Fliethmann, and Christiane Weller. St. Ingbert: Röhrig Universitätsverlag, 2010.

Priestley, Joseph. *Disquisitions Relating to Matter and Spirit*. London: For J. Johnson, 1777.

Reber, Natalie. *Studien zum Motiv des Doppelgängers bei Dostojevkij und E.T.A. Hoffmann*. Giessen: Wilhelm Schmitz, 1964.

Schelling, F. W. J. *Von der Weltseele*. Ed. Otto Weiss. Leipzig: Felix Meiner, 1911.

Schmid, Günther. *Chamisso als Naturforscher. Eine Bibliographie*. Leipzig: Köhler, 1942.

Schwann, Jürgen. *Vom "Faust" zum "Peter Schlemihl: Kohärenz und Kontinuität im Werk Adelbert von Chamissos*. Tübingen: Gunter Narr, 1984.

Solomon, Robert C. *Wicked Pleasures: Meditations on the Seven "Deadly" Sins*. Lanham: Rowman and Littlefield, 1999.

Wambach, Annemarie. "'Fortunati Wünschhütlein und Glückssäckel' in neuem Gewand: Adelbert von Chamissos *Peter Schlemihl.*" *The German Quarterly* 67.2 (1994): 173–84.

Webber, Andrew J. *The Doppelgänger: Double Visions in German Literature.* Oxford: Clarendon, 1996.

Author's Profile

Christa Knellwolf King teaches at Sultan Qaboos University, Oman. She is the author of *Faustus and the Promises of the New Science.* Her edited collections of essays include *The Cambridge History of Literary Criticism, Exoticism and the Culture of Exploration,* and *The Enlightenment World,* and she is completing a monograph on the role of naval travel accounts in the dissemination of imperial ideology. She is leading a research group, "Cognitive Studies of Culture," which concentrates on cognitive approaches to the interpretation of emotion.

Chapter 3

Lord Byron's Faustian Plays *Manfred* (1817), *Cain* (1821), and *The Deformed Transformed* (1822)

Frederick Burwick

Abstract

In his article, "Lord Byron's Faustian Plays *Manfred* (1817), *Cain* (1821), and *The Deformed Transformed* (1822)," Frederick Burwick examines the indebtedness of Byron's dramas to Goethe's *Faust*. The parallels between *Faust* and *Manfred* reside principally in repudiation of the pretenses of knowledge, the ruin of an innocent woman (Gretchen and Astarte), and the refusal to be morally governed by church or the so-called powers of evil (Mephistopheles and Arimanes). In *Cain* the titular hero, like Goethe's Faust with Mephistopheles, engages in probing debate with Lucifer over the power of the individual will. In the third play, *The Deformed Transformed*, Byron adopts as well the pact with the devil as crucial to the plot.

According to Robert Southey, Lord Byron, together with Percy Bysshe Shelley, promulgated a Satanic School of poetry through their exhibitions of "a Satanic spirit of pride and audacious impiety" (206). Both Shelley and Byron admired the achievement of Johann Wolfgang von Goethe: Shelley in his translation of the "Prologue in Heaven" ("Prolog im Himmel") and the "Walpurgis Night" ("Walpurgisnacht"); Byron in his appropriation of Faustian motifs in his plays *Manfred* (1817), *Cain* (1821), and *The Deformed Transformed* (1822). Like Goethe (*Faust* line 1112), Byron emphasized the internalized struggle; but unlike Goethe, the Byronic character is figured as an autobiographical projection. Like Goethe, and also like Christopher Marlowe, Byron inserted sardonic wit spiced with irony, sexual innuendo, and blasphemy. In appropriating Faust into the character of Manfred, Cain, and Arnold, Byron renders him excessively preoccupied with his own image and appearance, constantly aware of spectators and commanding their attention to watching. Although I am indebted to previous commentators, I choose to augment Byron's role in the English reception of Goethe by considering as well Goethe's reception of that reception (Butler; Chew; Parker; Robertson; Thorsley). According to Goethe, both Byron and the Byronic Faust are ambitious, clever, narcissistic, hypochondriacal, and too empirical. When Goethe in 1827 created his own Byronic character—Euphorion, the child of Faust and Helena (*Faust* lines 9588–961)—these were the predominant attributes.

During the summer of 1816, when Byron, John Polidori, Percy Bysshe Shelley, and Mary Shelley were gathered at the Villa Diodati, they were joined by another visitor from England, Matthew Gregory Lewis. Byron of course was working on *Manfred*, and Lewis translated for him parts of Goethe's *Faust* (Butler 29). Byron already knew the excerpts translated by Germaine de Staël (181–226). He dedicated *Sardanapalus* (1821) and *Werner* (1822) "to the Illustrious Goethe," and in acknowledging the sources for *The Deformed Transformed* declared that the incomplete drama poem was founded partly on *The Three Brothers* (1803) by Joshua Pickersgill "and partly on the 'Faust' of the great Goethe" (*Deformed* 605).

With historical roots in the Faust legend of the early sixteenth century, the adaptations by Goethe, Byron, and others share a plot in which the protagonist, questing for knowledge or power, risks his soul (Parker; Chew). In the first of Byron's three versions, Manfred makes no pact with the devil and thus in death denies the demons any hold over his spirit. In Byron's second version, Cain seeks a knowledge of death, supplied to him by Lucifer. In the third, Byron engages in none of the discussion of good and evil that recurs in the earlier two plays; rather, he literally incorporates that discussion in the transformation of physical deformity into godlike physical beauty. In all three, Byron disrupts the concept of the Greek *kalon* and denies any abiding unity of the good, true, and beautiful. Act 2 of *Manfred* ends with his encounter with Astarte, and act 3 commences just before sunset. Alone in his tower, Manfred declares,

> There is a calm upon me
> Inexplicable stillness! which till now
> Did not belong to what I knew of life.
> If that I did not know Philosophy
> To be of all our vanities the motliest,
> The merest word that ever fooled the ear
> From out the schoolman's jargon, I should deem
> The golden secret, the sought "Kalon," found,
> And seated in my soul. It will not last,
> But it is well to have known it, though but once:
> It hath enlarged my thoughts with a new sense,
> And I within my tablets would note down
> That there is such a feeling. (3.1.6–18)

The classical concept of the ideal is altered in two significant ways: it is only a feeling and it will not last. Although Goethe chose to mediate rather than utterly reject the claims of ideal beauty, he too affirmed the persistent interaction of knowing and feeling, permanence and change.

Manfred opens, as did Goethe's *Faust* (1808) and Marlowe's *Doctor Faustus* (published 1604), with a scene of abjuration. "Settle thy studies Faustus," Marlowe's character tells himself, "and beginne / To sound the depth of that thou wilt professe" (1.1.1–2). Aristotle's Analytics, Galen's Medicine, Justinian's Law are put aside, for Faustus will now devote his mind to mastering necromancy (1.1.1–60). Goethe's Faust similarly dismisses his study of the traditional disciplines—Philosophy, Law, Medicine, Theology—as having failed to bring him closer to the knowledge he seeks (lines 354–59). The abjuration scene occurs in other early plays. In Robert Greene's *Friar Bacon and Friar Bungay* (1594), the faculty charges Friar Bacon for having turned to magic, a trespass he readily confesses:

> What art can worke, the frolicke frier knowes,
> And therefore will I turne my Magicke bookes,
> And straine out Nigromancie to the deepe. (1.2.226–28)

In Shakespeare's *The Tempest* (1611), Prospero's abjuration in the final act is not to adopt but to foreswear magic:

> But this rough magic
> I here abjure . . .
>   . . . I'll break my staff,
> Bury it certain fathoms in the earth,
> And deeper than did ever plummet sound
> I'll drown my book. (5.1.50–57)

Manfred's abjuration of philosophy and science is preceded by his declaration of his ceaseless watching, a vigil which is a leitmotif in all his subsequent encounters. The abjuration of all previous endeavors which "availed not" is followed by the conjuration of the spiritual powers of the universe. Manfred's vigil is a mode of introspection, a constant monitoring of thought and feeling. Manfred seeks to enlist into this egocentric vigil each of those whom he meets in the ensuing scenes. "Look on me," he tells the Chamois Hunter (2.1.42). To the Witch of the Alps his request is that she "look on me in my sleep, / Or watch my watchings" (2.2.129–30). To the Phantom of Astarte he says, "Look on me!" (2.4.120). To the Abbot of St. Maurice, the request is again repeated: "Look on me!" (3.1.138) and "Look upon me!" (3.1.149).

Manfred introduces his abjuration with a broad indictment of all knowledge. In the Hall of Arimanes, the First Destiny declares that Manfred's aspirations have taught him the wisdom of hell: "That knowledge is not happiness" (2.4.59–62). Manfred commands that truth already in the opening lines when he reframes the words of Genesis (2:9,17) to define the futility and fatality of knowing.

> Sorrow is Knowledge: they who know the most
> Must mourn the deepest o'er the fatal truth,
> The Tree of Knowledge is not that of Life. (1.1.10–12)

In *Cain* Byron will again address the significance of these two trees of Eden. Manfred is less concerned with knowing good and evil in consequence of eating the forbidden fruit, as he is with the revelation of forbidden knowledge. Manfred dismisses the three major endeavors of his life: first, the mastery of "Philosophy and science, and the springs / Of wonder and wisdom of the world." Even though his mind had the "power to make these subject to itself . . . they avail not." So too the consequences of good works "availed not," and the ability to vanquish foes with military power "availed not." In this limbo of ineffectuality, there remains no moral constancy or stability. "Good, or evil, life, / Power, passions, all I see in other beings" have "since that all-nameless hour" (1.1.13–25) lost their meaning. That hour, as Manfred reveals in ensuing scenes, was the hour of Astarte's death.

The three-part abjuration is followed by three attempts at conjuration: first he conjures with a "written charm," and then by the "sign, Which makes you tremble." When neither charm nor sign arouse the spirits, he utters a third incantation, "By the strong curse which is upon my soul" (1.1.28–49). This spell calls forth seven spirits (1.1.50–131), first the four elements: air ("From my mansion in the cloud"), earth (dwelling in the mountains, compelling glacier and avalanche), fire (volcanic force, "pillowed on fire, And the lakes of bitumen"), water ("In the blue depth . . . Where the wave hath no strife"); then the three conditions: energy ("I am the rider of the wind, The stirrer of the storm"), darkness ("My dwelling is the shadow of the night"), and light (more particularly, Lucifer, "The star which rules thy destiny"). The spirits declare themselves ready to receive Manfred's command. To Manfred's request for "forgetfulness," the spirits reply that they "can but give thee that which we possess." The forgetfulness that Manfred desires is an end to his unrelenting vigil, the image of "that which is most within me" (1.1.132–50). When he then calls upon the spirits to assume some form that he may behold them, the seventh spirit, the star of his destiny, assumes the shape of Astarte. Manfred faints, and a voice recites an incantational curse,

> By thy brotherhood of Cain,
> I call upon thee! and I compel
> Thyself to be thy proper hell! (1.1.250–52)

As readers of Goethe's *Faust* will recognize, there are parallels to Faust's contemplation of the sign of the macrocosm, his conjuration of the Earth Spirit (lines 450–513), and Faust's spell from the *Clavicula Salomonis* to call for the spirits of the Four Elements, Fire, Water, Air, and Earth (lines 1257–291). From Goethe, Byron borrowed as well the incantation of the Spirits spoken over the slumbering Faust (lines 1447–505).

Byron, of course, had other sources that were less, or not at all, relevant to Goethe's work. Both drew frequently from the Bible. Goethe paid little attention to

John Milton, but Byron cited thrice in *Manfred* the declaration by Satan in *Paradise Lost* (1664) that "The mind is its own place, and it itself / Can make a Heaven of Hell, a Hell of Heaven," lines already echoed in the incantation, "Thyself to be thy proper hell!" (1.254–55). In the scenes with the Chamois Hunter, Byron defines the Swiss sense of liberty with allusions to Wilhelm Tell (Giddey 179–90). For the scene with the Witch of the Alps Byron drew from the legend of Tannhäuser, the celebrated medieval minnesinger who was captivated by the Venus of the Mountain (Tieck; Homer, *Odyssey* 4, 5). For the scene in the Hall of Arimanes Byron may again draw from Milton's description of Satan with the fallen angels in Pandemonium, but Milton introduced no mortal interloper defying Satan's reign.

When Manfred awakens from the trance, he must acknowledge the inefficacy of his conjuration.

> The spirits I have raised abandon me,
> The spells which I have studied baffle me,
> The remedy I recked of tortured me. (1.2.1–3)

They too have "avail'd not." Worse, he has been taunted by the Seventh Spirit, who assumed the form of Astarte. Marlowe had his Mephistopheles first introduce "a Devil dressed like a woman, with fireworks" (2.2.145–48), and Faustus is subsequently granted his desire for the embrace of Helen of Troy (5.1.96–118). Goethe's Faust, too, is tantalized by the image of Helen who appears in the witch's magic mirror (lines 2429–447). More than the influence of Helen on Faust, either in Marlowe or in Goethe, Astarte exerts her sway in *Manfred* beyond the solitary scene in which she appears only to bid him farewell.

Half the lines in *Manfred* belong to Manfred himself; the other characters, with the exception of Astarte, have no abiding role in the plot, appear only in one or two scenes, and function to reveal aspects of Manfred's character. Thus the Chamois-Hunter, living at one with the sublimity of Alpine nature, represents the Swiss spirit of liberty and independence and the ethos of patience in adversity. At a distance he perceives in Manfred one who is "Proud as a free-born peasant," but on closer approach recognizes a "madman" about to leap from the cliff. At the moment when Goethe's Faust raises the lethal dose of opiate poison to his lip, the church-bells and a choir of angels interrupt his suicidal act (lines 686–743). A more aggressive intervention is necessary to halt the suicidal leap of Manfred, whom the Chamois-Hunter seizes with the chastising words, "Stain not our pure vales with thy guilty blood" (1.2.111). Manfred confesses, as he will again and again, the origin of that guilt:

> my blood! the pure warm stream
> Which ran in the veins of my fathers, and in ours
> When we were in our youth, and had one heart,
> And loved each other as we should not love,
> And this was shed: but still it rises up,
> Colouring the clouds, that shut me out from Heaven,
> Where thou art not—and I shall never be. (2.1.24–30)

Recognizing Manfred as the victim of "some half-maddening sin," the Chamois-Hunter urges him to exercise "heavenly patience." When Manfred scorns the advice as useful only for "brutes of burden," the Chamois-Hunter replies that he would not share Manfred's order "for the free fame / Of William Tell," and whatever his sin, "it must be borne, and these wild starts are useless" (2.1.31–41). "Look on me," Manfred answers. He bears his pain by maintaining his vigil, and watching his own thoughts, "I look within" (2.1.42, 72).

Confessing his fatal embrace and the injuries that befell those who loved him (1.1.84–87), Manfred departs from the Chamois-Hunter and descends to the foot of an Alpine waterfall. Beneath the sunbow hovering in the mists of the cataract arises the Witch of the Alps, to whom he again confesses the loss of Astarte from whom he once more requests forgetfulness. In relating his love for Astarte, Manfred reveals a narcissistic fascination with the mirrored image he perceives in the traits and features of his female companion. Astarte, Manfred declares, "was like me in lineaments." This most harmonious of all possible heterosexual relationships is undermined by gender differences, cultural taboos, and familial or social opposition: "I loved her, and destroy'd her! / Not with my hand, but heart—which broke her heart" (2.2.111–21).

Although Byron could have found in Goethe's *Wilhelm Meisters Lehrjahre* (1795–96), the tale of the incestuous love of Mignon's parents, the harper and his sister (Ammerlahn; Becker), brother-sister incest in Manfred's confession was understood by contemporary readers to be Byron's own confession of his illicit relationship with his half-sister, Augusta Mary Byron. Almost exactly five years older than Byron, she first spent time with him while he was at Harrow School in 1804. Augusta wrote to him regularly and helped ease his distress over his quarrels with his mother. On August 17, 1807, Augusta married her cousin, Colonel George Leigh, and had a number of children by him, but Byron was acknowledged as father of her daughter, Elizabeth Medora Leigh. Two years later, on April 25, 1816, his marriage to Annabelle Milbank fell apart and Byron departed from England amidst rumors of incest with his half-sister.

The rumors seemed to be confirmed a year later in *Manfred* (published June 16, 1817) in the implied incestuous relationship between the Count and Astarte (Glass). The titillating gossip was repeatedly revived. Just as *Childe Harold* and *Don Juan* attracted attention for their presumed autobiographical revelations, the character of Manfred was deemed to be a thinly disguised dramatization of a forbidden love between Byron and his half-sister. There was an electric buzz of excitement as the audience waited for the curtain to rise on the premier performance of *Manfred* at Covent Garden (October 29, 1834). The buzz was hushed when the audience witnessed one last spectator take her place in one of the central boxes. The Honorable Augusta Leigh had arrived to watch the play that fueled the stories of incest. Twenty years had passed since the birth of their daughter (April 15, 1814), and ten years since the poet's death at Missolonghi (April 19, 1824), but the old scandals were as lively as ever.

Reiterating his need for spectator participation in his suffering, Manfred tells the Witch of the Alps to "look on me in my sleep, / Or watch my watching" (2.2.129–130). She assures him that she can secure the forgetfulness that he desires, but it will require "obedience to my will" and a surrender to her bidding. Manfred scorns the offer. In his soliloquy that closes the scene, Manfred declares his intention to call the dead, as David had the Witch of Endor summon the ghost of Samuel (1 Sam. 28) or Pausanias had his priests call the spirit of Cleonice (2.2.178–192), so that he could ask her forgiveness (Plutarch, 2, ch. 6). In the brief scene on the summit of the Jungfrau Mountain, the Destinies and Nemesis anticipate the night of "our great festival" (2.3.15), an event that suggests a parallel to the Walpurgis Night in Goethe's *Faust* (Chew 174–78). The ensuing scene has nothing of the witches' orgy atop the Brocken, nothing, that is, other than one essential feature: Faust beholds an apparition of Gretchen (lines 4183–205).

The realm of evil into which Manfred intrudes, as already noted, borrows little from the Pandemonium of Milton's Satan. The emphasis is rather on the bold defiance of the presumed sovereignty of Arimanes. Manfred, like Prometheus defying Jupiter, refuses to "Bow down and worship" (2.4.29–49). Arimanes, who speaks but one word, grants the request to call up the dead. Nemesis calls forth the spirit of Astarte. "Look on me," he tells her, but thrice repeats his more urgent plea, "Speak to me!" (2.4.117–50). Like Pausanias calling the spirit of Cleonice, Manfred wants Astarte's forgiveness, and like Cleonice, Astarte replies with the revelation of his impending death. Thrice she utters his name; thrice she bids him farewell. Her sole message: "Tomorrow ends thine earthly ills" (2.4.150–57).

Act 3 opens, as cited above, with Manfred reflecting on the *kalon* as transitory illusion. He is visited by the Abbot of St. Maurice, who comes to save Manfred's soul. Manfred tells him that there is no charm in prayer, no purification in penitence. As Milton's Satan declared, the mind can "make a Hell of Heaven." His fate, Manfred insists, is a matter exclusively between himself and heaven, and he wants neither church nor priest as his mediator. To behold one who has aged more than a mortal life time, he instructs the Abbot, "Look on me!" And to observe one who has experienced a full range of the maladies of fate, "Look on me!" (3.1.138, 149). In the next short scene, Manfred watches the sinking sun and declares himself ready to follow. Then in the third scene, the servants Herbert and Manuel recall former days—Manfred's youth and his devotion to Astarte. The word "sister" remains, as it does throughout the play, unspoken.

In the final scene, the Abbot returns, but again his offer of prayer is spurned. When the spirits come to claim Manfred's immortal soul, the Abbot makes a futile effort to exorcise them. Manfred, however, rejects their claim. His power, he tells them, "Was purchased by no compact with thy crew," rather by his own "length of watching, strength of mind, and skill" (3.4.114–16). "Back to thy hell!" he commands them, "Thou hast no power upon me." Just as he rejected the mediation of church and priest, he denies the claims of hell's minions. The declaration of Milton's Satan that "The mind is its own place, and it itself / Can make a Heaven of Hell, a

Hell of Heaven" (1.254–55), as I have previously observed, has already been echoed in the lines, "I call upon thee! and compel / Thyself to be thy proper hell!" (1.1.252), and again in the lines, "The innate tortures of that deep Despair, / Which is Remorse without the fear of hell, / But all in all sufficient to itself / Would make a hell of Heaven" (3.1.70–73). The words of Milton's Satan are repeated for the third time:

> The Mind which is immortal makes itself
> Requital for its good or evil thoughts,—
> Is its own origin of ill and end—
> And its own place and time. (3.4.129–32)

The demons are driven off. The Abbot remains at Manfred's side, still urging him to a final prayer. Instead, Manfred bids farewell with a simple statement: "Old man! tis not so difficult to die" (3.4.151).

In *Manfred*, Byron challenges the authority of the clerisy to arbitrate or mediate over questions of individual conscience. It may be a play of guilty self-persecution, but it is not a play of moral absolutes. Indeed, the demand to watch and to look up gives weight to bearing witness and giving testimony rather than to judging, praising, or condemning. The thrice repeated phrase "good or evil" (1.1.21; 2.2.202; 3.4.130) holds those opposites in balance. While Byron in *Manfred* reveals his awareness of Goethe's *Faust* in many incidents, he does not create in the spirit of Lucifer, the star of Manfred's destiny, a seducer or evil companion. *Manfred* has no counterpart to Mephistopheles. That counterpart, however, is fully developed in both *Cain* and *The Deformed Transformed*. In the relationship between Cain and Lucifer Byron emphasizes the risk-taking of intellectual curiosity tempered by an indomitable will, whereas the drama between Arnold and the Stranger exposes gradual corruption and perversion. The description of the serpent in Eden provides an apt motto to *Cain*: "Now the Serpent was more subtil than any beast of the field which the Lord God had made" (Gen 3:1).

Although Manfred declares himself ready to kneel with Arimanes to "The overruling Infinite—the Maker" (2.4.48), and the Abbot expresses his faith in Heaven, Byron's *Manfred* offers no further confirmation of a divine paradise. The existence of hell is sustained by the reign of Arimanes and by the demons who seek to take possession of Manfred's soul. From beginning to end the play never questions a spiritual afterlife. In *Cain*, however, death is a condition completely unknown, therefore the finality of death or the possibility of a future after death are unimagined rather than imponderable. Precisely because of his utter lack of experience, Cain at the outset has little depth of character. In comparison to Manfred or Arnold, he seems awkwardly shallow. In the course of the play, Cain acquires the insights that enable him to challenge the adversary from hell. Defiance of authority, a defining characteristic of the "Byronic hero," is certainly prominent in Cain's behavior, but the wrongs and injustices he claims to oppose seem more the reactions of a petulant child than the motives of one suffering cruel oppression. Another defining characteristic, shared with Goethe's Faust, is the quest for knowledge, especially forbidden knowledge or knowledge presumed to lie beyond mortal comprehension (Thorslev 176–84). Lucifer has no difficult task in nurturing Cain's resentments, but he finds it more difficult to cope with Cain's persistent questioning.

The play opens with the family offering a prayer of thanksgiving to God. Cain refuses to participate because he has nothing for which to be thankful. When Adam reminds him that he should be thankful for life, Cain replies that he is also doomed to death. Eve interprets Cain's response as a further consequence of their trespass for having eaten the fruit of the forbidden tree. Cain blames his parents for not having eaten the fruit of both trees. To Adam's accusation that he speaks the "serpent's words," Cain answers that the serpent spoke the truth:

> it *was* the Tree of Knowledge;
> It *was* the Tree of Life: knowledge is good,
> And Life is good; and how can both be evil? (1.1.36–38)

As Cain explains in his ensuing soliloquy, he regards his mortality as an unjust punishment for Adam and Eve's transgression in the Garden of Eden. Goethe has Mephistopheles revisit the serpent's seduction of Eve when he dons Faust's academic robes and taunts a student. "All theory is grey," he tells the student, "and green / The golden tree of life" ("Grau, teurer Freund, ist alle Theorie. Und grün des Lebens goldner Baum" [lines 2038–39]). And when the student begs that the Doctor write in his album, Mephistopheles inscribes the words that the serpent spoke to Eve, urging her to eat the forbidden fruit: "ye shall be as God, knowing good and evil" ("Eritis sicut Deus scientes bonum et malum" [Gen 3:5; line 2048]).

In *Cain*, as in *Manfred*, the credo of Milton's Satan is reaffirmed: "the mind is its own place." As Lucifer phrases it, "Nothing can / Quench the mind, if the mind will be itself / And centre of surrounding things—'tis made / To sway" (1.1.213–16). In arguing the capacity of mind to make its own hell or heaven, Lucifer also instantiates the consequences of "original sin." Just as the present and future progeny of Adam and Eve are all heirs to the primal sin of their disobedience in eating the forbidden fruit, so too all inherit the effects of having consumed "the fatal apple" of knowledge. The *Ursünde* of humanity is itself not the first cause, but rather the effect of another *Ursünde*: Lucifer's rivalry against God (Schmidt 15–17, 81–83). Goethe links the two by exhibiting the malcontent and melancholy that Faust shares with Mephistopheles (Schmidt 95–107). Byron dramatizes the defiant malcontent in parallel passages in the opening scene when Cain refuses to join in prayers (Parker); at the end of act 2, Lucifer insists on his equality with God: "I have a victor—true; but no superior. / Homage he has from all—but none from me" (2.2.429–30).

Cain has signed no pact with Lucifer, nor need he. The *Ursünde* renders any pact superfluous. Told by the serpent of Eden that eating the fruit of the tree of knowledge would open her eyes so that she would become wise and know good and evil, Eve chose to eat the fruit, and she gave it to Adam as well. In the biblical account, the immediate result is that Adam and Eve knew that they were naked and that they must hide their nakedness (Gen 3:1–7). Ignoring the condition of sexual shame,

Byron emphasizes instead the advent of love. From the love of Adam and Eve are born four children, Cain, Abel, and their sisters Adah and Zillah. Cain takes Adah as his wife, and Abel is wed to Zillah. Cain and Adah have a son and daughter, "My little Enoch! and his lisping sister!" (1.1.438).

The incest that works dark and destructive consequences in *Manfred* is irrelevant here. The contest between good and evil, between life and death, gives way to a more crucial contest between love and knowledge. Lucifer commands in the realm of "science / And sin." He lacks all capacity to love. He demands that Cain choose one or the other. Manfred, in his opening monologue, declared that "Sorrow is knowledge" (1.1.10). Lucifer, under Cain's persistent questioning, must confess that knowledge has not made him happy (1.1.121–22). As Adah readily senses, Lucifer's own unhappiness compels him to destroy happiness in others (1.1.518–19). Affirming knowledge as his choice and Lucifer as his guide, Cain is soon aware of his delusion in supposing the "quest for knowledge" was the "road to happiness" (2.2.230–33). Correlative to his incapacity to feel happiness is Lucifer's inability to love. Cain repeats the question: "Dost thou love nothing?" Lucifer attempts to define love as weakness and a burden: "I pity thee who lovest what must perish." Cain's quick response, "And I thee who lov'st nothing" (2.2.337–38), turns that deficiency back upon Lucifer. For his part, Cain never falters in his love of Adah.

A malcontent and a rebel, Cain nevertheless shows a loving tenderness toward his sister/wife. Nor did his tutelage under Lucifer undermine Cain's sensibility. When Lucifer prepares him for his return home, he encourages him to "multiply the race of Adam, / Eat, drink, toil, tremble, laugh, weep, sleep, and die." Because these are precisely the same human activities that he would probably have indulged even if he had never met Lucifer, Cain rightly asks what he was supposed to learn from Lucifer's teaching. That knowledge, Lucifer replies, is "to know thyself." When Cain responds, "I seem / Nothing," Lucifer congratulates him on a lesson well learned. Cain recognizes the mockery of Lucifer's words, but he comprehends their bitter truth only after he strikes the blow that kills his brother.

Cain's Faustian lust to know (*Wissensbegierde*) is directed to the mystery of mortality and the nature of death, a phenomenon not yet witnessed by the exiles from Eden. In act 1, he recalls keeping watch for the arrival "Of this almighty Death, who is, it seems, / Inevitable" (1.1.258–59). Lucifer assures him that Death "has no shape; but will absorb all things" (1.1.262). To teach Cain a knowledge of death, Lucifer leads him into the "Abyss of Space," where God's catastrophes are heaped, the remnants and revenants of extinct life forms (O'Connor). Buried in the geological layers beneath Eden are the fossil records of eons of life and death (2.2.132–44). Lucifer can show him the death, but cannot lead him there and bring him back again. The revelation that death is but a "prelude" gives Cain the hope that "it leads to something definite" (2.2.413).

When Cain returns to his family in act 3 he bears with him Lucifer's troublesome paradox that life is nothing, but death "leads to something definite." At the climax of the play, Cain murders Abel. The play concludes with Cain's banish-

ment, worse than the loss of Eden because it is darkened by crime against life
itself. The misery of his plight is deepened by the awareness that the suffering
belongs to all his progeny. In murdering his brother Abel, Cain exhibits the consequences of having chosen knowledge over love: love can quell the fires of anger
and rage; knowledge cannot. Immediately repentant, Cain bends over his dead
brother's body: "Oh! for a word more of that gentle voice, / That I may bear to hear
my own again!" And he refers to his preceding thoughts, to the anger of frustration
which had driven him to murder: "I am awake at last—a dreary dream / Had mad-
dened me" (3.1.356–79).

Goethe was impressed by the richness of thought and feeling which Byron
gave to a character who possessed little distinguishing identity in the biblical narrative. His motive for killing his brother, as presented in Genesis, "appears petty and
base" (Chew 120). Byron has developed Cain's character independent of his source.
Goethe may well be right that Byron derived his psychological portrait from his
own "hypochondriacal" introspection. So carefully has Byron developed the several
causes, that when Cain is provoked to sudden anger by his brother's relentless im-
portunity, that atrocity seems so fully explained that it is almost excused (Chew 121).

Similar to Manfred's refusal to bow before Arimanes, or to accept the prayers
of the Abbot, Cain defies both Lucifer and God. "That which I am, I am," Cain
declares, "I did not seek / For life, nor did I make myself" (3.1.509–10). His words
are defiantly independent, but he does not shirk responsibility. He is not trapped,
as Goethe suggests, in sheer negative defiance. Goethe had Mephistopheles define
himself in terms of such negation: "I am the spirit that always negates" ("Ich bin der
Geist, der stets verneint") (line 1338). Cain participated more than Goethe acknowledged in the dynamic quest of Faust. It may well be true that Lucifer as well as Cain
is a "Byronic Hero" (Thorslev 183), but Manfred and Cain rise above the morass of
negativity. Cain, in the most earnest prayer of the play, begs to be able to give his life
to return that of his brother.

Goethe shared the popular interpretation that Byron was an autobiographical
poet and the heroes of the plays and the romances were lightly disguised versions of
himself. As already noted, Goethe described this mode of nurturing the pathological
imagination as "clever" yet "hypochondriacal": "This strange clever poet absorbed
my *Faust* and, hypochondriacally, extracted the strangest nourishment from it. He
fitted the motives to his own purpose and his own manner, so that none remained the
same" ("Dieser seltsame, geistreiche Dichter hat meinen *Faust* in sich aufgenommen
und, hypochondrisch, die seltsamste Nahrung daraus gezogen. Er hat die seinen Zwe-
cken zusagenden Motive auf eigene Weise benutzt, so daß keins mehr dasselbige ist"
[*Werke* 13:640]). The mental sickness exhibited by Byron's characters was consistent
with Goethe's more comprehensive discrimination of the Classical as healthy and
the Romantic as sick ("Das Klassische nenne ich das Gesunde und das Romantische
das Kranke") (*Einzelnheiten* nr. 1031). In spite of finding the diseased mind of the
Byronic character a depressing experience, Goethe expressed highest admiration of
the literary accomplishment: "The reconstruction affects so much of the whole, that

one could hold highly interesting lectures on it and on the similarities and dissimilarities with the model, whereby I cannot deny that at the end I am disturbed by the dreary glow of a boundless, deep despair. The discomfort that one feels is nevertheless accompanied always by admiration and esteem" ("Diese Umbildung ist so aus dem Ganzen, daß man darüber und über die Ähnlichkeit und Unähnlichkeit mit dem Vorbild höchst interessante Vorlesungen halten könnte, wobei ich freilich nicht läugne, daß uns die düstere Gluth einer gränzelosen, reichen Verzweiflung am Ende lästig wird. Doch ist der Verdruß, dem [*sic*] man empfindet, immer mit Bewunderung und Hochachtung verknüpft" [*Werke* 13:640]). Describing Byron as "a talent born to self-torment" ("zu eigener Qual geborenen Talents"), Goethe goes on to explain that Byron/Manfred was haunted by the spirits of two women: Astarte and the nameless and formless Voice. He hints that the identity of the one is revealed only in whispers, and the other is the abiding guilt he bears from a youthful love affair in Florence, when the women's returning husband discovers the affair and murders his wife (*Werke* 13:640–41). Edward Bulwer Lytton observes that, "although Goethe's murder-story about Byron is ludicrously untrue, yet the fact that such a story was circulated, and could be seriously repeated by such a man as Goethe without being resented by Byron himself, offers significant illustration both of what Byron was and what he appeared to his contemporaries" (*Works* 434). Goethe closes the review with a translation of the monologue, "We are the fools of Time and Terror" (*Werke* 13:641–42), following the encounter with the Witch of the Alps (2.2.164–209).

Goethe's observations on *Cain* were not a review, but a response to a review in the *Moniteur* (October 30, 1823) of the French translation and commentary by Antoine Fabre d'Olivet (1767–1825). The numerous errors in Byron's *Cain*, Fabre d'Olivet contended, were derived in part from his reliance on the error-ridden translation of the King James Bible, which Byron then further distorted. Adam was too weak and subservient; Eve too violent and vindictive. Indeed, all of Byron's characters were badly conceived and guilty of specious arguments and perverted ideas, most especially the reiterations of Manicheism (Steffan 409–14). Goethe admitted that he had not read Fabre d'Olivet, but was thoroughly convinced by the counterarguments of the anonymous reviewer in the *Moniteur*. At issue was Byron's representation of two crucial events in act 3: the motivation for murdering Abel, and the mother's curse. Cain returns to his family "more excited," Goethe states, "but not worse than he was" ("So kehrt er zu den Seinigen zurück, aufgeregter, obgleich nicht schlimmer, als er war" [*Werke* 13:643–45]). The excitement is the new awareness of the vast prehistory of life on the planet, a sense of life forms that arose and passed away during the eons prior to the appearance of Adam and Eve in Eden.

Death remains, as before, a mystery, but Cain is now even more thoroughly repulsed by his brother's ritual of animal sacrifice. Abel brings to the altar "The firstlings of the flock, and fat thereof— / A shepherd's humble offering" (3.1.215–16). Cain prepares a sacrifice of fruits and grains. Byron's stage direction describes the ensuing contrast:

The fire upon the altar of Abel kindles into a column of the brightest flame, and ascends to heaven; while a whirlwind throws down the altar of Cain, and scatters the fruits abroad upon the earth.

Not upset by the wind, Cain observes that the scattering of the fruit is good, for "Their seed will bear fresh fruit there ere the summer" (3.1.282–83). Abel, however, declares that Cain has angered God and must now build another altar and pray for forgiveness. Angered by his brother's demand that he prepare a blood sacrifice, Cain tells Abel that his God shall have his sacrifice. The motivation for Cain's murderous act, Goethe maintains, could not have been prepared with more attentive development of the psychological nature of the character. Establishing the motives for a character's action could be achieved through precisely the sort of hypochondriacal projection that Byron often indulged. Such was the argument in *Wilhelm Meisters Theatralische Sendung* (1777–85). As I have observed elsewhere, Goethe critiques the advocacy of an actor identifying with a role. Defining Hamlet as a sensitive young man in an intolerable situation, Wilhelm Meister indulges his own self-image (317). Byron's Cain, too, is a self-image: "We say no more than that the scene in which Abel is killed, is most exquisitely led up to; and what follows is equally great and inestimable. There lies Abel! This is death, of which we have heard so much, the race of man knows just as little about it as before" ("Mehr sagen wir nicht, als daß die Scene, in welcher Abel umkommt, auf das köstlichste motivirt ist; und so ist auch die Folgende gleich groß und unschätzbar. Da liegt nun Abel! Das ist nun der Tod! von dem so viel die Rede war, und das Menschengeschlecht weiß eben so wenig davon als vorher" [*Werke* 13:645]).

Defending Byron against charges of blasphemy and heresy, Goethe contends that throughout *Cain* there runs "a kind of presentiment of the coming of a Saviour" ("eine Art Ahnung auf einen Erlöser" [*Werke* 13:645]). The New Testament references, however, are of questionable orthodoxy, as when the dying Abel anticipates the words of Christ on the cross; "Oh, God! receive thy servant, and / Forgive his slayer, for he knew not what / He did" (3.1.318–20); "Father, forgive them; for they know not what they do" (Lk 23:34). The critic in the *Moniteur* was perfectly right, Goethe concurs, in defending the propriety and purpose of Eve's curse in the final scene. Her anger and outrage are the consequence of her own sin and fall. "Of the scene with the parents, where Eve finally curses the speechless Cain, a scene which our western neighbor has so admirably singled out for praise, there is nothing more to be said; we can only approach the close with admiration and reverence" ("Von der Scene mit dem Eltern, worin Eva zuletzt dem verstummten Kain flucht, die unser westlicher Nachbar so trefflich günstig heraushebt, bleibt uns nichts zu sagen übrig; wir haben uns nur mit Bewunderung und Ehrfurcht dem Schlusse zu nähern" [*Werke* 13:645]).

As Cain recognized in the opening scene, his parents' only blessings and prayers were sad substitutes for the paradise they had lost. As Cain and Adah depart with their two children, Adah laments that Abel has left no children who may have been a "fountain for a gentler race." Her farewell is a blessing to Abel: "Peace be with him," to which Cain adds his own sense of ever-banished peace: "But with *me*!" Goethe agreed with his daughter-in-law, Ottilie von Goethe, who claimed that Cain's last three words contained "everything that can be said religiously and morally in the world" ("alles was religiös und sittlich in der Welt gesagt werden könne" [*Werke* 13:645]).

When Byron commenced work on *The Deformed Transformed*, Shelley dismissed the early draft as "a bad imitation of *Faust*" (Medwin 151). Byron himself had difficulties in achieving a dramatic representation of Arnold's transformation. In Goethe's judgment the problem arose from an excessive empiricism. Byron would not allow words to stimulate and inspire the visual imagination, but persisted in trying to anchor every image and idea in some physical reference. In *The Deformed Transformed*, Goethe recognized once again Byron's persistent engagement of *Faust*: "His Devil is derived from my Mephistopheles, but he is no mere imitation; rather, all is thoroughly original and new; everything is concise, capable, and clever. . . . If it were not for the hypochondrical and negative in his works, Byron would be as great as Shakespeare" ("Sein Teufel ist aus meinem Mephistopheles hervorgegangen, aber es ist keine Nachahmung, es ist alles durchaus originell und neu, und alles knapp, tüchtig und geistreich. . . . Ihm ist nichts im wege als das Hypochondrische und Negative und er wäre so groß wie Shakespeare" [Eckermann Nov. 8, 1826]). Eckermann recalls an earlier conversation in which Goethe asserted that "Lord Byron has too much empiria" ("Lord Byron habe zu viel Empirie"). Admitting that he was unsure of Goethe's meaning, he presumed that Goethe observed in Byron's work an over-abundant attention to empirical phenomena, a reliance on the senses and sensory associations.

Because of his great talent for representation ("sein großes Talent der Darstellung"), Byron allowed the descriptive to become his "speaking organ" ("redendes Organ"). Eckermann thus concludes that Goethe must have meant that "Lord Byron had too much empiricism, and not because he presented to our eyes too much actual life, but because his higher poetic nature seemed to be silenced, or even displaced by his empirical manner of thought" ("Lord Byron habe zu viel Empirie, und zwar nicht, weil er zuviel wirkliches Leben uns vor die Augen führte, sondern weil seine höhere poetische Natur zu schweigen, ja von einer empirischen Denkungsweise ausgetrieben zu sein schien" [Eckermann Nov. 8, 1826]). Three weeks later, when Eckermann informed Goethe that he has now read Byron's *Deformed Transformed*, Goethe shared his opinion that the first scene was great, even poetically great, while he declined to praise as poetical those dealing with the conquest of Rome, although he conceded that must be considered clever ("Das übrige, wo es . . . zur Belagerung Roms geht, will ich nicht als poetisch rühmen, allein man muß gestehen, daß es geistreich ist" [Eckermann Nov. 29, 1826]).

The word that I have been translating as "clever" ("geistreich") is the word most often repeated in the cluster of adjectives that Goethe bestowed upon Byron and the Byronic Faust. As a word that damns with its faint praise, "clever" is among the less redeeming qualities that can be affirmed even when true poetry has been undermined by the negative, hypochondriacal, and too empirical. With the implication that cleverness is implemented by negativity and an excess of empirical detail,

Eckermann responds that "it is no art to be clever when one has respect for nothing" ("es ist keine Kunst geistreich sein, wenn man vor nichts Respekt hat"). Goethe agrees "that the poet says more than one would want; he tells truth, yet one does not feel good about it, and would rather that he kept his mouth shut. There are things in the world, which the poet had better cover up than expose; but this is Byron's character and one would destroy him, if one would have him otherwise" ("daß der Poet mehr sagt als man möchte; er sagt Wahrheit, allein es wird einem nicht wohl dabei und man sähe lieber, daß er den Mund hielt. Es gibt Dinge in der Welt, die der Dichter besser überhüllet als aufdeckt; doch dies ist eben Byrons Charakter und man würde ihn vernichten, wenn man ihn anders wollte" [Eckermann Nov. 29, 1826]). The more details the poet assembles, the easier his task in adding ridicule and scorn to the heap. Thus it is concluded that Byron is "clever in the highest degree" ("im höchsten Grade geistreich"), and that cleverness is pertinently expressed by Caesar: "The Devil speaks truth much oftener than he's deemed, / He hath an ignorant audience" (*Deformed* 2.3.150–51). These lines, Goethe asserts, are "just as great and free as any ever spoken by my Mephistopheles" ("ebenso groß und frei als mein Mephistopheles irgend etwas gesagt hat" [Eckermann Nov. 29, 1826]).

Among the minor incidents from Goethe's *Faust*, Byron too has an *ignis-fatuus* summoned to demonic service. When Faust and Mephistopheles are ascending the Brocken by night, an *ignis-fatuus* ("Irrlicht") is summoned to light the way (lines 3855–70). The *ignis-fatuus* is conjured as "the wisp on the morass" in the Incantation spoken over Manfred when he falls in a swoon (1.1.195). When the Stranger implants Arnold into the beautiful body of Achilles, the empty carcass of the deformed body falls to the ground. The Stranger then summons a "little, marshy spark of flame" (*Deformed* 1.1.479) to reanimate the lifeless body as the Stranger's new residence (Chew 146–47). In the lines immediately following, a page arrives with four coal-black horses (*Deformed* 1.1.511), a reminder that Mephistopheles, too, called upon black horses to carry him and Faust to the prison where Gretchen awaited execution (line 4399).

Byron's previous plays provided little development of a Mephistophelean character. In *Manfred*, Lucifer, the star of Manfred's destiny, remained an essentially abstract and symbolic character. In *Cain*, the character of Lucifer was derived from Milton's Satan, but like Mephistopheles adopted a mortal companion. The Stranger and Caesar in *The Deformed Transformed* (1822), however, provide a much closer appropriation of Mephistopheles and Faust. As in Goethe's *Faust*, the Stranger mingles admiration and scorn in appraising Arnold's aspirations and desires. For his part, Arnold is a very different sort of Byronic Faust, constructed no less hypochondriacally out of Byron's personal torments. The voice of Byron's mother, Catherine Gordon, who taunted him in childhood as "a lame brat" (Galt 23–30), may have been rhetorically aggrandized in Eve's curse of Cain (3.1.419–43), but it was echoed more directly in the voice of Bertha, Arnold's mother, who curses him as a deformed club-footed hunchback and regrets that she once gave suckle to such an abortion. Byron's sensitivity to the deformity of his right foot (MacCarthy 35) gave him occasion to develop sympathy for his cruelly derided and abused club-footed and hunched-back character. The maltreatment of Arnold as a social outcast was apparently intended as a broader critique of social oppression and inhumanity (Robinson). Arnold's denunciation of intolerance soon collapses into his self-centered despair over his own disabled body. Like Faust holding aloft the opiate phial (lines 686–736), or Manfred preparing to leap from the mountain precipice (1.2.13–109), Arnold contemplates suicide to escape his torment.

About to impale himself on his knife, Arnold is interrupted by a Stranger who offers to trade his misshapen form for the body of any of the great heroes of the past. The deformed protagonist, the appearance of the devil, the transformed body, and even Arnold's name were borrowed from Joshua Pickersgill's *The Three Brothers* (Varnhagen 12). In Byron's adaptation there follows a procession of mythic and historical figures until Arnold chooses at last the ideal body of Achilles, hero of the Trojan War. Arnold, wary that he must enter a pact and sign away his soul, is reassured by the Stranger: "You shall have no bond / But your own will, no contract save your deeds" (1.1.151–52). Once again Byron rejects the convention of a pact with the devil. "My past power," Manfred proudly declared to the demons, "Was purchased by no compact with thy crew" (3.4.113–14). Cain, too, refused allegiance to Lucifer (1.1.302–19). More than either Manfred or Cain, Arnold seems hell-bound by his own will.

Arnold's body is transformed into the shape of Achilles, and the Stranger enters into Arnold's former body. This physical exchange no sooner takes place than the Stranger notes that psychological changes are taking place as well. Byron once again disassembles the Greek *kalon*, the beautiful is neither good nor true. In his beautiful body, Arnold becomes a thorough narcissist, unconcerned with the conditions and feelings of others, obliviousness to any personal responsibility beyond self-aggrandizement. The progression of events ultimately makes Arnold a less sympathetic character, while the Stranger, in Arnold's deformed body, gains admiration and respect in his identity as Caesar. The crucial aspect of this exchange of bodies is that Byron welds them together as inseparable companions.

Byron's intention, had he completed this fragmentary draft, may have been to reveal to Arnold what he might have accomplished in his deformed body and what he failed to achieve in his heroic body. No such awareness arises. Arnold changes in other respects, becoming at least in external appearance more like the character of the heroic form he occupies: bold, resourceful, respected, but utterly lacking in conscience. Caesar, in the body of the crippled hunchback, is witty, sardonic, cunning, more like Mephistopheles than any other character Byron created. He exercises the cynicism and mockery of Goethe's Mephistopheles, but without his subtlety and commanding power (Chew 147–48). Byron's Caesar waits and watches. A new direction of the plot emerges with the introduction of Olimpia and her death and resurrection at the end of part 2.

The scene at the opening of part 3 is "*A Castle in the Apennines, surrounded by a wild but smiling Country. Chorus of Peasants singing before the Gates.*" The festive song and dance replicate the sort of scene, "Before the Gate" ("Vor dem

Tor") (*Faust* lines 808–1577), that Goethe had used as a lively contrast to the dusky isolation of Faust's study. In chorus the peasants sing that "The wars are over" and "The bride and her lover" are united. Arnold expects Olimpia to love and admire him as much as he loves and admires himself. Instead her response is cold, loveless, unreciprocating. The old adage, "Be careful what you wish for," was reformulated by Goethe, who predicted a satiating plenty: "What one wishes for in youth, one has in abundance [too much of] in age" ("Was man in der Jugend wünscht, hat man im Alter die Fülle" [*Werke* 9:170]). Caesar has given Arnold the body of Achilles, has resurrected his assassinated bride, and clearly in part 3 Caesar will arrange for Arnold to be "possessed" by Olimpia. The fragment ends here, and Byron provided no explicit clues to its completion. One possibility, suggested by Caesar when he rescued Olimpia from death, is that he might become a rival. Goethe had Mephistopheles engage in a comic seduction of Martha while Faust was wooing Gretchen (lines 2865–3034). Byron might have implicated Caesar in a serious seduction. Rather than a love rivalry, Byron might have pursued the dead-bride motif, as if Olimpia were a soulless resurrection, an embodied Astarte. Arnold might thus be possessed by an Olimpia become a vampire bride, as in Goethe's "Die Braut von Corinth" (1797).

However Byron might have chosen to complete *The Deformed Transformed*, it is clear that he was on the juncture of addressing once more a conflict between love and knowledge. Manfred's quest for knowledge turned to a quest for the lost Astarte, whose momentary resurrection promised an end to his earthly struggle. In *Cain*, Adah's cry, "Choose love," is ignored by her husband, who departs with Lucifer on a quest for knowledge. The leitmotif in *The Deformed Transformed* is Arnold's desire for love and power. He blames his deformed body for the abuse and scorn he suffered. In part I he is granted the beautiful body of Achilles. In part 2 his desire for power is fulfilled. But his physical form does not suffice to secure love. In part 3, Olympia is introduced for the intended dramatization of the theme of love, but the reader is left with no clear insight into how the fragment might have been completed.

Writing the Helena episode in *Faust*, part 2, Goethe announced in 1827 that he intended the union of Faust and Helena to result in the birth of a beautiful child, Euphorion, whose progress toward maturity would exhibit in the confluence of his parentage more and more the characteristics of Byron (*Faust* lines 9588–961). In creating in Euphorion his own conception of the Byronic character, and at the same time the offspring of Faust and Helena, Goethe attended to the Byronic attributes that he had already identified as predominant. Euphorion would have his mother's beauty, his father's quest for knowledge, and mixed with these he would have Byron's narcissistic ego, hypochondriacal fantasies, and empirical distractions. A spirited youth, he would charm all with his beauty. His wild spirit would drive him to become increasingly bold in his flight until like Icarus he fell to his death (Eckermann July 5, 1827). The account of Byron's appropriations from Goethe's *Faust* in the characters and situations of his three Faustian plays is certainly interesting in itself, but it is more fully understood in the context of Goethe's reception of Byron's reworking of his own Faustian themes.

Goethe's essay on the death of Byron (*Werke* 13:646–48) is a fine tribute to the poet whom he admired most among the contemporary English writers, but he achieved something more personal and more pertinent in his portrait of Euphorion. Goethe said that he conceived his idea for Euphorion's fate upon hearing the news of Byron's death at Missolonghi. The resulting episode is a fitting summation of a complex instance of the reception and counter-reception between two of the best known poets of their age.

Works Cited

Ammerlahn, Hellmut. "Mignons nachgetragene Vorgeschichte und das Inzestmotiv: Zur Genese und Symbolik der Goetheschen Geniusgestalten." *Monatshefte* 64.1 (1972): 15–24.

Anon. *Le Moniteur universel* 393 (October 30, 1823), 1277–78.

Bakewell, Michael, and Melissa Bakewell. *Augusta Leigh: Byron's Half-Sister.* London: Chatto & Windus, 2000.

Becker, Hans Joachim. "Inzestmotive in Goethes Roman 'Wilhelm Meisters Lehrjahre.'" *Jahrbuch der Österreichischen Goethe-Gesellschaft* 111–13 (2007–2009): 197–203.

Bulwer Lytton, Edward. *Works of Edward Bulwer Lytton.* New York: Peter Fenelon Collier, 1880.

Burwick, Frederick. "Shakespeare and Germany." *Shakespeare in the Nineteenth Century.* Ed. Gail Marshall. Cambridge: Cambridge UP, 2012. 313–31.

Butler, E. M. *Byron and Goethe: Analysis of a Passion.* London: Bowes and Bowes, 1956.

Byron, George Gordon. *Poetical Works.* London: Oxford UP, 1967.

Byron, George Gordon. *Byron's Letters and Journals.* Ed. Leslie A. Marchand. Cambridge: Harvard UP, 1973–82.

Chew, Samuel C. *The Dramas of Lord Byron.* Göttingen: Vandenhoeck & Ruprecht, 1915.

Coleridge, Samuel Taylor. *Collected Letters.* Ed. Earl Leslie Griggs. Oxford: Clarendon, 1956–71.

Eckermann, Johann Peter. *Gespräche mit Goethe in den letzten Jahren seines Lebens.* Ed. H. H. Houben. Wiesbaden: F. A. Brockhaus, 1959.

Fabre d'Olivet, Antoine. *Caïn, mystère dramatique en trois actes.* Paris: Servier, 1823.

Galt, John. *The Life of Lord Byron.* London: Henry Colburn and Richard Bentley, 1830.

Giddey, Ernest. "Byron and Switzerland: Byron's Political Dimension." *Byron's Political and Cultural Influence in Nineteenth-Century Europe: A Symposium.* Ed. Paul Graham Trueblood. Atlantic Highlands: Humanities, 1981. 179–90.

Gilmour, Ian. *The Making of the Poets: Byron and Shelley in Their Time.* New York: Carroll & Graf, 2004.

Glass, Loren. "Blood and Affection: The Poetics of Incest in *Manfred* and *Parisina*." *Studies in Romanticism* 34.2 (1995): 211–26.

Goethe, Johann Wolfgang von. *Einzelnheiten, Maximen und Reflexionen*. Augsburg: in der Buchdruckerey der J. G. Cotta'schen Buchhandlung, 1833.

Goethe, Johann Wolfgang von. *Faust, der Tragödie erster und zweiter Teil*. Ed. Erich Trunz. Hamburg: Christian Wegner Verlag, 1966.

Goethe, Johann Wolfgang von. *Sämmtliche Werke*. Ed. Karl Goedecke. Stuttgart: J. G. Cotta, 1872.

Greene, Robert. *Friar Bacon and Friar Bungay*. London: Printed for The Malone Society by J. Johnson at Oxford UP, 1926.

Homer. *The Odyssey*. Trans. Richard Lattimore. New York: Harper & Row, 1965.

MacCarthy, Fiona. *Byron: Life and Legend*. London: John Murray, 2002.

Marlowe, Christopher. *Doctor Faustus, 1604–1616. Parallel Texts*. Ed. W. W. Greg. Oxford: Clarendon, 1950.

Medwin, Thomas. *Conversations of Lord Byron*. London: H. Colburn, 1824.

Milton, John. *Paradise Lost*. Ed. Merritt Hughes. New York: Odyssey, 1935.

O'Connor, Ralph. "Mammoths and Maggots: Byron and the Geology of Cuvier." *Romanticism* 5.1 (1999): 26–42.

Parker, Fred "Between Satan and Mephistopheles: Byron and the Devil." *Cambridge Quarterly* 35.1 (2006): 1–29.

Pickersgill, Joshua. *The Three Brothers*. London: Printed for J. Stockdale, 1803.

Plutarch. *Lives*. Ed. Bernadotte Perrin. Cambridge: Harvard UP, 1914.

Robertson, J. G., ed. *Goethe and Byron*. London: Publications of the English Goethe Society, 1925.

Robinson, Charles E. "The Devil as Doppelgänger in *The Deformed Transformed*: The Sources and Meaning of Byron's Unfinished Drama." *Bulletin of the New York Public Library* 74.3 (1970): 177–202.

Schmidt, Jochen. *Goethes* Faust, Erster und Zweiter Teil*: Grundlagen—Werk—Wirkung*. Munich: Beck, 1999.

Shakespeare, William. *The Complete Works of Shakespeare*. Ed. Hardin Craig. Chicago: Scott, Foresman, 1951.

Southey, Robert. Preface. *A Vision of Judgement* (1821). Vol. 10. *Poetical Works*. London: Longman, Orme, Brown, Green, & Longmans, 1838. 206–56.

Staël, Germaine de. *Germany*. Trans. Francis Hodgson. Ed. William Lamb. London: John Murray, 1813.

Steffan, Truman Guy. *Lord Byron's Cain. Twelve Essays and a Text with Variants and Annotations*. Austin: U of Texas P, 1968.

Stokoe, F. W. *German Influence in the English Romantic Period, 1788–1818*. Cambridge: Cambridge UP, 1926.

Thorslev, Peter. *The Byronic Hero, Types and Prototypes*. Minneapolis: U of Minnesota P, 1962.

Tieck, Ludwig. *Romantische Dichtungen*. Jena: Frommann, 1799.

Varnhagen, Hermann. *Über Byrons dramatisches Bruchstück "Der umgestaltete Missgestaltete."* Erlangen: Junge, 1905.

Author's Profile

Frederick Burwick, author and editor of thirty-three books and one hundred and fifty articles, has worked extensively in British drama and Anglo-German literary relations. Recent monographs include *Romantic Drama: Acting and Reacting*; *Playing to the Crowd, London Popular Theatre, 1780-1830*; *British Drama of the Industrial Revolution*; and, with Manushag N. Powell, *British Pirates in Print and Performance*. He is also coeditor of *Faustus from the German of Goethe. Translated by Samuel Taylor Coleridge* and editor of *The Oxford Handbook of Samuel Taylor Coleridge*.

Chapter 4

Heine's *Doctor Faust, a Ballet Poem*

Beate I. Allert

Abstract

In her article, "Heine's *Doctor Faust, a Ballet Poem*," Beate I. Allert examines Heinrich Heine's version of the Faust theme, which he called a libretto for a ballet, a "*Tanzpoem,*" based on traditional Faust stories. Heine's adaptation of the Faust legend is distinctive in presenting Faust's accomplice as the female Mephistophela. For Heine's *Faust* there is no final redemption, no uplifting to any heavenly or otherworldly realm; rather, the protagonist is pulled down into the earth and punished for his broken contract. Heine's ballet offers an alternative to Goethe's *Faust*, drawing on earlier sources. The production history of the libretto makes us aware of intertextual cultural histories between France, Germany, and England.

In 1851 the fifty-four-year-old Heinrich Heine, a German writer living in Paris since 1831, published in Hamburg *Der Doktor Faust: Ein Tanzpoem nebst kuriosen Berichten über Teufel, Hexen und Dichtkunst* (*Doctor Faust, a Dance Poem*). This was the first German edition of the scenario, which had been published earlier in French as *Le Légende du Docteur Jean Faust* (1847), but without Heine's long explanatory letter to Benjamin Lumley, the "Explanations" ("Erläuterungen"), included in subsequent editions. According to Gerhard Weiss, who discusses the complicated history of the various versions of the text, the translation was done by Heine's friend August Gathy (54–56).

Heine's "dance-poem" had been commissioned by Lumley, who, since 1842, had been manager of the opera house, Her Majesty's Theatre, in the Haymarket, London. While "libretto" in modern English usually refers to the text of the words sung in an opera, it can also be used, as it is here, to refer to the text or scenario of a ballet. Observing that ballet scenarios of literature are unusual, Robert E. Stiefel regards *Doctor Faust, a Ballet Poem* and the slightly earlier *Die Göttin Diana* (1846) as "outlines, blueprints, sketches—imagination ordered, but not realized" (187). He comments that Heine's use of the term "libretto of a ballet" ("Libretto eines Balletts") (*Doktor Faust* 5) is a "misnomer." But because it is the term Heine chose to use, it is the one adopted here. The libretto was in fact meant as the blueprint for an actual performance, at the same time giving much interpretive freedom to the stage director and the actors. This shift of perspective from audience to performers is one of the innovative features of Heine's text and is significant in my reading of *Doctor Faust, a Ballet Poem*.

Heine had been recommended to Lumley by Théophile Gautier as someone with the talent to produce ballet librettos for Lumley's stage productions. Gautier had achieved international success with his spectacularly popular ballet, *Giselle* (first performed in 1841), the idea for which, as he acknowledged, came from Heine's *De l'Allemagne* (Heine *Oeuvres* V–VI 2: 146–47). On Gautier's recommendation, Heine contacted Lumley in 1846, and later that same year Lumley asked Heine to write a scenario for a ballet based on the story of Faust. Heine worked on this commission during the winter of 1846–47 and sent the finished result to Lumley. For various reasons, Lumley never staged the work, although Heine was handsomely paid for his efforts (6000 francs or £240.00 [*Doctor Faust* 80]).

In accordance with Lumley's mandate, Heine had conceived of an innovative adaptation of the Faust legend. Heine knew that any modern interpretation of the story was likely to be compared with Goethe's masterful recasting of the Faust materials and chose to emphasize different sources. He admired Goethe's marvelous poetic achievement in *Faust*, but preferred to rely on older and more marginalized sources while at the same time conceiving of the presentation in a completely different medium. In conceiving of a ballet, Heine had to forego language and focus instead on movement, rhythm, and dance. But even under these circumstances he felt under the shadow of Goethe and realized that the success of his work would much depend on the skill of the actors. They would have to be able to dance the "most wonderful figures" ("wunderlichsten Figuren") as when Faust "dances a brilliant pas de deux with Mephistophela and to the joy of his fellow artists also dashes around about with them in the strangest figures" ("tanzt ein brillantes Pas de deux mit Mephistophela, und zur Freude seiner Kunstgenossinnen fliegt er auch mit ihnen umher in den wunderlichsten Figuren") (*Doktor Faust* 14). This appears to be a deliberate allusion to a phrase in Goethe's *Dichtung and Wahrheit* (*Poetry and Truth*), in which Goethe discusses dance and the "wonderful movements [figures]" ("wunderliche Bewegungen") of the participants (*Meinem Leben* 421).

Whereas Goethe draws attention to movements both literally onstage and metaphorically, Heine focuses on dance performance and the difficulties of the human body in limited space. The printed text consists of a compilation of Heine's stage directions and his scenario for the ballet, an open-ended multidisciplinary form, but nonverbal in its execution, even if the participants have to receive their instructions in written or oral form. Heine was less interested in an audience response than in how the dancers in the ballet would understand their directions. Concerned about their movements and the stage production, he deliberately left space for the performers to interpret how to carry out their swift and elegant moves.

It took Goethe almost a lifetime to write his *Faust,* but Heine claimed to have written his version in only one month, albeit under pressure. According to Heine, the work was based on careful research. Stiefel, one of the few who have chosen to interpret *Doctor Faust, a Ballet Poem*, suggests that Heine was eager to draw on earlier Faust sources rather than rely on Goethe's version. The sudden transitions from hell to paradise also suggest that he may have been influenced by *Orfeo ed Euridice* (*Orpheus and Eurydice*) (1762) by Christoph Willibald Gluck, as well as Berlioz's *La Damnation de Faust* (*The Damnation of Faust*) (Stiefel 191).

Heine departs significantly from Goethe's work. Clearly, there are stark differences concerning genre and gender roles, such as Heine's making Mephistopheles female and presenting Faust less as a scholar. The most obvious distinction is that Heine does not offer any rescue to Faust in the end. His version does not conclude with a move upward in the sense of Goethe's dictum, "The Eternal Feminine pulls us upward" ("Das Ewig-Weibliche /Zieht uns hinan") (*Faust* lines 12110–11). Rather, following pre-Goethean versions of the story, Heine's Faust is pulled down into the earth in the final movements of the ballet. In the last act he has become a medical doctor (although a charlatan) who offers cures to the sick and is about to get happily married when he is punished by Mephistophela for all his earlier transgressions and in conformance with the agreement he made with her when he signed a document in his own blood in the opening act.

Heine's commentary on Goethe's *Faust* in his "Erläuterungen" and statements about his own intentions reveal that although he admired Goethe's version, especially the Helena scene in the part 2, he wanted to return to earlier sources. Heine favored the Spies Faust Book, *Historia von D. Johann Fausten* (1587), rather than the version published in Hamburg in 1589 by Georg Rudolff Widman, and its subsequent versions, which he found too sentimental. Heine was interested in promoting marginalized versions of the Faust legend, including the Polish tradition concerning the nobleman Pan Twardowski, who was said to have studied magic at the University of Kraków and sold his soul in exchange for knowledge (36, 38). Adam Mickiewicz, the Polish national poet, composed the ballad "Pani Twardowska" in 1822, which first appeared in German translation in 1836, and in 1828 the Russian composer Alexey Nikolayevich Verstovsky premiered his opera, *Pan Tvardovsky* (libretto by Mikhail Nikolayevich Zagoskin), both of which would have been known to Heine. It is obvious in Heine's "Erläuterungen" that he is aware of a tension between Faust's legendary pursuit of knowledge and the indulgent life of the senses which his Faust eventually chooses, even to the point of altering the protagonist's state of mind.

Heine indicates that Marlowe's *Doctor Faustus* (published 1604), various British comedies, and French puppet shows all had some influence on his Faust narrative. What is decisive, he argues, is whatever is deeply engrained in the consciousness of the people who ever saw or had contact with any Faust-related street theater, to which Heine most wants to return. He remains closer to Marlowe than to Goethe, for the former offered quite the opposite to the uplifting and poetic rescue of Faust at the end of Goethe's *Faust II*, which Heine did not like. However, he placed himself in a dialogue with Goethe, sharing some of the same experiences of the Faust story from the street puppet theater in Strasbourg and elsewhere, which still presented the play as an exemplum illustrating the dire consequences of seeking after the forbidden. Goethe had expressed his recollection of the Strasbourg puppet play of Faust (*Dichtung* 1:18, 10:445) (see also Berghahn 160–69).

Even though Heine's ballet adaptation was somewhat didactic, it nevertheless appears as modern as Goethe's *Faust* in that the latter's didacticism was also not overt. Since Heine tells his story in the form of dance, he turns to the visual, rhythmic, and acoustic, using nonverbal hints, gesticulations, and expressions, so that the narrative becomes cryptic and fragmentary, a sequence of signs to be deciphered. Heine's approach to the adaptation must be understood in the context of a long and complicated history of artistic incubation, conception, and production, along with related dialogues between Heine and his producers. The real-world complications of theater production were another influence. No matter how impractical the execution of Heine's vision may have seemed to the outside world, it was clearly something that he thought was achievable, and he trusted that the dancers and the stage director would be capable of bringing his Faust ballet to performance.

When Heine wrote to his publisher, Julius Campe, in 1847, that *Doctor Faust* is a "poem which has from ballet only the form but is otherwise one of my greatest and most highly poetic productions" ("Gedicht welches vom Ballet nur die Form hat, sonst aber eine meiner größten und hochpoetischsten Produktionen ist") (*Doktor Faust* 82), he does not seem to be humorous or strategically "hyperbolic," as Stiefel claims (187). Rather, I think that Heine truly felt that in essence this work had captured something different which was most relevant and implicit in the *Zeitgeist*, having to do with a real need for change while reflecting on the impossibility of escaping outdated meanings and engrained patterns. The images in *Doctor Faust* are in a sense opaque. New meanings that are apparently offered never completely erase old ones that were there before. Heine appears to be expressing how hard it is to attain newly set goals in life. In his "Erläuterungen" he confesses how he struggled to express metamorphosis. In this sense *Doctor Faust, a Ballet Poem* is a palimpsest, a document written over a previously existing text which, while something of it has been ostensibly erased, is still there lingering to disrupt the text written over it. Implicit in this work is the experience of recollecting past statements, a repeated rewriting, counteracting, an erasing, editing, and false adapting via translation. Heine's *Doctor Faust* is in the end a document of multiple reconstructions and the poet's hope that those who do not keep contracts in life, no matter with whom, even with one's self, will be punished eventually.

But what were the real-world complications of theater production that ultimately meant that *Doctor Faust* was never staged? Gerhard Weiss shows that Heine's initial substructure of his Faust play involved the folklore figure of the *Wili* which he had mentioned in *De l'Allemagne* (1835). The *Wili* are young women who are engaged to be married but die before their wedding day. However, this concept had already been appropriated by Gautier and was now associated with his work. It was not going to be possible for Heine to reclaim it and make it central in his own work on Faust. The best Heine was able to do was to reverse the gender of the *Wili* figure and make it Faust who is engaged yet does not get to dance at his wedding celebration. But this was hardly likely to be as appealing as the *Wili*s of *Giselle.*

Gautier's ballet, *Giselle, ou les Wilis*, had its premiere on June 28, 1841. Carlotta Grisi was a sensation in the lead role of Giselle and Heine praised her (as well as Gautier) in an enthusiastic review in the *Augsburger Allgemeine* (February 7, 1842) (Weiss 41). At the same time, however, Heine felt as if he had lost control of something which was his own and he wanted to gain it back. *Giselle* went on to be a hit in London, in 1842, when Lumley produced it at Her Majesty's Theatre on March 12, again with Grisi as the principal ballerina. Grisi was accompanied by her husband, Jules Perrot, who had been one of Lumley's ballet masters since 1842 and was to prove to be Heine's particular bête noire. In January 1846 Heine sent Lumley the libretto for his ballet *Die Göttin Diana*. Lumley thanked Heine politely for the work, but announced that he was postponing its production to the following year. He sent Heine 2000 francs and promised to pay the same amount when the ballet was performed subsequently, and noted that he would be interested in his ideas for a Faust piece (Weiss 42).

In November 1846 Heine sent a draft of *Doctor Faust, a Ballet Poem* to Lumley, who asked for some clarifications, which Heine provided in the "Erläuterungen." A French translation of *Doctor Faust* was made by August Gathy and privately printed as *Le Légende du Docteur Jean Faust* (1847), which is the source of all following French versions of the text. Copies of Gathy's translation were sent to London and were used in the initial preparations for a premiere. Heine was prepared to follow in order to participate in the audience, but was informed that because of unforeseen technical difficulties, the production of *Doctor Faust, a Ballet Poem* was delayed indefinitely and that it was being replaced on the program with Perrot's new ballet *Les Éléments* (Weiss 42–48).

Heine tried again in 1849 to interest Lumley in the project but to no avail. Nor did the dramatist Heinrich Laube have any more success with his plans to stage the ballet in Vienna or Berlin in 1850. Finally in the summer of 1851 Heine sent a further revised version of the libretto and the "Erläuterungen" to his publisher Julius Campe in Hamburg. The printing history of this first edition is complicated because Campe sent it to two printers, but Heine made significant corrections only to the proofs of one of them (Weiss 49–52; Heine, *Doktor Faust* 65–66).

Doctor Faust, a Ballet Poem

Heine's dance-poem is five acts in length. The curtain rises on a dimly lit study piled with books and objects of alchemy and anatomy. The clock strikes midnight and we notice Dr. Faust wearing sixteenth-century academic robes. He takes a large grimoire, lights some candles, and draws magical circles on the floor. The room gets completely dark. There is thunder and lightning and from the floor a flaming red tiger arises. Faust seems to dominate the tiger and it sinks back into the ground. After a second incantation indicated only by gestures, there is another bolt of lightning. A huge, agile snake spirals up from the floor making hissing sounds. Faust laughs and scoffs so that the snake crawls timidly back into the ground. This is Faust at the height of his powers controlling the serpent at will, in stark contrast to his fate at the end of the fifth act. Faust then continues his amazing magic. All of a sudden, the darkness vanishes and we see uncountable lights and hear dance music. Something emerges from the ground, a colorful flower basket. A ballet dancer, Mephistophela, steps out of the basket, performing the most banal pirouettes. The effect of these amazing images is a touch of annoyance. Rather than being amazed and truly impressed by what he now sees, Faust apparently already knows the artificiality of it all. But soon he finds the apparition appealing.

Golden Venetian mirrors, bas-reliefs, and artworks surround Faust, all chaotically spectral and lustrously beautiful. Whatever the ballerina touches with her wand undergoes transformation, yet the initial form of the objects does not disappear, as when the scholar's dark globe begins to glow. Though tempted, Faust refuses the parchment she offers and demands to see aspects of hell. Monstrous creatures appear, which a touch of Mephistophela's wand changes into dancers. Visuality is cancelled out by mutability and metamorphosis and the only thing that seems to be predictable is motion itself. Faust is enchanted by this spectacle until he realizes that none of these figures actually matches his taste. Finally he sees in a mirror the reflection of a woman dressed in court dress. He approaches the image, desiring what he sees, but the woman is contemptuous toward him. When an ape transforms into a handsome dancer and begins to approach the woman in the mirror, she responds to the dancer, smiling and stretching her arms towards him. Watching this, Faust becomes jealous and despairs. Again, a tap of the wand is effective, and the dancer sinks into the ground, returning to his ape shape and leaving his ballet costume on the floor. Having been tempted, Faust now agrees to sign the parchment with his blood from one of his veins. Taking up the discarded ballet costume, Faust is assisted into it by the wanton corps de ballet of hell, perhaps an ironic allusion to "The Eternal Feminine pulls us upward" ("Das Ewig-Weibliche / Zieht uns hinan") from the end of Goethe's *Faust* (lines 12110–11). Given dancing lessons by Mephistophela and the other dancers, Faust rapidly learns to be an excellent dancer. Desiring the attractive female figure in the mirror, he dances for her and she appears to respond positively to his gestures. But Mephistophela pulls him away from the mirror and, touching it with her magic wand, makes it vanish. The dance lessons continue.

Critics have noticed correctly that the appearance of the devil in female form, Mephistophela rather than Mephistopheles, is the most noteworthy innovation in *Doctor Faust, a Ballet Poem* compared to all the other previous versions. This shift of gender is indeed remarkable and with it Heine adds another aspect to figurations of the feminine in Faust. In his discussion of this topic, Ellis Dye shows how the feminine in Goethe's *Faust* is associated with physicality, Eros, domesticity, divinity, fertility, agency, origin, and destiny. Heine's conception of the Mephisto figure as female complicates some of these aspects, and I would also like to draw attention to the fact that whatever she touches changes and gets transformed but in such a way that whatever underlying meaning there was does not get completely erased or replaced. Elements of the previous remain strangely lingering. What underpins Heine's Faust ballet, it seems, is the horror of recurrent images that actually are timeless and defy their specific meaning in the context in which they were initially used. Heine seems to be in search of real change but then encounters the camouflage of old figures already known, thus defying transformation in a true sense. Although Faust seems to be striving for something new, he appears to be caught in a cycle of repeated and familiar objects and events. We can conclude that the role of Mephistophela is to control and to tease Faust. It is not Mephistophela whom he desires, but rather the fleeting image which only she is able to control. Mephistophela can project or erase as she likes whatever gives Faust pleasure. She seduces him into a world of simulacra, which she brings about just like any image in a film. As soon as the image is perceived by the desiring male she erases it immediately, thus making him a fool of the first order. With her images she can control Faust.

By changing Mephistopheles into Mephistophela, Heine challenges gender roles and hybridizes form. His work is neither tragedy nor comedy but a mixture of both. It is a palimpsest, an overwriting of hybrid elements, drawing on traces of various Faust traditions. The original contribution of Heine's work resides in how it enables us to reflect not only on the adaptation for dance, but equally on the importance and fluidity of images and the evanescence of time. Images exist ultimately only in the mind of the beholder and can change meaning any moment.

In act 2, the setting changes to a large plaza in front of a castle. A Duke and his Duchess are attending a Rococo pastoral play. That which had been an image or reflection in the first act is here manifested in the flesh, but in some ways no less unreal and unattainable. The Duchess, who resembles the woman in the mirror, is wearing a golden shoe on her left foot. As soon as Faust and Mephistophela arrive, the Arcadian performers vanish and are immediately replaced by a troupe of Mephistophela's infernal ballerinas, accompanied by jubilant fanfares. Mephistophela flirts with the Duke and Faust with the Duchess. Faust shows off his skill in black magic by calling up the figure of King David. A wagon drawn by Levites arises from the ground carrying the Ark of the Covenant, before which King David dances in a costume worthy of a king from a deck of cards. Behind the Ark are some of the Duke's bodyguards, dressed as Polish Jews. All these caricatures vanish to great applause, whereupon Faust and Mephistophela dance a brilliant pas de deux. The Duke and the Duchess leave their thrones to make up a dramatic quadrille in which Faust and the Duchess become even more captivated with each other. Faust recognizes that she represents a witch by the "devil's mark" on her neck. He makes a rendezvous with her to meet at the next sabbat. Although she denies his suspicions, Faust indicates that her golden shoe implies she is a remarkable witch. After another display of Faust's magic, the quadrille resumes, and Faust and the Duchess declare their love for each other. Seeing this, the Duke leaps up to kill Faust, but the magician uses the magic wand to inflict horns on the Duke's head. Faust and Mephistophela escape from the ensuing chaos on two black horses.

Mephistophela has fulfilled the letter of her part of the bargain by giving Faust access to the mysterious woman in the mirror. They are even able to pledge their love to one another, but the fine print did not guarantee that they would live happily ever after. As Paris was betrayed by Aphrodite, so Faust is betrayed by Mephistophela. Faced with an angry husband and his enraged supporters, Faust finds his life in danger until Mephistophela takes him to safety at the last moment. Here Mephistophela, who represents the world of visual imagination and art, comes to rescue Faust after his struggle to perform the intricate dance of a world that exhausted him. Levels of fiction and reality become unstable and the problem of Faust seems to have lost control albeit in a world of playfulness and without any harmful intentions which are suddenly of major personal and political consequence. Heine may have come to the realization that even the world of art is one that cannot avoid politics and that images are powerful and potentially destructive.

The third act presents the nocturnal setting of a sabbat, among trees illuminated by strange lamps. A large black goat with a human face and a burning candle placed between its horns stands on a pedestal in the middle of the stage. A man and a woman walk back and forth in front of the pedestal each holding a blazing torch as "they bow to the rear of the goat" ("sie verbeugen sich vor der Rückseite des Bocks") (19). The scene is surrounded by terraces which form an amphitheater in which the nobility of the underworld are sitting. Musicians with faces of birds perch in the trees, and the space below is filled with dancers. Their costumes are reminiscent of various regions and time periods. The scene resembles a masquerade ball, with many masked figures. Everything appears to be bizarre. New guests come riding through the air "on broomsticks, manure forks, cooking ladles, as well as on wolfs and cats" ("auf Besenstielen, Mistgabeln, Kochlöffeln, auch auf Wölfen und Katzen") (19). These figures mingle with the dancing group and the Duchess arrives on a monstrous bat, barely dressed but with a golden shoe on her right foot. She is impatiently looking for someone. Finally she sees Faust with Mephistophela flying in on black horses. Faust and the Duchess fly into each other's arms dancing wildly. Mephistophela has meanwhile also found her expected partner, a gaunt nobleman in black Spanish-caped garment. When Faust and his partner dance passionately, Mephistophela and her partner, in contrast, are ironic in their mock gallantry. The four of them then take torches and join the "Ronde." Faust and the Duchess, delirious with love, disappear behind the trees on the right of the stage. The ring dance comes to an end and many more populate the stage to worship the goat, including officials. Faust and the Duchess reappear but Faust's face is stricken and he now firmly rejects her. Three Moors in golden heraldic costumes come to return her to her husband and drag her away. She is seen dancing a minuet with the goat in slow, measured steps. The goat's face has the melancholic expression of a fallen angel and the extreme boredom of an arrogant prince. There is despair in every gesture of the Duchess. Faust who has watched all this with disgust is rejoined by Mephistophela. He now has a deep yearning "for the purely beautiful, for Greek harmony, for the selfless, noble personalities of the Homeric springtime of the world" ("nach dem Reinschönen, nach den griechisher Harmonie, nach den uneigennützig edlen Gestalten der Homerischen Frühlingswelt") (21).

Mephistophela touches the ground with her magic wand and the image of Helena of Troy appears and then quickly vanishes. This classical model of beauty excites Faust's desire, which he makes known to Mephistophela. After she summons the magic horses, she flies off with Faust. As they depart the Duchess reappears and, seeing her lover vanishing, swoons to the ground. She is carried off as if spoils of war by ugly mocking figures. The round dance of the witches resumes but is interrupted by the piercing clang of a little bell and of an organ-choral which parodies ecclesiastical music. All gather around where the black goat burns in wild flames and even after the curtain has fallen one can still hear "horrible, burlesque wanton sounds" ("grausenhaft burlesken Freveltöne") (22).

Act 4 is set on an island in an archipelago; one glimpses to the left the bright emerald colored ocean and the turquoise blue sky. This is an ideal landscape bathed in sunny daylight. The vegetation and architecture are Greek as described in the *Odyssey*. White statues rest in the shadow of pines and laurels, and large marble vases hold marvelous plants. The trees are garlanded with flowers and there are crystal waterfalls. To the right is the temple of Venus, whose statue shimmers through the colonnades. On the stage are young men in their white festival attire and young women in the scanty dresses of nymphs, their heads bedecked with roses and myrtle.

Faust and Mephistophela burst into this idyllic world flying on their black horses. They exchange their medieval clothing for Greek garments. Having been welcomed by Queen Helena, Faust sits with her on a throne, whereas Mephistophela dances as a maenad with the most unrestrained postures. Helena's maidens understand this example of desire and join in the dance, swaying as maenads. The young men chase away the young women, and dance a military pantomime. Cupids armed with bows and arrows and riding swans join the heroic pastorale. The Duchess arrives on her monstrous bat and, like one of the Furies, approaches the throne where Faust and Helena are sitting. She casts the most dreadful reproaches on both of them and Mephistophela resumes her maenad dance along with Helena's maidens. The Duchess gets so angry that she brandishes the magic wand, uttering direst imprecations. The sky turns pitch black with thunder and lightning. The sea floods the entire island, which becomes horribly transformed. Mephistophela again brings the black horses, and she and Faust escape.

Heine's account of Queen Helena seems to be magical and appealing, in the beginning, but upon a closer look we see that the apparent beauty is indeed only a skeleton and a sign of death. Heine shifts the focus of *Doctor Faust, a Ballet Poem* to include not only a feminized Mephistophela but also an awareness that human actions have an impact on nature and the environment. How could happiness of the couple be maintained if their environment is destroyed? This is perhaps Heine's comment on the destructiveness of the Seven Years' War and his vision of a perfect utopian landscape that would allow for peace and happiness. Yet the imagery seems to suggest that the notion of personal happiness is not possible in a world that witnesses injustice. Heine draws attention to the individual responsibility that all human actions entail. Social affairs may no longer be "natural" in the world, but they could still be beautiful, if such human qualities as responsibility and love could persist. This seems to express Heine's utopian stance and it presents Faust in a rather reflective mode. Yet the ideals of Weimar Classicism do not satisfy Heine. The notion of multiple planes of reality, such as the departure to another plane at the end of the act, suggests that the classical ideas are no longer convincing.

Act 5 opens in front of a Gothic cathedral during the annual market. The participants in the festivities include the mayor and his wife along with their young blonde daughter. The erudite Doctor Faust appears in the gold-braided costume of a mountebank. Surrounded by patients who want remedies from him, he has a magic potion that heals and induces a desire to dance. In the midst of all the wild dancing, Faust approaches the mayor's daughter and declares his love for her. The naive beauty assents to his marriage proposal. Forgotten are the doubts and the effusive painful pleasures of an arrogant spirit, and Faust glows with inner bliss. When the wedding procession sets off for the church, however, Mephistophela intervenes and demands that Faust leave with her. Through Mephistophela's enchantment it becomes dark as night and the most terrible thunderstorm breaks out. Mephistophela produces the fateful parchment, dancing around Faust scornfully. The princes of hell suddenly arise from the ground, mocking Faust, whom Mephistophela, now changed into a "horrible snake" ("gräßliche Schlange") (29), strangles in a wild embrace, an image which invokes both the serpent in the Garden of Eden, symbolic of evil (Gen 3.1), and the serpent, in classical mythology, by which Laocoön and his sons are strangled because he has violated the rules of his priesthood by marrying and having children. The entire group then sinks into the ground under a roar of flames "while the sound of bells and the chords of the organ resound from the dome and summon to pious, Christian prayer" ("während das Glockengeläute und die Orgelklänge, die vom Dome her ertönen, zu frommen, christlichen Gebeten auffordern") (29).

In this act, Faust is represented as a doctor of medicine with a capacity to help people. Heine's Faust seems on the brink of finding happiness in life but is denied the blessing of the church that would have sanctioned his new life cycle. The final intervention of Mephistophela in the form of a snake reminds us not only of the Fall of humankind in the Garden of Eden, but also of the return of forces that Faust set in motion at the beginning of the ballet, which now prove so dangerous that they will destroy him. The play remains an exemplum not only as a warning against hubris and ignorance but also of the dangers of forgetfulness and the consequences which arise when old scripts are forgotten but not erased. Rejecting the Romantics' return to the state of false harmony, Heine creates an ending that is much more "grounded."

Neither an escape to the higher planes of idealism and high art nor a rescue via adoption of a new identity seems plausible for Heine.

Conclusion

Heine's *Doctor Faust, a Ballet Poem* is perhaps less about the question of whether change is really possible than the danger of forgetting what happened in the past. Goethe's *Faust* concerns the search for a fulfilled moment that would make the wish for happiness obsolete. Goethe has the Eternal Feminine rescue Faust after all his transgressions on earth, and it seems that he can escape hell. In *Doctor Faust*, on the other hand, the attempt to achieve the mastery of forgetting is just as impossible as the ability to achieve total change from one existence to another. Faust cannot detach from the social boundaries definitive of his existence and the stolen meanings that he has tried to hide under a veil of amnesia. Whereas Lessing probes the boundaries of the Enlightenment and, parallel to Goethe and his Classicism, is concerned with setting standards for ethical action and for freedom from a predictable myth, Heine challenges Classicism and Romanticism at the same time. He parodies Faust as much as all the fake relationships and superficial flirtations into which the scholar falls. Faust becomes tired of the masquerades and upheavals of the first four acts. He wants to marry, yet he must fulfill the contract he signed thoughtlessly, in the first act, when under the spell of the image in the mirror. The past cannot be erased and eventually catches up with him. The female characters in the ballet are eerie and prone to be incarnations not of the devil as the old legend may have had it, but rather of the Salamander or a fiery spirit that has fable-like qualities and will not vanish under the cover of new personalities. The persistence of the old and reappearance of the past are decisive. Although Heine projects strong images of a positive utopia in the fourth act, they are ultimately not realizable. Mephistophela, a medium of a gender-specific other, constrains Faust by means of his own unforgettable compromises which have, as Heine seems aware, not only artistic and performance-related consequences, but also political and painfully personal ones.

Works Cited

Berghahn, Klaus L. "Transformations of the Faust Theme." *Lives of Faust: The Faust Theme in Literature and Music. A Reader*. Ed. Lorna Fitzsimmons. Berlin: De Gruyter, 2008. 160–69.

Cerf, Steven. "The Faust Theme in Twentieth-Century Opera." *Lives of Faust: The Faust Theme in Literature and Music. A Reader*. Ed. Lorna Fitzsimmons. Berlin: De Gruyter, 2008. 461–72.

Dye, Ellis. "Figurations of the Feminine in Goethe's *Faust*." *A Companion to Goethe's Faust Parts I and II*. Ed. Paul Bishop. Rochester: Camden House, 2001. 95–121.

Goethe, Johann Wolfgang von. *Aus meinem Leben: Dichtung und Wahrheit*. Ed. Peter Sprengel. Munich: Carl Hanser 1985.

Goethe, Johann Wolfgang von. *Faust: Texte*. Ed. Albrecht Schöne. Frankfurt: Deutscher Klassiker Verlag, 1994.

Heine, Heinrich. *Der Doktor Faust: Ein Tanzpoem nebst kuriosen Berichten über Teufel, Hexen und Dichtkunst*. Ed. Joseph A. Kruse. Stuttgart: Philipp Reclam, 2007.

Heine, Heinrich. *Doctor Faust, a Ballet Poem. The Sword and the Flame: Selections from Heinrich Heine's Prose*. Ed. Alfred Werner. Trans. Charles Godfrey Leland. New York: Thomas Yoseloff, 1960. 503–40.

Heine, Heinrich. *Le Légende du Docteur Jean Faust*. Paris: Gerdès, [1847].

Heine, Heinrich. *Oeuvres de Henri Heine V–VI. De l'Allemagne 1–2*. Paris: Eugène Renduel, 1835.

Stiefel, Robert E. "Heine's Ballet Scenarios. An Interpretation." *The Germanic Review* 44.3 (1969): 186–98.

Wiese, Benno von. "Mephistophela und Faust. Zur Interpretation von Heines Tanzpoem 'Der Doktor Faustus.'" *Herkommen und Erneuerung: Essays für Oskar Seidlin*. Ed. Gerald Gillespie and Edgar Lohner. Tübingen: Niemeyer, 1976. 225–40.

Weiss, Gerhard. "Die Entstehung von Heines 'Doktor Faust': Ein Beispiel deutsch-english-franzözischer Freundschaft." *Heine-Jahrbuch* 5 (1966): 41–57.

Author's Profile

Beate I. Allert teaches German, Comparative Literature, and Film Studies at Purdue University. She has published three books, *Comparative Cinema* (2008*), Languages of Visuality: Crossings between Science, Art, Politics, and Literature (*1996), and *Die Metapher und ihre Krise: Zur Dynamik der "Bilderschrift" Jean Pauls* (1987), as well as numerous articles, especially on eighteenth- and nineteenth-century German and European literature. She is currently in the process of completing a book manuscript on G. E. Lessing.

Chapter 5

Thomas Mann's *Doctor Faustus* as Political Document

Ehrhard Bahr

Abstract

In his article, "Thomas Mann's *Doctor Faustus* as Political Document," Ehrhard Bahr argues that although Mann's version of the Faust legend, published in 1947, was designated as a novel, it served the author also as a vehicle for an individual and national confession as well as a political document. Mann compares Germany to Faust and sees his nation involved in a pact with the devil that led to its corruption and final destruction. He considers music as the most typical art form for Germany and characterizes it as a compulsive obsession that drove his Faust figure as a composer to self-destruction. The autobiographical aspects of the novel reflect Mann's preoccupation with Richard Wagner and Friedrich Nietzsche. His Faust figure has a mental breakdown when he introduces his most successful composition. Until his death he lives a life of dementia like Nietzsche. The question of grace is raised at the end, but not answered.

Thomas Mann wrote his novel *Doktor Faustus: Das Leben des deutschen Tonsetzers Adrian Leverkühn, erzählt von einem Freunde* (*Doctor Faustus: The Life of the German Composer Adrian Leverkühn as Told by a Friend*) in Los Angeles during World War II. Although clearly designated as fiction, it is also an individual and national confession as well as a political document. The novelist used the sixteenth-century chapbook of D. Faustus as matrix for his analysis of the German mentality that led to Nazi rule in Germany in 1933 and World War II in 1939. In a lecture entitled "Germany and the Germans," delivered at the Library of Congress in May 1945, only three weeks after Germany's unconditional surrender, Mann compared Germany to

Faust and saw the nation "literally being carried off by the Devil." This verdict made a lot of sense to his contemporary audience. It did not pay much attention to his declaration that Faust "would have to be musical, if [he] is to be the representative of the German soul." Mann blamed the "musicality of the German soul" for the German disdain of the political realm (Mann, "Germany" 51–52). His audience did not realize that Mann was presenting the major theses of the novel that took him two more years to finish. Rather than a professor of theology, like the protagonist of the chapbook, Mann's Faust figure is a composer. Relating the Faust legend to music allowed the novelist to blame musicality for the German catastrophe in politics. This interpretation turned Mann's *Doctor Faustus* into a book of reckoning not only of his nation's history, but also of his own biography.

As a young man Thomas Mann was primarily attracted by music, "the most German of the arts" ("die deutscheste der Künste"), as he defined it later (*Werke* 11:227), while literature was only his second interest. He heard his mother play the piano and was introduced to the German *Lied*, as represented by Franz Schubert, Robert Schumann, Johannes Brahms, and Hugo Wolf. But the central attraction to him was Richard Wagner. He regularly attended the productions of Wagner's operas at the city theater of his home town, Lübeck. In his reminiscences, Mann called his early encounter with Wagner's music "the most important chapter of his life" (*Werke* 11:418). When he moved to Munich in 1894, he continued his visits to productions of Wagner operas at the two local opera houses. His first and only visit to Bayreuth occurred in 1909.

Many critics have written of Mann's idolatry of Wagner and they are right to emphasize its influence on his literary production, which can be found not only in the titles of his novellas such as *Tristan* and "Wälsungenblut" ("The Blood of the Walsungs"), but also in the body of his major novels, such as *Buddenbrooks*, *Königliche Hoheit* (*Royal Highness*), and *Joseph und seine Brüder* (*Joseph and His Brothers*). But in spite of this evidence, there is also Mann's critique of Wagner, documented by his Wagner crisis between 1909 and 1911, which can be attributed to his reading of Friedrich Nietzsche's scathing critique of the composer whom he had first admired as a prototype of the modern artist. The notes for a major essay on art and intellect that Mann had planned to write in 1911 are full of invectives against Wagner. His Wagner crisis was actually "a permanent crisis" (Vaget, "Mann" 312). Nietzsche provided the "double perspective" on Wagner that Mann maintained for the rest of his life, but he did not fool himself when he camouflaged his preference for Wagner behind his "enthusiastic ambivalence" ("enthusiastische Ambivalenz") for the idol of his youth who continued to be his secret passion (*Werke* 10:928).

It is an example of the bitter irony of history that Thomas Mann was driven into exile in 1933 by his study on "The Sufferings and Greatness of Richard Wagner," which riled the representatives of the Wagner cult in Munich. They considered it a defamation of the composer who had been chosen to serve as the iconic artist of the Nazi regime. They issued a "Protest of the Richard Wagner-City Munich," signed, among others, by the leading composers of the post-Wagner era, Hans Pfitzner and

Richard Strauss. Thomas Mann was unaware of the commotion about his essay, because he was on a lecture tour abroad in Holland, Belgium, and France to deliver his cosmopolitan assessment of the composer. Warned by his children not to return home to Munich, Mann and his wife extended their vacation in Switzerland for the next five years, until they immigrated to the United States in 1938.

Germany's Wagnerians had split into a cosmopolitan and a nationalistic faction. The latter was also motivated by anti-Semitism. The heirs of the Wagner family had welcomed Adolf Hitler in Bayreuth as early as 1923 and made the annual festival into a meeting place for the enemies of the Weimar Republic. The Munich protest against Thomas Mann was an extension of the German nationalism and anti-Semitism that had its roots in Wagner's writings, but had now become the official ideology of the Nazi government, which came into office in 1933.

Thomas Mann acknowledged that there was much Nazi ideology in the Bayreuth Wagner cult (Mann, *Im Schatten* 145; *Werke* 10:926). In the United States he defended Wagner as an artist, but attacked his cooptation by the Nazis in an article entitled "In Defense of Wagner: A Letter on the German Culture that Produced both Wagner and Hitler," published in *Common Sense* in January 1940. He denied that he had claimed Wagner as representative of the "good" Germany in contrast to the "evil" Germany of Hitler and admitted that not only Wagner's writings, but also his music, showed some of the characteristics of National Socialism that he condemned. In conclusion he declared that Germany must be defeated in order to reactivate its social virtues and enable it to join again the family of European states (*Werke* 13:351–59).

When Mann began working on his Faust novel in 1943, he discarded Wagner from his concept of German musicality. Although his essays on the composer had served him well to rehearse and hone his arguments about the role of music in Germany and the problem of German identity, he considered Wagner no longer central to his new project. The composer is occasionally mentioned in *Doctor Faustus*, but has no symbolic function. Mann was able to decouple his concept of German musicality from his preoccupation with Wagner and applied it to the problem of German fascism at hand. While the majority of exiles from Hitler's Germany considered themselves representatives of the "Other Germany," that is, the "good" Germany, Mann declared in his lecture on "Germany and the Germans" at the Library of Congress in 1945 that "there are *not* two Germanys, a good one and a bad one, but only one, whose best turned into evil through devilish cunning. Wicked Germany is merely good Germany gone astray, good Germany in misfortune, in guilt, and ruin" (64). Thomas Mann felt responsible, if not guilty, for the downfall of the Weimar Republic. Although he had supported the new democracy in a public lecture in 1922 and warned of the dangers of the Hitler party in 1930 and 1932, he had a conservative nationalist past, as documented by his essay "Thoughts in War" of 1914 and his comprehensive *Betrachtungen eines Unpolitischen* (*Reflections of a Nonpolitical Man*) of 1918, which extolled the superiority of German culture in comparison to Western civilization (*Werke* 13:527–45). For this reason, he rejected the two Germanys theory of his fellow exiles in favor of the identity of the good and evil Germany. It is important to notice that Mann had first developed this concept in his Wagner essay of January 1940, when he said that Germany was a menace not because it was evil, but especially because it was also good at the same time (*Werke* 13:358).

When Mann began working on *Doctor Faustus* in March 1943, he dug up a three-line draft from 1904 about a syphilitic artist "who becomes close to a pure, sweet young girl and shoots himself before the wedding" (Kurzke 462). This outline dealt with Mann's concept of the artist and his guilt feelings about sexual involvements, but it lacked the historical and political dimensions that Mann considered essential for his novel of the 1940s. By the end of the nineteenth century the figure of Goethe's Faust had become representative of the national character in German ideology and his *Faust* was considered the paradigmatic German drama. Any German writer of rank felt challenged by Goethe's work. For Mann's draft of 1904 with the figure of the "pure, sweet young girl," resembling Margarete, Goethe's Faust drama of 1808 might still have served as a model. But for his novel of 1947 Mann chose the 1587 chapbook of Doctor Faustus as master narrative. The negative ending of the *Historia von D. Johann Fausten* appeared more appropriate to him for his fictional account of Germany's twentieth-century history than the redemptive drama by Goethe.

The German chapbook by an anonymous author tells the story of a young man of peasant origin, who is supported by his uncle to study theology and obtain the degree of Doctor of Theology. Unsatisfied with his life at the university and the study of theology, Faust makes a pact with a devil named Mephostophiles, giving him his soul in exchange for the devil's services on earth for twenty-four years. After a life full of travel adventures and magic tricks, such as conjuring the image of Helen of Troy and consorting with her as his concubine, Faust is condemned and carried off to hell. His gruesome ending takes place after a meal with his students in a tavern, where he begs his students to bury him, for he died "both a good and bad Christian." The chapbook provided an example of Luther's theology of grace, explaining that Faust's major sin was his denial of divine grace. Faust believed that his sins were too great to be forgiven. His belief that he had gone too far in making a pact with the devil was considered an example of sinful pride.

Mann followed Faust's life story as it appears in the chapbook, except for the name of his protagonist and his profession: his Faust figure is called Adrian Leverkühn and he is a composer. He also grows up on a farm, run by his parents. His well-to-do uncle in the city supports him in his study of theology which he finally renounces in favor of a career as a modern composer. He makes a pact with the devil by willfully contracting syphilis and is implicitly condemned in the end. Before Leverkühn succumbs to a paralytic stroke, he invites his friends to hear his last composition, entitled *The Lamentation of Dr. Faustus*. For this composition Leverkühn employs the same words as the chapbook character, when he asked his students to bury him: "For I die as both a wicked and good Christian" (511). Afflicted by dementia, Leverkühn dies ten years later, while his biographer and friend, named Serenus Zeitblom, prays that God may have mercy on his soul.

Leverkühn's paralytic stroke is a reference to Friedrich Nietzsche's life and the final ten years of general paresis in the care of his mother and sister. This motif is an example of the symbolic overdetermination that is characteristic of Mann's novel, which is not only a Faust novel, but also a Nietzsche novel. Leverkühn's family name is an allusion to Nietzsche's philosophy: "to live boldly." Mann employed episodes from Nietzsche's life for the plot of his Leverkühn story, such as, for example, his crucial encounter with a prostitute in a brothel in Leipzig in chapter 16, which follows almost verbatim a similar incident in Nietzsche's biography, told by his friend and fellow student Paul Deussen (Bergsten 57–62). Nietzsche's troublesome ménage à trois with Paul Rée and Lou Andreas-Salomé served as model for Leverkühn's unsuccessful marriage proposal to Marie Godeau, a Swiss stage designer. Nietzsche was known to idolize music and envisioned a career as a composer in his youth. There are even some forty-five musical compositions attributed to him. Mann's fictional composer dies on the same day as Nietzsche, although forty years later, on August 25, 1940 (Mann, *Faustus* 534).

Nietzsche was, like Wagner, a stellar model for Thomas Mann, but also a controversial figure in the history of National Socialism. Although the Nazi reception of Nietzsche was limited to a few key words, such as "superman" and "will to power," Mann was keenly aware of his negative legacy and endowed the devil of his Faust novel with Nietzschean arguments in favor of irrationalism as the basis for musical creativity.

It took Mann about two months of research before he began writing his novel on May 23, 1943. After he decided to use the chapbook of Dr. Faustus, he began reading about music (including letters by Hugo Wolff, Igor Stravinsky's memoirs, and a history of music by Paul Bekker), Friedrich Nietzsche, and sixteenth-century German intellectual history (Martin Luther, Albrecht Dürer, Ulrich von Hutten). At the same time, Mann recorded in his diary the events of World War II, as they happened in the Soviet Union, North Africa, and Nazi-occupied Europe. It was the time after the defeat at Stalingrad, the surrender of the German troops in Tunisia, the landing of American and British troops in Sicily, and continuous air raids of Berlin, Hamburg, and Cologne. The choice of Hugo Wolff and Stravinsky for his research indicated that Leverkühn was going to be a post-Wagnerian composer, while Nietzsche's life would provide the framework for the fictional composer's life history. The Nietzsche model is crucial for the interpretation of the novel, since it confirms that Mann never thought of using Arnold Schoenberg's biography as a model for his protagonist, but only his music.

Mann's research did not end in May 1943, but was continued during the following months, while he was writing the initial seven chapters. Most important for Leverkühn's position within the history of modern music was Mann's meeting with Theodor W. Adorno in July 1943. The German sociologist, philosopher, and musicologist had moved to Los Angeles in 1941 as a member of the Frankfurt Institute of Social Research in exile. Adorno's manuscript on "The Philosophy of Modern Music," which consisted at that time of only one chapter on Arnold Schoenberg (when the book was published under the title *Philosophie der neuen Musik* in Germany in

1949, Adorno had added a chapter on Igor Stravinsky) made a big impact on Mann. He realized that "here indeed was something important," as it dealt with modern music on a similar level that he envisioned for his novel. As Mann wrote later in his *Die Entstehung des Doktor Faustus* (*Story of a Novel*), Adorno's manuscript

> dealt with modern music both on an artistic and on a sociological plane. The spirit of it was remarkably forward looking, subtle and deep, and the whole thing had the strangest affinity to the idea of my book, to the "composition" in which I lived and moved and had my being. The decision was made of itself: "this was my man." (43)

> Ich fand eine artistisch-soziologische Situationskritik von grösster Fortgeschrittenheit, Feinheit und Tiefe, welche die eigentümlichste Affinität zur Idee meines Werkes, zu der "Komposition," hatte, in der ich lebte, an der ich webte. In mir entschied es sich: "Das ist mein Mann." (*Werke* 11:172)

Due to Adorno's influence, Mann's protagonist did not only become a modernist composer, but a twelve-tone composer. Mann had met Arnold Schoenberg as fellow exile at parties in Los Angeles and picked his brain. But he had not anticipated equipping his fictional composer with a mindset predetermined to composing with twelve tones. Mann felt at home in the realm of nineteenth-century music, but modern music was a foreign territory to him. He realized that he needed a sympathetic adviser. If it had not been for Adorno, his Faust novel would have taken a different course. Adorno's essay tracing the trajectory of modern music as an irreversible trend and relating it to early twentieth-century history convinced Mann to adopt this approach as a model for Leverkühn's professional development. In addition, Adorno provided Mann with the theory and vocabulary of modern music. Mann admitted that the analysis of composing with twelve-tones that appears in chapter 22 was based on Adorno's essay on Schoenberg. Furthermore, Adorno supplied Mann with descriptions of works that a musician like Leverkühn would compose. There are four such sketches available for comparison: a violin concerto in chapters 33 and 38, two chamber music compositions in chapter 43, and the cantata, *The Lamentation of Dr. Faustus*, in chapter 46 (Adorno and Mann 158–61). Adorno was indeed Mann's "privy councillor," as he liked to call him (Mann, *Tagebücher* 952).

Thomas Mann, who loved his fictional composer like no other character of his imagination, related Leverkühn's fate to the problem of German inwardness. Leverkühn was not designed as a fellow traveler of Nazism, but as a good German, "whose best turned into evil through devilish cunning." This was the final analysis of Mann's lecture on "Germany and the Germans," when he told his American audience in 1945 that "there are *not* two Germanys, a good one and a bad one. . . . wicked Germany is merely good Germany gone astray" (Mann, "Germany" 62). The only difference between Mann's national character analysis of 1945 and Leverkühn's qualities was the fact that the composer did not fall for the devil's cunning, but challenged the devil with his deliberate syphilitic infection. Leverkühn's pact was a pact

without the devil. His union with a prostitute named Esmeralda replaced the traditional pact. The devil does not appear in the real world of the novel, but only in
Leverkühn's own writings that reveal "the hidden Faustian program of his life" in
chapters 16 and 25 (Vaget, "German Music" 225–44). While the former chapter,
written in the sixteenth-century language of the Chapbook, contains Leverkühn's
description of his encounter with Esmeralda, a Leipzig prostitute, the latter chapter
includes the composer's transcript of a feverish dream in which the devil showed up
in various costumes. His visit was "intended merely for confirmation" of the pact
(264). Leverkühn's Faustian sin was emotional coldness and arrogance, or pride. His
career choices—first theology, then music—were made out of arrogance (90). What
the devil in Leverkühn's transcript demanded was that he renounce love: "Love is
forbidden you insofar as it warms. Your life shall be cold—hence you may love
no human" (264). Three episodes central to the plot serve to enforce this sentence:
the failure of Leverkühn's marriage proposal to Marie Godeau (chapters 39–42),
the gratuitous murder of his friend Rudi Schwerdtfeger by a jealous lover (chapter
42), and the tragic death of his five-year old nephew Nepomuk or Echo, who dies
of meningitis (chapters 44–45). Whenever Leverkühn violated this command, the
objects of his love were doomed. Only Serenus Zeitblom, his childhood friend and
narrator, was exempt from this fate, as the composer showed total indifference to
him, although Zeitblom loved him "with terror and tenderness, with indulgence and
doting admiration, seldom asking whether he in any way returned [his] feelings" (8).

The Esmeralda story is perhaps the only example of the influence of Goethe's
Faust. It raises the question of divine grace in a similar fashion as in Goethe's drama,
where it is embodied by the figures of Gretchen and the Mater Gloriosa as representations of the Eternal Feminine. In Mann's *Doctor Faustus* the Eternal Feminine
is introduced as a prostitute. Leverkühn fled from her touch in the Leipzig brothel,
but was irreversibly attracted by her. When he realized that she had left Leipzig, he
followed her to Pressburg in Hungary for the sexual union with "that ill-fated creature," as the narrator calls her. Realizing that "something resembling the bond of love
reigned here," the narrator informs the reader that Esmeralda warned Leverkühn
"against her body." He concludes that this warning was "an act of compassion, an act
. . . of love." Showing the same kind of love Leverkühn disregards Esmeralda's advice and contracts the syphilitic infection that is the cause of his dementia and early
death. In the eyes of the narrator, this is an act of "recklessly tempting God" and with
"a religious shudder" he resolves that in that embrace, "one party forfeited his salvation, the other found hers" (164–65). Esmeralda later marries a Hungarian nobleman
and reappears as Madame de Tolna, secretly supporting Leverkühn's music from a
distance as his most generous patron (411). Linking her to an exotic insect that his
father had shown him (17–18), he encodes her name as *Hetaera esmeralda* in the
tone sequence as h-e-a-e-es (in English notation: B-E-A-E-E-flat) in the most beautiful song of a cycle that constitutes his first serial experiment: "Oh sweet maiden, how
bad you are" (166). The Esmeralda subplot is of central importance to the theological
discourse of the book, as it involves the question of grace that Leverkühn—similar

to Goethe's Faust—may be granted through the intervention of this saintly figure, afflicted with the poison of syphilis (Vaget, "Mann" 185).

Mann designed his novel as an allegory of twentieth-century German history. The dates of events in Leverkühn's life correspond to historical moments in German history: his syphilitic infection in 1905 parallels the rise of Wilhelmine imperialism; the confirmation of the pact takes place before the outbreak of World War I; Leverkühn's mental collapse occurs in 1930, when the Nazi party had its first sensational victory in the German parliamentary elections; and his death takes place in 1940, one year after the beginning of World War II. Numerous critics have pointed out that the allegory does not work, but it has to be read in terms of an antimony, not an equation of Leverkühn = Germany. These antimonies signify that the allegorical composer is not to be identified with imperialist or fascist Germany, but instead to be related dialectically against this background. The burden of interpretation is put upon the individual reader who has to deal with the unresolved problem of the "identity of the nonidentical" (Bahr 263–64; Mann may have found the concept of "antinomies of allegory" in Walter Benjamin's *Ursprung des deutschen Trauerspiels* [1928], which he read in 1946).

The realism of the novel resides primarily with Leverkühn's friend Serenus Zeitblom. He is not only the narrator of the composer's biography, but also of his own life story as a representative of the inner emigration in Nazi Germany. Interposing "the medium of the 'friend'" between himself as author and his protagonist allowed Mann to write the novel as a dual biography (Mann, *Story* 31). This device enabled him to begin his narrative on the same day as Zeitblom, who puts his first lines on paper in his small study in Freising on the Isar, a small town in Nazi Germany, on May 23, 1943. The novel provides not only excerpts from the history of World War I and the Weimar Republic, but also an account of the last two years of World War II. Zeitblom is estranged not only from his two sons who serve the Führer, but also from the Nazi regime. For this reason he retired prematurely from his position as a teacher of Latin and Greek at the local high school and Catholic seminary, but his language is still interspersed with terms of Nazi propaganda, such as "our beleaguered Fortress Europe" (6, 267) or the "Allied invasion of France" for D-Day. Against his "conscience as a citizen," Zeitblom is more afraid of a German victory than of a German defeat (33–34). In September 1943 Zeitblom reports about the revival of the German submarine warfare, the student uprising in Munich, the destruction of German cities, the Soviet offensive, and the landing of Allied troops in Sicily (183–85). He realizes that the war is lost not only in terms of military strategy:

> It means that *we* in fact are lost—lost, our cause and soul, our faith and our history. Germany is done for, or will be done for. An unutterable collapse—economic, political, moral, and spiritual—in short, an all-embracing collapse looms ahead. (186)

> Es bedeutet tatsächlich, dass wir verloren sind, verloren unsere Sache und Seele, unser Glauben und unsere Geschichte. Es ist aus mit Deutschland, wird

aus mit ihm sein, ein unnennbarer Zusammenbruch, ökonomisch, politisch, moralisch und geistig, kurz allumfassend, zeichnet sich ab. (*Werke* 6:233)

Zeitblom mentions "unconditional surrender," the goal of the Allied war effort, but finds it unacceptable because of the German mentality that prefers the Wagnerian "red twilight of the gods" (*Götterdämmerungsröte*) to common sense (185). In April 1944, he writes about the battles for Odessa and Sebastopol in the Soviet Union and expresses fear about D-Day. The attack on the "European fortress"—"our prison, or perhaps our madhouse," as he calls it—is expected any day (267–68). Less than two months later, he records the Allied landing in France: "a technical and military feat of first, or simply of totally, new rank" (355). Germany's rocket-bomb, its "new retaliatory weapon," cannot disrupt or forestall the advance of the Allied armies. In the East, Soviet troops are taking strategic cities in Belorussia. Zeitblom realizes that enemy troops will soon enter German territory: "our sacred German soil! As if anything were still sacred about it" (355–56). Finally, in April 1945, Zeitblom reports that an American general has the inhabitants of Weimar, Goethe's former place of residence and the center of German classical culture,

> file past the crematoria of their local concentration camp [Buchenwald] and declares . . . that they, citizens who went about their business in seeming honesty and tried to know nothing, though at times the wind blew the stench of burned human flesh up their noses, declares that they share in the guilt for these horrors that are now laid bare and to which he forces them to direct their eyes. (505)

> die Bevölkerung von Weimar vor den Krematorien des dortigen Konzentrationslagers vorbeidefilieren und erklärt . . . diese Bürger, die in scheinbaren Ehren ihren Geschäften nachgingen und nichts zu wissen versuchten, obgleich der Wind ihnen den Stank verbrannten Menschenfleisches von dorther in die Nasen blies,—erkärt sie für mitschuldig an den nun blossgelegten Greueln, auf die er sie zwingt, die Augen zu richten. (*Werke* 6: 637)

Zeitblom sees himself, "in his mind's eye," among the crowd and expresses his revulsion at the "thick-walled torture chamber, into which Germany was transformed by a vile regime of conspirators sworn to nihilism." His final verdict acknowledges German "ignominy [lying] naked before the eyes of the world" (505) ("unsere Schmach vor den Augen der Welt" [638]). This historical account of the last two years of World War II is part of the novel's agenda of reckoning and is designed to preserve in writing and print the record of the war that was started by Germany and ended with its defeat in 1945.

An earlier chapter dealing with Leverkühn's membership in a Christian student fraternity documents German nationalism before World War I (chapter 14), while another chapter reveals Zeitblom's reservations about the reactionary ideas expressed at the round table sessions of the so-called Kridwiss circle during the 1920s (chapter 34). These discussions reveal the antidemocratic thinking among intellectuals of the Weimar Republic. Research has identified the members of the Kridwiss circle as historical persons of Munich society and confirmed their attachment to pre-Nazi ideology (Bergsten 27–34). The most radical ideas are expressed by Chaim Braisacher, modeled after the Jewish scholar Oskar Goldberg (1885–1953), whose book, *Der Wirklichkeit der Habräer* (*The Reality of the Hebrews*) of 1925, Mann had used as a source for his Joseph tetralogy.

The role of music in *Doctor Faustus* is best explained as a desire for hegemony in the arts that is comparable to Germany's drive for hegemony in international politics. The crucial scene for this interpretation is the historical exuberance at the beginning of World War I. Zeitblom describes it in retrospect as "liberation from a global stagnation . . . enthusiasm for the future, an appeal to duty and manliness—in short, a heroic festival" ("Befreiung aus der Welt-Stagnation . . . Zukunftsbegeisterung, Appell an Pflicht und Mannheit, kurz, als heroische Festivität" [399]) and employs the concept of "breakthrough" for the German violation of Belgian neutrality (316–18). It is the same concept that the devil had promised to Leverkühn in the realm of music during their conversation confirming the pact in 1912 (259). Leverkühn is anxious to achieve the "breakthrough" in the realm of modern music. Now Zeitblom has adopted the term for his purpose and explained its new meaning as "the breakthrough that would make [Germany] a dominant world power" ("Durchbruch . . . zur dominierenden Weltmacht" [402]). He is certain "that the hour of Germany's era had come" ("dass Deutschlands säkulare Stunde geschlagen habe" [401]) and enthusiastically marches off to war, even though he is fully aware of the ethical price paid for the "breakthrough." Leverkühn does not join the German armed forces. Telling his friend that he would not join him to conquer Paris, he suggests that the members of his generation are going in his place. It is important to notice that Leverkühn does not reject the political "breakthrough" as such, but claims it for his music. The failure of the German "breakthrough" in the Battle of the Marne in September 1914 does not discourage him from pursuing a similar goal in his realm (Vaget, "German Music" 233). On the contrary, he sacrifices the love for Marie Godeau, his intended wife, the friendship for Rudi Schwerdtfeger, and the affection for his nephew Nepomuk for his "breakthrough" in music. Intellectual interest is a stronger emotion for him than love.

Leverkühn's point of departure in modern music is a German immigrant composer, named Johann Conrad Beissel (1691–1768). Wendell Kretzschmar, his music teacher and the local organist in his home town, had introduced him to this eighteenth-century figure who had come to America in 1720 to settle in a semimonastic Anabaptist community in Ephrata in Pennsylvania. There he developed a system of musical notation of "masters" and "servants" notes for the religious hymns of his community. Leverkühn is intrigued by Beissel's sense of order (71–76). His system serves him as model for composing with twelve-tones. In 1910 Leverkühn presents his ideas for the first time to Zeitblom. It is a major step beyond his five-note code for the Esmeralda songs which he considers now too limited. The description of Leverkühn's discovery in chapter 22 is an analysis of twelve-tone music (205–08).

It was not surprising that Arnold Schoenberg considered it an infringement upon his intellectual property and Mann had to accommodate the composer later with a note at the end of the novel that protected his original invention (535; for the controversy between Mann and Schoenberg see Schoenberg).

Some critics have claimed that Mann's image of Leverkühn as an artist was influenced by Adorno's characterization of twelve-tone composers as subservient to the musical material in his *Philosophy of Modern Music* (Cobley 54–55). Others have argued more convincingly that Mann deviated from Adorno because he needed an artist who expressed his subjectivity in the works that he created. Self-reckoning required an artist who was in anguish over his pact with the devil (Kraus 177). Thus, Leverkühn communicated his feelings in his music like any other well-known nineteenth-century composer.

Leverkühn's fictitious compositions between 1910 and 1930 show the development and perfection of his new style. At the end of his career he achieves his "breakthrough" with *The Lamentation of Doctor Faustus*, his symphonic cantata of 1930. He selects the words of the 1587 *Historia von D. Johann Fausten*—"For I die as both a wicked and good Christian"—as general musical theme for the cantata (511). The twelve syllables of this sentence ingeniously fit the composition that expresses with twelve tones in word and music Faust's final oration to his students.

Zeitblom provides an analysis of Leverkühn's Faust work as the inverse of Beethoven's "Ode to Joy": namely, an "Ode to Sorrow." This negation of Beethoven's optimistic composition makes *The Lamentation of Doctor Faustus* into the ultimate "revocation" of the solace of art that the modern composer denounces after the death of Nepomuk. Leverkühn conceives his last composition as the Ninth Symphony's "counterpart in a most melancholy sense of the word" (514). Beethoven's symphony is negated by Leverkühn's work not only formally, but also thematically. The Faust cantata is "a negation of the religious," but not a denial of religion. Zeitblom further elaborates that a work dealing with the devil as tempter, with apostasy, and with damnation must be a religious work, but its religiosity can only be explained ex nihilo (514). Leverkühn's Faust cantata does not allow any consolation, appeasement, or redemption until the very end. Zeitblom interprets the final tone—the high G of a cello—as "hope beyond hopelessness, the transcendence of despair" ("Hoffnung jenseits der Hoffnungslosigkeit"). As Leverkühn's devoted friend he perceives it as "the dying note of sorrow" and believes that "its meaning changes, it stands as a light in the night" (515) ("der Ausklang der Trauer . . . wandelt den Sinn, steht als ein Licht in der Nacht" [*Werke* 6:651]).

But this final "breakthrough" is not a cause for celebration, since it constitutes Leverkühn's mental breakdown according to the Faustian program of his life. As his role model Faust had invited his students for a farewell dinner, Leverkühn assembles his friends at his home in a village outside of Munich for a private premiere of his cantata on his piano. Addressing his audience in the sixteenth-century language of the Chapbook as his "esteemable, peculiarly beloved brethren and sisters," he confesses that he has been "wed with Satan" for the term of twenty-four years (521). He admits that he has made the devil his companion, in order "to go beyond and break through" (524), and expresses the hope that what he completed "in wickedness can yet be good by grace" (526). He considers himself responsible for the murder of his friend Rudi Schwerdtfeger and the death of his nephew, saying that he sits before his audience "also as a murderer" (525). In conclusion he utters the words of the Chapbook that sealed the fate of the sixteenth-century Faust: "My sin is larger than that it can be forgiven me" (526). As his guests leave him in dismay, Leverkühn collapses at the piano. His landlady, a simple peasant woman, holds the unconscious man in her lap and declares that grace may not be available for the sinner, but there is enough for "real human understanding" (527). Zeitblom ends his biography of Leverkühn with a prayer for his friend and country in May 1945, after Germany's unconditional surrender: "May God have mercy on your poor soul, my friend, my fatherland" (534) ("Gott sei eurer armen Seele gnädig, mein Freund, mein Vaterland" [676]).

To a large degree *Doctor Faustus* was for Thomas Mann a work of self-criticism. Richard Wagner and Friedrich Nietzsche were the "stellar icons" of his thought, as he had proclaimed in his conservative and nationalistic *Reflections of a Nonpolitical Man* of 1918. Wagner's absence as a symbolic figure in *Doctor Faustus* is evidence of Thomas Mann's revisionism. He distanced himself from Wagner's overwhelming influence. Detaching Wagner's name from his drive for the hegemony of German music, he adopted it as a negative tendency that ruined the life and career of his Faustian composer. Leverkühn's cold-hearted ambition was presented as an example of the good and evil qualities that led his nation to destruction. Nietzsche's influence was reduced by focusing on the tragic details of his biography rather than his philosophy. Mann's Faust character was conceived in terms of Nietzsche's disease and collapse.

In 1914, Mann got caught up in the war exuberance displayed by German intellectuals and published a number of aggressive war essays, among them an article entitled "Reflections in War," which defended Germany's war as a defense of its culture against French and English civilization and democracy. Mann explained German militarism as the manifestation of German morality. In his book-length treatise, *Reflections of a Nonpolitical Man*, published in 1918, shortly before Germany's surrender during World War I, he continued to claim the opposition German culture versus Western civilization as the cause of war. Chapters 30 and 31 of *Doctor Faustus* reflect this mentality, now criticized with hindsight by the narrator. Zeitblom admits his participation in "the general exaltation" at the beginning of World War I, but is now ready to claim a "subconscious stirring of critical doubts" (319).

Chapter 34 on the Kridwiss circle serves as an account of the antidemocratic thinking among the conservative intellectual elites of the Weimar Republic. They did not accept democracy because they considered this form of government forced upon Germany by the victorious Allies and therefore they promoted the country's move toward a modern dictatorship. These intellectuals are shown as representatives of a pre-Nazi ideology. They were not even adverse to "hygienic arguments" that advised the killing of "the feeble-minded and those incapable of survival." The narrator reports that it was Dr. Breisacher who advanced this "subtle point, greeted with general approval" (389). It is not surprising that Leverkühn's composition of that time was his oratorio *Apocalipsis cum figuris*, because it corresponded to the apocalyptic mentality that Zeitblom encountered at the Kridwiss circle.

Critics have deplored the absence of an indictment of anti-Semitism from these discussions. The novel's portrayal of "a Germany without anti-Semitism" has been viewed as one of the novel's most serious shortcomings (Vaget, "German Music" 238). Furthermore, there are two negatively drawn Jewish characters, Dr. Chaim Breisacher, modeled after Oskar Goldberg, and Saul Fitelberg, a concert agent from Paris, who tries to lure Leverkühn to a life of wealth and international fame. As a perceptive critic pointed out, Mann's presentation of Breisacher as a Jewish fascist was "at the very least . . . a case of almost perversely bad taste, at worst . . . a whitewash of German intellectuals" (Klüger 162). With regard to Fitelberg, family members had warned Thomas Mann about the anti-Semitic undertones in his description, but Mann insisted that this character stay for comic effect. The author's misunderstanding of his own work was particularly embarrassing in view of his "full knowledge of the Jewish catastrophe" (Klüger 162). Only one of the concentration camps was mentioned and that one not by its name ("Buchenwald"). Although the "hideousness" of the crimes exceeding "anything the human imagination can conceive" was reported, the full extent of the genocide at the other camps remained unremarked. The narrator appears almost more concerned about "the disgrace of these revelations" to the German nation than about the victims (505–06).

This attitude did not prevent Thomas Mann from indicting the German genocide of European Jews in public. He was perhaps the most outspoken critic among the exiles to indict the Germans for the extermination of European Jews. In September 1941, he spoke up against the crimes against "Poles and Jews" in his monthly radio address transmitted by the BBC to Germany. In November 1941, he mentioned the mass extermination by poison gas and in June 1942 he spoke of the "brutal mass murder [of Dutch Jews] at Mauthausen." In June 1943, Thomas Mann delivered a speech on "The Fall of the European Jews" before an audience of ten thousand in San Francisco, indicting the German "resolution for the total extermination of the European Jewry" (Mann, *Werke* 11:1016, 1021, 1042, 13:495; Kurzke 425–27).

The end of the novel dealing with the question of German responsibility and the question of grace for the protagonist as well as the nation represents the final demonstration of its function as a political document. Like the chapters on World War I and on the Kridwiss circle, the "Epilogue" is a reflection of Mann's political speeches and articles written after the unconditional surrender of Germany in May 1945. In an article entitled "The End," published in *The Free World* in 1945, Mann stressed German responsibility and warned against confusion with the concept of collective guilt (*Werke* 12:944–50).

Some passages from another article, first published in *The Nation* under the title "The Camps" in May 1945, were incorporated almost verbatim into chapter 46 of *Doctor Faustus*. The article appeared in German under the misleading title

"Thomas Mann and German Guilt," which made the author appear as a proponent of collective guilt, charging every German for the crimes committed by the Nazi regime (*Werke* 12: 951–53).

This false impression was reconfirmed when Mann rejected an invitation to return to Germany in September 1945 and listed as the reason the failure of the cultural elites under the Hitler regime. Speaking of the "odor of blood and shame" attached to the books published in Germany between 1933 and 1945, he suggested that they should be pulped. Mentioning the music performed in Nazi Germany, he called it a "scandal" that there were musicians and singers to perform Beethoven's opera *Fidelio* and an audience eager to listen to them (*Werke* 12:953–62; for the West German reaction, see Vaget, *Thomas Mann* 480–91). In the novel Zeitblom had hoped for a performance of *Fidelio* "to celebrate Germany's liberation, its liberation of itself" (509). But that did not happen, because Germany had to be liberated by the Allies.

Mann's novel was received with much resentment in West Germany, where it became available in 1948 (Beddow 97–104). German readers disregarded the frequent references to the question of grace and viewed the novel with suspicion as an indictment of collective guilt. One critic accused the novelist of having presented a "world without transcendence," even though the novel dealt with the conditions of divine grace in the twentieth century (Holthusen).

The question of damnation or salvation is central to any Faust story since Goethe's version. Thomas Mann left the question open. In the final paragraph of the novel the author takes over from Zeitblom as first-person narrator, focusing on the pact that the nation had signed with its blood. He sees Germany, with "a hand over one eye," plummeting "from despair to despair." Leverkühn's pact is no longer mentioned. The question of a miracle "that goes beyond faith" and will "bear the light of hope" is raised. Zeitblom is shown as "a lonely man," folding his hands and praying for God's mercy for the soul of his friend and fatherland (534). In his lecture on "Germany and the Germans" at the Library of Congress in May 1945, Thomas Mann answered the question of salvation more explicitly, when he changed the political tone of his speech and ventured his personal opinion that Germany's "misfortune is only the paradigm of the tragedy of human life. And the grace that Germany so sorely needs, all of us need it" (66).

Works Cited

Adorno, Theodor W. *Aesthetic Theory*. Ed. Gretel Adorno and Rolf Tiedemann. Trans. Robert Hullot-Kentor. Minneapolis: U of Minnesota P, 1997.

Adorno, Theodor W. *Philosophie der neuen Musik*. Frankfurt: Suhrkamp, 1997.

Adorno, Theodor W., and Thomas Mann. *Briefwechsel 1943–1955*. Ed. Christoph Gödde and Thomas Sprecher. Frankfurt: Suhrkamp, 2002.

Bahr, Ehrhard. *Weimar on the Pacific: German Exile Culture in Los Angeles and the Crisis of Modernism*. Berkeley: U of California P, 2007.

Beddow, Michael. *Thomas Mann:* Doctor Faustus. Cambridge: Cambridge UP, 1994.

Benjamin, Walter. *Ursprung des deutschen Trauerspiels*. Frankfurt: Suhrkamp, 1972.

Bergsten, Gunilla. *Thomas Mann's* Doctor Faustus: *The Sources and Structure of the Novel*. Trans. Krishna Winston. Chicago: U of Chicago P, 1969.

Cobley, Evelyn. "Avant-Garde Aesthetics and Fascist Politics: Thomas Mann's *Doctor Faustus* and Theodor W. Adorno's *Philosophy of Modern Music*." *New German Critique* 86 (2002): 43–70.

Füssel, Stephan, and Hans Joachim Kreutzer, eds. *Historia von D. Johann Fausten: Text des Druckes von 1587: Kritische Ausgabe mit den Zusatztexten der Wolfenbütteler Handschrift und der zeitgenössischen Drucke*. Stuttgart: Reclam, 1988.

Holthusen, Hans Egon. *Die Welt ohne Transzendenz: Eine Studie zu Thomas Manns* Doktor Faustus *und seinen Nebenschriften*. Hamburg: Ellermann, 1948.

Klüger, R. "Jewish Characters in Thomas Mann's Fiction." *Horizonte: Festschrift für Herbert Lehnert zum 65. Geburtstag*. Ed. Hannelore Mundt, Egon Schwartz, and William J. Lillyman. Tübingen: Niemeyer, 1990. 161–72.

Kraus, Justice. "Expression and Adorno's Avant-Garde: The Composer in *Doktor Faustus*." *The German Quarterly* 81.2 (2008): 170–84.

Kurzke, Hermann. *Thomas Mann: Life as a Work of Art. A Biography*. Trans. Leslie Wilson. Princeton: Princeton UP, 2002.

Mann, Thomas. *Doctor Faustus: The Life of the German Composer Adrian Leverkühn as Told by a Friend*. Trans. John E. Woods. New York: Vintage Books, 1999.

Mann, Thomas. "Germany and the Germans." *Thomas Mann's Addresses Delivered at the Library of Congress 1942–1949*. Washington, DC: Library of Congress, 1963. 45–66.

Mann, Thomas. *Gesammelte Werke in dreizehn Bänden*. Frankfurt: Fischer, 1974.

Mann, Thomas. *Im Schatten Wagners: Thomas Mann über Richard Wagner: Texte und Zeugnisse 1895–1955*. Frankfurt: Fischer, 1999.

Mann, Thomas. *Reflections of a Nonpolitical Man*. Trans. Walter D. Morris. New York: Ungar, 1983.

Mann, Thomas. *The Story of a Novel: The Genesis of* Doctor Faustus. Trans. Richard and Clara Winston. New York: Knopf, 1961.

Mann, Thomas. *Tagebücher 1946–1948*. Ed. Inge Jens. Frankfurt: Fischer, 1989.

Potter, Pamela Maxine. *Most German of the Arts: Musicology and Society from the Weimar Republic to the End of Hitler's Reich*. New Haven: Yale UP, 1998.

Schoenberg, E. Randol, ed. *Apropos* Doktor Faustus: *Briefwechsel Arnold Schönberg—Thomas Mann, Tagebücher und Aufsätze 1930–1951*. Vienna: Czernin, 2009.

Vaget, Hans Rudolf. "German Music and German Catastrophe: A Re-Reading of *Doctor Faustus*." *A Companion to the Works of Thomas Mann*. Ed. Herbert Lehnert and Eva Wessell. Rochester: Camden House, 2004. 225–44.

Vaget, Hans Rudolf. "Mann, Joyce, and the Question of Modernism in *Doctor Faustus*." *Thomas Mann's Doctor Faustus: A Novel at the Margin of Modernism*. Ed. Herbert Lehnert and Peter C. Pfeiffer. Columbia: Camden House, 1991. 167–91.

Vaget, Hans Rudolf. *Thomas Mann, der Amerikaner: Leben und Werk im amerikanischen Exil 1938–1952*. Frankfurt: Fischer, 2011.

Author's Profile

Ehrhard Bahr is a member of the Germanic Languages faculty at the University of California, Los Angeles. He is a former President of the Goethe Society of North America. His publications include *Weimar on the Pacific: German Exile Culture in Los Angeles and the Crisis of Modernism*; *The Novel as Archive: The Genesis, Reception, and Criticism of Goethe's Wilhelm Meisters Wanderjahre*; and *Georg Lukács*.

Chapter 6

D. J. Enright and the Faust Theme

Arnd Bohm

Abstract

In his article, "D. J. Enright and the Faust Theme," Arnd Bohm discusses the innovative use made of the Faust story by D. J. Enright, primarily in his poetic work, *A Faust Book* (1979). Enright was an English poet and critic who spent much of his career outside Britain, teaching at foreign universities. His first book on Faust, *Commentary on Goethe's* Faust (1949), was a straightforward guide to the play. However, *A Faust Book* is a creative work. It consists of short poems and texts in which Enright presents a humorous revision and updating of the Faust story. He relies mainly on Marlowe and Goethe, but also makes use of the original anonymous Faust Book in creating a composite Faust figure. In addition to the conventional characters, including Mephistopheles, Wagner, and Gretchen, Enright introduces Faust's parents and a woman named Meretrix. Allusions to such things as washing machines and sewing machines disrupt the temporal frame established by Marlowe and Goethe. Mentions of Hamlet, Milton's Eve, and Wordsworth's daffodils serve to bring Faust closer to English-speaking readers.

It is hard to imagine another foreign writer who has become so domesticated in the Anglo-American world of letters as Goethe, or a story that has become so firmly established in the canon as that of *Faust*. The relevant productivity of academic scholars is extensive, generally of a high quality, and reflected in the standard bibliographies as well as in journals such as *Publications of the English Goethe Society* and the *Goethe Yearbook*, to say nothing of the German-language journals and more general literary ones. Excellent new translations of various sorts are available, as Derek Glass's bibliography *Goethe in English* (2005) shows. Poets such as the American Randall Jarrell struggled to come to terms with Goethe and the Germans. The translation of "The Archangels' Song" (251–52) is hardly audible in the *Complete Works* above the horror of poems like "A Camp in the Prussian Forest" (167–68). Jarrell's involvement with Goethe included a translation of *Faust I* that was published in 1976. Karl Shapiro's "The Progress of Faust" is brutally cynical (123–24). Donald Barthelme's short story "Conversations with Goethe" depends for its satire upon readers familiar with at least the stereotypical view of him. Even for those who are not, there is nevertheless something hilarious in the spoofed dialogue, as in the conclusion: "Critics, Goethe said, are the cracked mirror in the grand ball-room of the creative spirit. No, I said, they were, rather, the extra baggage on the grand cabriolet of conceptual progress. 'Eckermann,' said Goethe, '*shut up*'" (76). Some traces are bizarre, such as the translation of "Das Tagebuch" published in 1968 in *Playboy* (Glass 147). Others reveal how deeply Goethe has penetrated the curriculum, as does James Young's brief history of the German society at Franklin and Marshall College (1941).

Among the more recent adaptations of the Faust story has been David Mamet's short two-act play, *Faustus*, which had a world premiere on February 28, 2004 in San Francisco, under Mamet's direction. The play's division into two acts mirrors the two parts of Goethe's *Faust*. The figures have been reduced to five: Faustus, his Wife and Son, a Friend, and a Magus. Other details are also borrowed from Goethe, but on the whole it is a different work. Here, the action opens in Faustus's home on the occasion of a birthday party planned for his son. The theme of the relationship between father and son is predominant and also tragic. Part 2 expands to include Earth, Heaven, and Hell. The idea that the child who died in *Faust I* and in *Faust II* has lived to early teenage years is a striking deviation from Goethe. Faustus, on the other hand, is the familiar seeker for knowledge and fame, admitting: "I covet fame. And, like the criminal I plead first, what have I done, and next, who suffered? Yes, I would have fame. For my works, and fame surpassing them, till Faustus's renown shines free of accomplishment" (21). Faustus loses his family after he swears his oath on their sake; they die, the boy of sickness and the wife of suicide. Faustus was not present at their ends, but only hears a report from the Friend. This Friend indicts Faustus ruthlessly: "Our petted philosopher—who burned with the thirst for truth. Who betrayed those who trusted him, parsing their love to tribute and then to oblivion. Our sick creation. False friend, inconstant husband, engorged obscene digest of self-reference" (75). His failure as a husband and as a father finally leave him outside heaven, as the gates are closed. His regrets for his actions are not sufficient to save him. He pleads in vain for God's mercy; there is no one to intercede on his behalf. Unlike Gretchen, who intervenes for Faust, the Wife pronounces him an "Unnatural vicious father" (92).

In England, Goethe never achieved again the fame he had held in the nineteenth century (Simpson). Scholars were secure in their roles as guardians of Goethe's reputation, but the public generally turned from him to German poets like Rilke. The forays into Goethe by poets such as Auden (718) betokened familiarity, albeit at a distance. Certainly the world wars did not win German literature ready sympathy.

A complex intertextual reworking binds John Banville's novella *Mefisto* (1986) to Goethe's play and to other elements of the discourse on Faust and Faustianism. Not the person but rather the scientist is central. For Banville, the key theme is that of striving for knowledge, which places *Mefisto* at the end of his multivolume series about scientists: *Dr. Copernicus*, *Kepler*, and *The Newton Letter*. Already *The Newton Letter* (1982), with its extensive borrowing from Hugo von Hofmannsthal's "Letter of Lord Chandos," indicated Banville's interest in the history of science. Here, as the title makes clear and as Banville has claimed, the main character Gabriel Swan is not explicitly a Faust. But woven throughout the novella are subtle allusions and hints about precursors from the tradition, as Yael Levin has shown. For example, the name Kasperl points to the tradition of the puppet theater in which the Faust story was transmitted (Levin 50). Like Goethe's *Faust*, the novella is divided into two sections. Readers who know the originals will recognize affinities to them. The conclusion echoes the realization of Goethe's Faust that the approach he has taken to unlock the secrets of the universe has been misguided and requires a new beginning, one more attuned to nature. Similarly, Gabriel resolves to start over: "I have begun to work again, tentatively. I have gone back to the very start, to the simplest things. Simple! I like that. It will be different this time, I think it will be different. I won't do as I used to, in the old days. No. In future, I will leave things, I will try to leave things, to chance" (234). As the culmination of what is virtually a history of ideas, this end underscores that Faustian striving for absolute knowledge is destined for a dead end. Banville's tragedy of epistemology nonetheless ends on the hopeful note that there could be a new beginning. The striving may be bootless, but this does not entail that the individual Faust figure is doomed irrevocably.

Enright's Faust

Against this background, the ongoing and close involvement of English poet D. J. Enright with Goethe stands out for its dedication to the Faust material. Enright wrote two books on Faust. One was published at the beginning of Enright's career, a commentary that first appeared in *Scrutiny* in 1945 and was printed by James Laughlin for New Directions in 1945 as *Commentary on Goethe's* Faust. The second appeared thirty years later as *A Faust Book* with Oxford University Press. As Leonard Forster noted, the collection of poems was less "a lyric cycle" and more "a series of dramatic tableaux capable of being presented on a stage" (142). Although separated from the first book by a lifetime of thinking, teaching, and writing, the group of poems too provided a kind of commentary, dealing with the main aspects of the Faust story down to the late twentieth century. The texts—not all are verse; some of them are in prose—are short, varying from chains of couplets to free verse. The titles resemble the chapter headings in the original Faust Book (*Historie* 55–57). They operate as captions that shed light on what follows, such as "Faust is soon bored" (*Faust Book* 24) or "Mephistopheles addresses the working class. Faust's aged parents are nonplussed" (31).These are frequently wry editorializing comments, establishing an extra level to the interpretation of the whole. They frame the action and lend something of the carnivalesque atmosphere to the events, as though a barker were speaking to the audience.

Before turning to the problems of Enright's treatment of Goethe and of Faust, a brief biographical note is needed, not least because it sheds light on his position. Dennis Joseph Enright was born in 1920 in Warwickshire. After excelling at school, he attended Cambridge University. The autobiographical poems of *The Terrible Shears: Scenes from a Twenties Childhood* (1973) afford glimpses of a British lower middle-class life in the interwar period—sometimes dreadful, sometimes darkly humorous, mostly bleak. For an intelligent child of limited means, ironies were everywhere, even if bitter. Central lines from a short text, "Class," recall how the status quo was maintained: "The wife of a teacher at school (she was / Mother of one of my classmates) was / Genuinely enraged when I won a scholarship. / She stopped me in the street, to tell me / (With a loudness I supposed was upper-class) / That Cambridge was not for the likes of me, nor was / Long hair, nor the verse I wrote for the school mag" (*The Terrible Shears* 64). Made wary and wiser by life, Enright clung to the values of decency, hard work, and justice as he built a career teaching English literature abroad. Although his mood was mellowed by his sense of humor when compared with the generally bleak outlook of Britain in the 1950s, Enright continued to hold to the middle-class ideal of hard work as the path to achievement. His route was indirect, taking him abroad to lecture at universities outside the usual circles of British academics. His lecture in Singapore on "Robert Graves and the Decline of Modernism" gave rise to a nationalist reply in the newspaper *Straits Times* defending cultural autonomy. Eventually Enright returned home, where he remained something of an outsider. From 1970–72 he was a coeditor of *Encounter*, then director at the publisher Chatto and Windus from 1974 to 1982, as well as Honorary Professor of English at the University of Warwick (1975–80). Even including reprints and editing, Enright's output of some sixty books is an indication of his tireless dedication to the world of letters, even if he did not achieve wide fame. Once he had placed himself outside the boundaries of the domestic literary system, it proved difficult to reenter. Some honors did come his way. His contribution was recognized in 1981 when he received the Queen's Gold Medal for Poetry and in 1991 when he was granted an Order of the British Empire (OBE). Enright died on the last day of 2002 in London (Harding; Morrison).

Enright's two major publications on the Faust theme belong to two different categories, yet their starting positions do demonstrate parallels. Both might be said to share what Enright once said about his commentary on Goethe, namely, they have a kind of impudence (Enright, *Interplay* 37). The term is a bit strong. What distinguishes Enright is his willingness to be autonomous in his interpretations and frank in his judgments. He has taken previous scholarship into account, but offers a reading, particularly of Goethe's *Faust*, that avoids traditional opinions. For example, Enright has limited use for the so-called *Urfaust* and follows instead texts authorized by Goethe:

the sad thing is that critics have spent so much time and labor in the study of the earlier versions that when they come to the culminating *First Part* their approach is vitiated, they deplore that such and such should have been omitted, or added, or altered; and the fact that Goethe's literary use of the legend should have changed seems to them sufficient proof of artistic (or philosophical) uncertainty. (Enright, *Commentary* 17)

The "critics" he opposes remain anonymous.

    The full implications of Enright's analysis in the commentary have thus far not been embraced by Goethe scholarship. Approaching Goethe from an English context, Enright was not blinkered by adulation of Goethe. Neither the German nor the Anglo-American side is quite open to the suggestion that Goethe meant to debunk the pretensions of rank, particularly arbitrary rank. Equally neglected has been the substance of Enright's *A Faust Book*. Divided almost equally into two parts and thereby mirroring the division of Goethe's drama, the texts present problems on how to deal with them. There are all sorts of variations in form, length, and tone, ranging over the entire field of Faust stories and beyond. The attempt to reduce everything to a simple formula leads to the unhelpful observation, attributed to Heine as a motto, that "Everyone should write a Faust of his own" (vi).

    The first edition of the poems had no other editorial notes than the three mottoes, one each from Heine, Valéry, and Goethe. The second version in 1997 has succinct yet suggestive introductory words about *Paradise Lost* and the Faust material. While of limited utility, the comments do offer some tantalizing hints, such as: "Faust's sin corresponds to that of Adam and Eve. . . . This sin — if sin it is — was committed by Faust more deliberately, as would be expected of a discontented and ambitious scholar of his time, thirsting for deeper knowledge, whether forbidden or not, and the power it would bring him" (*Telling Tales* ix). Enright claims a right to complicate the literary Faust via the liberties of the lyric sequence. Anything goes: "While continuing to exploit possibilities for comedy and even slapstick, a modern treatment is more likely to dwell on science and technology—which once would have been deemed 'forbidden knowledge'— and their equivocal consequences, the 'necromantic' entertainment offered by television and video, and the sort of bleak prophecies uttered by Mephistopheles" (*Telling Tales* x). Mephistopheles has been wittily revised and updated, to make him reflect the contemporary world's views of what is permitted and what is diabolical. The conclusion reflects the contemporary world governed by impersonal, disembodied fiat. Carefully guarding his tongue in one cheek, Enright concludes by pronouncing somewhat mysteriously that "it doesn't do to make light of the devil" (*Telling Tales* xi). Just what that would mean in the fading years of the terrible twentieth century remains to give us thought.

    Enright's attitude places a shimmer of mockery over the entire set of poems, yet the problems of the Faust story remain serious and provocative. Quick skimming could misdirect readers into taking *A Faust Book* as little more than a series of jibes at a story of major gravity. Enright accepts that Marlowe and Goethe have both produced works whose treatments were intended to be taken seriously:

> Even so, the man had to be duly punished and dragged down into hell: wherever Marlowe's personal sympathies lay, this made a tremendous finale. Goethe, an indefatigable seeker after knowledge and a believer in its holiness, couldn't possibly follow suit, and at the end of his huge and heterogeneous work he went to some pains, not to say dodgy devices, to redeem his hero, ending with a mystical extravaganza which my Mephistopheles derides for its lack of realism and relevance. (*Telling Tales* xi)

Just because we have different premises than previous ages accepted does not allow us to make light of them, or to pretend that we necessarily still share their beliefs. Each age receives, absorbs and transforms the Faust material according to current methods and convictions.

Overall, the events of the poems follow the order set by Goethe's work, from the initial encounter between Faust and Mephistopheles down to their breaking up. Some scenes are taken from other sources, such as Marlowe's play, where Faust is forbidden to marry (Enright, *Faust Book* 23) or where he bids his friends farewell (73). The goodbye is common to both Marlowe and the earlier Faust Book, so some scenes may have more than one link connected to them. Enright approaches the play chronologically in the commentary and in the poetic cycle. First, he is ready to acknowledge and accept the priorities of earlier versions, such as the Faust Book of 1587 and Marlowe's *Tragicall History of Doctor Faustus*. Immediately the difference with German philologists is clear: while they too were aware of earlier works, they long insisted that Goethe had created his version more or less independently. Nevertheless, they intensely pursued references to evidence of the "historical Faust," eager to show that he had been a German original. Rather than dwelling on things for which the evidence was, at best, thin, Enright concentrates on the study of the Goethean texts. His methodology appears to be a strong rebuke to generations of Goethe scholars: "I really think that the person who comes to Faust with no scholarly preconceptions will have the best chance of comprehending what the play is about—which suggests that the neglect experienced by the work during recent years may finally prove to have done it a considerable service" (Enright, *Commentary* 19). The approach could come across as a provocation, but at stake was actually a challenge to the standards of learning, which too often lose readers and themselves in questions about details such as the nature of Faust's relationship to Paracelsus.

Enright's commentary is, however, filled with relevant details that will be of interest and help to ordinary readers, guiding them without excessive shows of learning, so the objection against "scholarly preconceptions" has to be taken cautiously. An alert reader who follows the text has to be able to make sense of an admittedly complex work. Enright's purpose then is to be a friendly guide, "to go straight through the play, making whatever point seems called for as I reach it" (Enright, *Commentary* 6). The passages he translated into clear English are further indication that the aim is to provide readers with access to the text, even at the risk of undermining its status as a masterpiece.

The first poem, with its title "Dr Faust discourses on the subject of training and heredity," is typical of the approach Enright will take. It is short but carefully constructed. The shift between the names Faust and Faustus indicates that Enright is not particularly concerned about the layers of the story's versions. At times the German elements predominate; then again the figure is tied to the English tradition as passed on by Marlowe. It is Mephistopheles, not Faust, who meets with the undergraduate and sardonically introduces the hypocrisies of university life. Faustus compares the students' learning ability negatively with that of the poodle. Ironically, the professor who mocks the students is himself not very wise or cunning. He fails to see through the poodle's disguise. He relies upon clichés to do his thinking for him and never penetrates to the truth. The dog's "toothy smile" is double-edged: it could be friendly, or it could be a foreshadowing of how Mephistopheles is out to devour Faust's life and soul. The mention of Easter is a gesture to its function in Goethe's play, where it saves Faust from drinking poison and where it introduces the memory of Christ's presence in personal and world salvation. All of this is lost on Faust, even though he is supposed to have studied theology and should make the appropriate associations.

The use of the word heredity in the poem's title has its own implications. Modern readers think immediately of genetics and the discoveries made after Mendel, but those are all matters hidden in the sixteenth century. Faust's discourse hardly measures up to modern science. His manner reflects the confidence of the age of pedantry, adhering to Aristotelianism, not the anxieties and doubts of actual investigations of the world. Thus, even though not aware of the poodle's true identity, Faust simply gives it a name, and a harmless diminutive at that. The allusion to Adam's naming is reduced to a trifle. Mephistopheles makes ambiguous signs, wagging a tail and giving a toothy grin. These are not honest revelations, just as he does not actually identify himself to Goethe's Faust.

The presence of the dog continues in the next two poems. Faust in his study recites an updated version of his famous soliloquy of complaint about the defects of learning: "Divinity talks all the time of better times to come, / Science invents false limbs and true explosives, / And Alchemy turns lead to lead at vast expense; / Art thrills with piggish gods and puffy goddesses, / While Law invokes the laws its lawyers legalize, / And Logic says it all depends on what you mean" (*Faust Book* 2). The revisions make the limitations of the various disciplines reach down to our present era. Some barbs are sharp, as in the reference to how science has promoted the tools of warfare. Faust will come close to an insight into the part played by Aristotelianism in all this, but schooled in abstract thinking as a mode of research, he quickly turns to unanswerable questions: "Then what is life . . . / Except a slower form of suicide?" (2). As before, Faust ignores the teachings of Christianity and leaves an opening for the Mephistophelean dog to pipe up and offer a "'small service'" about suicide. The response in the next poem to Faust's question is a jumble mingling superstition and arcane lore. A wise or prudent Faust should be alerted by all this to his dire situation, especially when God is turned by anagram into a dog ("every god has its day" [3]).

After the opening poems which are strongly evocative of Goethe's play, with some borrowing from Marlowe, there is a shift. The fifth poem reproduces part of the text of the pact signed by Faustus in Marlowe's version. However, it has been modified by the insertion of parenthetical editorial comments:

> Being of sound mind (and all that mumbo-jumbo), I (name in full) by these presents (already?) do covenant and grant, in consideration of 24 (Twenty-Four) years of service by Mephistopheles, the which (which?) shall bring me anything, or do for me whatsoever, that I give them (names of Lucifer and self) full power to do with me at their pleasure, to rule, to send, fetch, or carry me (that should cover everything) or mine, be it either body, soul, flesh, blood, or goods (curious expression), into their habitation, be it wheresoever (how discreet!). (*Faust Book* 5)

The first phrase "being of sound mind" is an addition that domesticates the contract for English audiences with a familiar bit of legalese. But the thrust of most of the comments works in an opposite direction to distance readers from an easy, uncritical acceptance of the jargon used by lawyers and the legal system. Apparently little has changed over the centuries even if the ossified formulas generally go unquestioned; only small modifications are needed to make a modern document out of the archaic original.

One of the themes Enright emphasizes is politics, connecting to the conditions of the twentieth century. Mephistopheles declares himself to be "a man of the people" even though he remains "a Prince's man" (*Faust Book* 7). As one might expect, his notion of democracy is diabolical. Liberty is the freedom to choose pornography. The whole process of democracy is, from a satanic perspective, useful for trapping unwary innocents: "The process may be time-consuming, / But in the end it eats up . . . more than time" (7). These are harsh judgements, but anyone who had seen the evils wrought in the name of democracy, from communism to fascism, must grant that there is some validity to them.

Another poem mocks the promises proffered to the proletariat. Mephistopheles holds out the ideal of universal literacy and educational opportunities. On the surface, it will look as if the children of the working class have improved opportunities and will live better lives. The reality, however, is that nothing has changed or will change: "And they shall then discover / That correct spelling is held cheap / That the best people hire scriveners / And books are no longer read" (31). One cannot help but think that these lines reflect the reality and the disappointments of Enright's own career. Although he had risen through education and scholarships, in the end he remained out of fashion, ignored for the most part as a marginal figure.

An explicit indictment of the global political reality comes in a report on "The Political Achievements of Faust." There are clear references to the twentieth century and the various improvement projects undertaken by developing countries: "He furnished the Z Republic with a / Computer called Rational Government. / Its rule was just, taxes were abolished, / Crime dwindled, the economy flourished— / And the good citizens were bored to tears" (*Faust Book* 61). Faust's efforts, even when successful, do not make people contented. He grows angry and bitter, but Mephistopheles merely smiles to see the frustrated outcomes. Another bleak poem forecasts that change will yield forms that look better but accomplish little. The concluding lines take aim at the domination of the world by capitalism: "only those prophecies are genuine / which show a profit" (66).

Neither Marlowe nor Goethe provides a full context for either Faust's or his own era. For Marlowe, the sixteenth century was an age of global exploration and incipient colonial expansion. There are traces of this when Faustus announces his intention to become "great emperor of the world" (Marlowe 276). Goethe also excludes most details of the globalization visible in the eighteenth century. Enright, by contrast, weaves in evidence that the industrial revolution is underway. In one poem, Faust dreams about a woman who "Was the proud owner of a mighty and intricate engine, / A Washing Machine, which cleansed and rinsed one's linen" (*Faust Book* 55). One of the most extraordinary episodes is the disruption of the received Faust story by the introduction of a Gretchen at a modernized spinning wheel, namely, a sewing machine. It is important to recall how the literary critic brings to bear all sorts of external knowledge when reading any work. An unavoidable hermeneutic catch is that whether it is wished or not, every current reading always takes place marked by the present. Sometimes this is deliberately articulated, as when Mephistopheles quotes the name of Freud. At other times, the temporal jumbling disrupts the illusion of the text's atemporality, its pastness. This happens to devastating effect in the poem "Gretchen at the Sewing-Machine" (57–58). The translation into English is close to the German original yet sharpened, emphasizing Gretchen's frankness about her condition and her helplessness: "My stomach is sore, / My peace is fled, / I wish I'd been careful, / I wish I was wed" (58). A comparison with the poetically nuanced German shows how Enright has intensified things: "My peace is gone— / my heart is sore— / I shall find it never. / No, never more" (Goethe, *Goethe's* Faust: Part I 125) ("Meine Ruh' ist hin / Mein Herz ist schwer; / Ich finde sie nimmer / Und nimmermehr" [Goethe, *Werke* 3 lines 3374–77]).The use of the indicative instead of the subjunctive highlights Gretchen's lack of sophistication, signaling as well the care with which Enright has worked. This makes the replacement of the spinning wheel by a sewing machine quite startling. As Leonard Forster comments, Germans with whom he discussed the poem were taken aback (148). Their response comes from their reception of Goethe, of *Faust*, and of Gretchen's situation. However, this is impervious to Goethe's concern for work and technology and their impact in his own time. The industrial revolution, with its destruction of traditional trades, was looming; a careful observer like Goethe sensed change coming, as when he was writing *Iphigenie auf Tauris*. His exclamation in a letter to Charlotte von Stein is well known: "Here the drama just will not advance. It is accursed: the King of Tauris is supposed to talk as though no stocking-weaver in Apolda were starving" ("Hier will das Drama gar nicht fort . . . der König von Tauris soll reden, als wenn kein Strumpfwürker in Apolda hungerte" [Goethe, *Werke* 5 403]). Whether Gretchen is suffering at a spinning wheel, as women had for millennia, and as they would in front of the sewing machine, was ultimately of little consequence. Women's basic condition would repeat over and over again, either to the music of the spinning wheel or to the rhythms of the machine. The vagaries of technological change serve to underscore how little progress could alter Gretchen's fate.

Recognizing that Enright's interpretive approach reflects his political views also gives another side to the commentary. Far from being just any random reading of the play, Enright operates with a precise hierarchy of participants. At the top is God, who is treated with remarkable generosity. Below him are the angels and Mephistopheles, with Faust below them but slightly ahead of other humans in the play. Off to one side, perhaps on the plane of the angels, is the voice of the commentator (close to but not identical with Enright's own voice). The readers could be on Faust's level, with whom they sympathize and from whom they can learn. Such hierarchical sorting proves crucial for grasping Goethe's argument as Enright sees it: "Will Faust (as a representative man) under temptation and, more than that, during the enactment of evil, still retain his divine acknowledgment of the distinction between good and evil?" (Enright, *Commentary* 19). Whereas Goethe resisted ranking because of his situation at the Weimar court, Enright was sensitized to its importance because of his upbringing in a society that professed equality but maintained class boundaries. Seeing this aspect also makes it possible to discern moments of comedy. One is that God's place at the top is tested by the events. At the same time, Mephistopheles's slippery function, and the genuine chance he will move down the ladder, increase our readiness to sympathize with him (Enright, *Commentary* 142–43). The world of struggle becomes an arena where everyone, from top to bottom, must contend.

The episodes with Gretchen-Margarete are closely connected to Goethe's text, yet they are subtly adapted. "Faust and Gretchen walk in the garden" is darkened, intensified (*Faust Book* 21–22). Faust's denials are translated into blunt negatives: "Do I believe in God you ask. / You're a natural philosopher! / Can anyone say he believes in God? / What is meant by *God*? / What is meant by *believe*? / What is meant by *I*? / Can we employ these words any more?" (21). The weight of these plain questions partakes of Faust's directness yet gains because he is open and frank about his nonbelief. The poem is complemented by the episode, original to Enright, where Gretchen touches and then loses her cross. Faust seems to have had something to do with it, as his irony confirms: "It's too good for you? / Nonsense, my sweet—nothing's too good . . . / Oh dear, the chain's broken— / Where can the cross have got to? It can't have gone too far" (22). The final line plays with the idiom of going too far as the equivalent of getting out of hand, serving as a reminder that everything said and shown in texts about Faust occludes sinister underlying meanings.

Enright's love of language shows in frequent word play, of which the following are some examples: "Adam and his madam paid a price" (*Faust Book* 8); "Your famulus / Grows familiar!" (8); "Take care of your running head, and / Your tailpiece will take care of itself" (10); "Number seven—go to heaven" (15); "*The Story of O* by Oh!" (20); "Remove the sin from penis and there's not much left, / Is there? You might as well take Origen's tip" (41); "How alchemy shall yield to chemists, aspiration to / aspirin, barbs to barbiturates, aesthetics to / anaesthetics, whores to hormones, heroines to heroin"(65); "You think we policemen are boobies, ha ha!" (67). Not everyone takes these games all that seriously, seeing them primarily as signs of "rather donnish wit and a relish for the quirks of language" (Harding 100). However, in addition to annoying the establishment of high-brow literature, these games underscore how irreverent the Faust theme can be. The jokes often also require sudden insights into deeper backgrounds to the issues. The ludic quality recalls something that is too rarely granted to Goethe's *Faust*, namely, the pervasive slipperiness of language. Critics prefer words to mean just what they say and tend to resist Goethe's own poetic awareness of the many ways language shifts shape at every opportunity (Bohm). Indeed, how could *Faust* be a significant, serious work of literature without puns, after they had been used by writers of the stature of Chaucer and Shakespeare (Joseph; Partridge)?

As a demonstration of linguistic fun, Enright introduces Meretrix, a character primarily his own. She is a popular woman at "Spicy Spiess's / In downtown Wittenberg": "There Faust met a go-go dancer / Called Meretrix, big bust, long legs, / Lusted after by university wits / And city aldermen alike" (*Faust Book* 25). She reappears later, notably in the next poem, where ribaldry sets the tone: "This talk of naked made him think of Meretrix' bare thighs" (26). There is a clever allusion in all this to the classicists, who might recall that a "meretrix" in Latin was a common prostitute (Georges 2: 892). The quatrain "Faust considers the subject of souls" continues on the same fixations: "Gretchen has a large soul and small breasts / Meretrix, great big breasts and a tiny soul / Breasts are of this world: Faust loves them / Faust loves not souls, especially large ones" (28). Nothing of Meretrix is found in Goethe's *Faust*—and yet, the explicit references to the body and to desires may seem compatible with what we are told about Faust and his likings.

One aspect of Faust's desires highlighted by Enright are the sexual ones. Mephistopheles has the world searched for obscene books for Faust's gratification (20). The joke is that reading about sex is only a distant imitation of the actual thing. As always, Faust the pedant does not really get to reality; the charade of seducing Gretchen confirms this. Nor is the relationship with Helen able to concentrate on the corporeal. Faust's language deals with issues of immortality and the soul, rather removed from the details of eroticism. The lines "Sweet Helen, make me immortal with a kiss!" and "Thy lips such forth my soul: see where it flies" (37) are taken from Marlowe (330). Helen is also not interested in sex. Mephistopheles realizes that virtual sex is not going to advance the campaign to subvert Faust. An affair with the student might do the trick, but Faust balks (41). When she is gone, all Faust retains is a prurient curiosity as when Mephistopheles tells a story of having seduced Pilate's wife. Faust eagerly asks, "And what did you do? Did you do it?" (53). When Mephistopheles teases him with a description of her ear, he brushes it aside. Mephistopheles reveals the precedent in the attempt on Eve, who "had a fine ear too, sort of pink and innocent" (54). Faust dismisses the reference too. He has quite missed the allusion to the episode from Milton's *Paradise Lost* in which Satan's whispering in her ear plays an important role in the plot (IV lines 800–805). The repeated mention of ear does not alert Faust to the ways in which Mephistopheles has been talking to him, even though aurality was suspect as a means by which temptation could enter consciousness. It is further evidence that Faust is not nearly as learned in theology as he pretends.

The scenes with Faust's parents are again invented but plausible. The parents as imagined by Enright are touching in their honest simplicity and ridiculous in their vanity about their son the professor. They leave as innocent as they came, mouthing platitudes: "'I wouldn't mind him being rich, / As long as he was honest,' said the father. / 'I wouldn't mind him being poor, / As long as he was happy' said the mother" (32). Of course, Faust must have had parents, but both Marlowe and Goethe are virtually silent about them. Enright's common decency introduces the parents, for everyone has parents at some time, but he gently mocks their failure to be adroit in the ways of the world. The suggestion that they have some sort of connection to the figures of Philemon and Baucis is tempting to explore, but really lacks any firm ground.

Perhaps the most startling intrusions are the references to William Wordsworth's daffodils, which have no place in the Faust story. They are introduced in "Mephistopheles and the primrose" by Mephistopheles: "Mind you, / He also made a host of golden daffodils, / To mention but a few" (39). Any English reader should recognize the phrase; the references in "Faust and the daffodils" give definitely familiar images: "'What a crowd of golden daffodils!' He exclaimed. 'Or even a host. . .' / The daffodils tossed their heads again. / 'One might say you were fluttering / And dancing in the breeze'" (40). The purpose of these references is initially unclear, until one remembers how they originally represented the power of the recalling imagination. The power of imagining would seem to fit well with the episode in question, which involves the appearance of Helen of Troy. No matter how real she appears to Faust, in fact she is only a fantasy brought back to life by him. The English poem stresses the extent to which Faust acts like a Romantic, quite the opposite of the author Goethe.

The Faust who is presented by Enright is, in a word, more of a human being than his prototypes. Whereas they were concentrated images of cosmic significance, this one is humble; at the end he even thanks Mephistopheles. In his farewell address he stutters and wanders about aimlessly, speaking to "trusty and well-beloved friends" about "murder and lechery" (73). His bumbling and ineffectual striving are more representative of a mundane human being who finds himself in affairs he never quite understands. He is perhaps incompetent, but not evil. His end resembles that in Goethe's play more than it elaborates on the gruesome fate given to Marlowe's Faustus.

It would be daunting to nominate Enright as a member of the illustrious group that includes Marlowe, Goethe, and Thomas Mann as authors who have raised Faust to global significance. While Enright has other claims for broader recognition than he receives, his contribution to the elaboration of the Faust story will remain tangential. Yet at the same time it would be shortsighted to disregard him when considering the pattern and complexities of the literary discussion of Faust. Whether as commentator or as an original poet, Enright has given his special perspective voice and thus ought to be heard. Certainly his place in the Anglo-American reception of Faust in the middle of the twentieth century deserves to be known. A lifetime spent in reading, thinking, and teaching about Faust and his fellows sheds unique light, makes us see anew what might become. Faust no longer belongs just to the Germans and to their often skewed perspective. Enright serves as a clear reminder that many writers, such as Thomas Disch (*Camp Concentration*), Mikhail Bulgakov (*The Master and Margarita*), and Vladimir Nabokov (*Lolita*), are among those who have enriched our understanding of the Faust story by telling us things we had overlooked or not heard before about it.

Works Cited

Auden, W. H. *Collected Poems*. Ed. Edward Mendelson. New York: Random House, 1991.

Banville, John. *Mefisto*. London: Random House, 1993.

Barthelme, Donald. *Overnight to Many Distant Cities*. New York: Viking Penguin, 1985.

Bohm, Arnd. "Naming Goethe's Faust: A Matter of Significance." *Deutsche Vierteljahrsschrift für Literaturwissenschaft und Geistesgeschichte* 80.3 (2006): 408–34.

Disch, Thomas M. *Camp Concentration*. New York: Bantam, 1980.

Enright, D. J. *Commentary on Goethe's Faust*. New York: New Directions, 1949.

Enright, D. J. *A Faust Book*. Oxford: Oxford UP, 1979.

Enright, D. J. *Interplay: A Kind of Commonplace Book*. Oxford: Oxford UP, 1995.

Enright, D. J. *Telling Tales:* Paradise Illustrated & A Faust Book. Oxford: Oxford UP, 1997.

Enright, D. J. *The Terrible Shears: Scenes from a Twenties Childhood*. London: Chatto & Windus, 1975.

Forster, Leonard. "*A Faust Book*." *Life by Other Means: Essays on D. J. Enright*. Ed. Jacqueline Simms. Oxford: Oxford UP, 1990. 144–49.

Georges, Karl Ernst. *Ausführliches Lateinisch-Deutsches Handwörterbuch*. Ed. Heinrich Georges. Darmstadt: Wissenschaftliche Buchgesellschaft, 1998.

Glass, Derek. *Goethe in English: A Bibliography of the Translations in the Twentieth Century*. Leeds: Maney Publishing, 2005.

Goethe, Johann Wolfgang von. *Faust Part 1*. Trans. Randall Jarrell. New York: Farrar, Straus and Giroux, 2000.

Goethe, Johann Wolfgang von. *Goethe's* Faust: Part I. Trans. C. F. MacIntyre. New York: New Directions, 1957.

Goethe, Johann Wolfgang von. *Werke*. Vol. 3.1. Ed. Erich Trunz. Munich: Deutscher Taschenbuch Verlag, 1982.

Goethe, Johann Wolfgang von. *Werke: Hamburger Ausgabe, Band 5: Dramatische Dichtungen III*. Ed. Lieselotte Blumenthal and Eberhard Haufe. Munich: Deutscher Taschenbuch Verlag, 1982.

Harding, Anthony John. "D. J. Enright." *Poets of Great Britain and Ireland, 1945–1960*. Ed. Vincent B. Sherry. Detroit: Gale, 1984. 95–101.

The Historie of the Damnable Life and Deserved Death of Doctor John Faustus. *Lives of Faust: The Faust Theme in Literature and Music. A Reader.* Ed. Lorna Fitzsimmons. Berlin: De Gruyter, 2008. 53–142.

Jarrell, Randall. *The Complete Poems*. New York: Farrar, Straus & Giroux, 1990.

Joseph, Gerhard. "Chaucer's Coinage: Foreign Exchange and the Puns of the 'Shipman's Tale.'" *Chaucer Review* 17.4 (1983): 341–57.

Levin, Yael. "Thinking outside the Hermeneutic Circle: Mephistophelean Intertextuality in John Banville's *Mefisto*." *Partial Answers* 7.1 (2009): 45–59.

Mamet, David. *Faustus*. New York: Vintage, 2004.

Marlowe, Christopher. *The Complete Plays*. Ed. J. B. Steane. London: Penguin, 1986.

Milton, John. *The Poems of John Milton*. Ed. John Carey and Alastair Fowler. London: Longmans, 1968.

Morrison, Blake. "D. J. Enright [obituary]." *The Guardian*. January 1, 2003. <http://www.guardian.co.uk/news/2003/jan/01/guardianobituraries.books>.

Nabokov, Vladimir. *The Annotated* Lolita. Ed. Alfred Appel, Jr. New York: Random House, 1991.

Partridge, Eric. *Shakespeare's Bawdy*. London: Routledge & Kegan Paul, 1968.

Shapiro, Karl. *Selected Poems*. New York: Vintage Books, 1973.

Simpson, James. "The Authority of Culture: Some Reflections on the Reception of a Classic." *Goethe and the English-Speaking World: Essays from the Cambridge Symposium for his 250th Anniversary*. Eds. Nicholas Boyle and John Guthrie. Rochester: Camden House, 2002. 185–98.

Young, Henry James. *Historical Account of the Goethean Literary Society of Franklin and Marshall College*. Lancaster: Franklin and Marshall College, 1941.

Author's Profile

Arnd Bohm teaches English at Carleton University, Ottawa, Canada. His publications in German literature include articles on Goethe, Herder, Schiller, Wieland, and Celan. His book, *Goethe's* Faust *and European Epic: Forgetting the Future*, appeared in 2007. In addition to an ongoing interest in German literature, his interests include English literature since 1750, Anglo-German literary relations, comparative literature, poetry, and ecocriticism. He is currently working on Nabokov's *Lolita*.

Chapter 7

Is My *Doktor Faustus* the Last Opera?

Konrad Boehmer

Abstract

In his article, "Is My *Doktor Faustus* the Last Opera?" Dutch composer Konrad Boehmer discusses the genesis, composition, and production of his "anti-opera" *Doktor Faustus* (1985). Although repelled by Goethe's *Faust* as a schoolboy, Boehmer later became familiar with Hanns Eisler's Faust libretto and decided to work on the theme. To do so, Boehmer realized that he would have to redefine the relation between "Material" and "Darstellungslogik" and create a revisionist perspective on the historical Faustus. He opted to synthesize historical methods and new serial strategies. The result treats traditional elements of opera ironically: an overture, two male protagonists, and a miracle, but one without redemption. In conceiving the plot, Boehmer interjects Trithemius and Hans Böhm in his adaptation of material on the historical Faustus. The libretto was composed by Flemish writer Hugo Claus. Boehmer mentions some of the difficulties encountered during production of the opera, and concludes with a glance at his subsequent work on the Faust theme.

Mythology

After Jesus of Nazareth, Faustus is the last mythological figure in our history. They both have one thing in common: their real life has nothing to do with their mythological survival. The Jesus mythology has evolved into a gigantic institution (after two thousand years in full decline); the Faust mythology has obsessed European literature and the arts for over five hundred years. Richard Wagner's attempt to compose a "Jesus" opera failed. My *Doktor Faustus* (Doctor Faustus) was a modest attempt to reduce a myth to its historical nucleus and to write the last "opera" of our history.

A last opera? The twentieth century is full of those promises which came from the suprematists and the futurists in the first instance and later on from the authors of happenings, inspired by John Cage's *Theatre Piece* (from 1952). Though in some of those concepts elements of traditional opera were used, they all rejected the concept of the genre, replacing it by symbolic or purely ritual actions with completely unconnected elements, as in Cage's pieces or similar happenings. From a European viewpoint, these attempts are more reminiscent of the kinds of music theater which preceded opera (the medieval liturgic drama or the Renaissance intermedia). Should a "last opera" follow those strategies, or should it keep to the genre it wants to terminate? I think that this last option is the most dialectic one, because it offers the possibility to end the historic genre by making use of its inner contradictions and thus further its inner erosion. The Faust theme lends itself perfectly to such an approach.

My *Faust* Childhood

When I was a schoolboy at the Cologne Apostel-Gymnasium, Goethe's *Faust* was a compulsory lecture. The teacher of German language presented Goethe's play as the most Christian message: whatever you do, God will forgive you if you do so with good intentions. When reading the text, I was horrified: Faust asks Mephistopheles, at the end of part 2, to "clean up" a vast area (for a gigantic reclamation project). Mephistopheles interferes and the peaceful Philemon and Baucis are burned to ashes. Though I had no idea about the Holocaust at this time, the very fact that Faust only reprimands Mephistopheles, and nothing more, horrified me. Philemon and Baucis could have been my grandparents, whom I loved and admired very much.

For a long time, I completely abandoned Faust and was disgusted with Goethe, whom I suspected to be a first ideologist of ruthless imperialism. Faust, the reckless project developer, is rewarded with a place in paradise, and Goethe's final "Whoever strives with all his might, that man we can redeem" neglects the simple question of for what purpose or for whom this striving is undertaken. Napoleon, Stalin, or even the Austro-German Führer strove with all their might too. Who would like to sit next to them in paradise? I remember that around the time of my final examination, I dreamt of composing Maurice Maeterlinck's *The Blind*, a kind of anti-Faust, but it stayed a dream. Obtaining the rights to compose that text was much too expensive for a nineteen-year-old schoolboy.

The Reconversion

During the late sixties—when our generation was in turmoil because of the horrors of the Vietnam War—I stumbled on a completely different version of Faust. An East German friend had succeeded in sending me the libretto of the Faust opera that Hanns Eisler had written. Due to Stalinist aesthetical restrictions (which were

Figure 8.1. Score of *Doktor Faustus*, 1, creation of the homunculus, composed by Konrad Boehmer.

already extremely effective in the *German* Democratic Republic [GDR] at the end of the fifties), Eisler had been prevented from composing his own wonderful text. After having read the libretto, I naively decided to compose it. My letters to the East German (GDR) institutions to obtain the license never got any response. During a long car trip with the writer and historian Alexander von Plato, we talked about Faust. Alexander drew my attention to the numerous Faust dramas after Goethe, from Lenau to Grabbe, from Lunacharsky (Lenin's minister of culture) to Mikhail Bulgakov's *The Master and Margarita*. As Eisler had already brought Faustus back to his historical roots, I restarted thinking about my project.

Faust, above all, attracted me as a completely ambiguous figure, in historical as well as psychological terms. In Faust's times, when the radically developing new economic structures steadily changed the psychic constitutions of the involved actors, we should not be astonished that this left its traces in Faust's psychic system too. Though deeply linked to the Middle Ages by all his alchemist experiments, his relation with the outer world is more like the quite modern behavior of a contemporary banker who sells hot air with a cold-blooded face. Let us not forget another important fact of those times: this was the era where the arts got an independent status as both an object of nearly religious adoration and as object of commercial speculation. No wonder that I banish Faustus in the empire of the arts at the end of my musical theater. This process of aesthetic heroization is typical of modern culture.

An Opera?

Where Eisler's project had been prevented by a group of East German Stalinist diehards, the very thought of composing a Faust "opera" in Western Europe seemed from the first a hopeless adventure, not only because of the possibly controversial approach to the Faust legend, but also for strictly musical reasons. Since the rise of extensive serial techniques (in the beginning of the second half of the twentieth century), the unilateral emphasis on what Schoenberg once called "Materiallogik" (logic inherent to the material) seemed to stand in an antagonistic relation to the other Schoenbergian definition of a "Darstellungslogik" (logic of representation). Indeed, from the very few "operas" which have emerged from the so called avant-garde circles of that time, only one has remained in the repertoire: Bernd Alois Zimmermann's *Die Soldaten*. Thus my decision to nevertheless develop the Faust motive implied two steps: a) a redefinition of the relation between "Material" and "Darstellungslogik" (call it a rehabilitation of this relation), and b) a different, nonidealistic view on the historic figure of Faustus.

The problem of the "logic inherent to the material" is relatively easy to explain. It mainly consists of a careful translation of the inner tendencies of musical "material" into forms which, as it were, represent the personal behavior of the composer within the chosen material coordinates. The "logic of representation" is a much more intricate problem, because in this case any musical texture or structure has to be developed in close relation with an extra-musical datum: a word, a text, a drama, an image, or a sequence of images. Where, in the first case, the composer's activity is directly concentrated on the articulation of musical *sense,* in the second he has to wrestle with extra-musical significations. From Monteverdi until our time, these significations have considerably changed in meaning, attitude, and even inner structure. Setting a text by Jack Kerouac in the style of, for example, Schubert or Wagner would be a complete anachronism. When he has to deal with a dramatic text, the composer has to deal with another problem: shall he emphasize the signification or the inner "sense" of the single words (losing the general tendency of the text), or should he try to capture its general meaning, risking the subordination of the "weight" of the single word? This problem is as old as Monteverdi, but it manifests itself on every occasion in a new light.

The Two Logic Approaches

The easiest solution to Schoenberg's antithesis might be the integration of all aspects of music theater into an all-englobing serial concept. Every verbal utterance, every movement, light, or color would be subordinated to a set of "series" or "parameters." That might have been Stockhausen's dream for his liturgical rocket *Licht,* but the mere idea of singers producing series of permutated letters or syllables and adapting to a serially organized stage set was—and still is—a horror to me. Moreover, a Neoplatonic conception of modern music theater seems a *contradictio in adjecto* to me. One conceives a drama in music (instead of a string quartet or electronic music), because one wants to reflect at least one aspect of the surrounding world. Obtruding a Pythagorean serialism on such a project may be conceived as an attempt to get the entire universe under control, but it is in any case a false universe (as in Stockhausen's case, who derived his entire *Licht* plot from the absurd cosmic ideologies of the "bible" of the "Urantia" sect).

   Another option to lead Schoenberg's concept of the two treatments of musical material to a synthesis would be a glance back on the solution which Alban Berg has achieved in his *Wozzeck.* This option also causes severe problems. Alban Berg's idea to conciliate structural models from the instrumental music of the classic era with the dramatic gestures of Georg Büchner's text relies on two facts: Berg himself is still rooted in the classic-romantic traditions and Büchner's text is in fact a lyric drama, allowing much more musical freedom than other types of tragedy. If one agrees that in musical drama music has to create the unity, whereas it has at the same time to take into account the diversity emerging from the plot and its protagonists, one can devise lots of solutions without copying historic models. This does not mean that the composer has to cut himself off from history itself (as did some initiators of serial music fifty years ago). No dramatic composer can avoid "historical colors" (as per the French writer Michel Butor): they are active in dramatic works since Monteverdi and certainly until B. A. Zimmermann. One does certainly not have to have recourse to Stravinsky and his "historic" chameleon tactics. Whatever the composer decides, his conclusions should be in accordance with the dramatic impetus of the plot.

I chose a synthesis between (historical) "evolutionary" methods and new methods coming forth from new kinds of serial strategies. The "original" idea came after a long (and, I have to confess, quite dionysiac) night. Walking home, I translated the name "Faust" into the names of the notes of the gamut: F-A-S is clear—if one applies the north European names S would be "Es" = E^b). The letters "U" and "T" can be derived from the Latin names of the gamut and be synthesized to the tone "C." What a horror: the nucleus of a material to be developed would be a chord of the dominant seventh, the most banal harmony of all. Look at this "nucleus" as a symbolon which can only be developed in all possible directions: horizontal, vertical, tonal, or serial. This means that possible historical colors can be derived from the initial material and that this same material can be developed into numerous directions. In this way the same basic motive can be used as a leitmotiv or, in a more abstract manner, as a basic structure.

I am not the kind of composer who publicly analyses his compositional techniques. It seems completely irrelevant to me whether a piece is serial, stochastic, atonal, or so forth. As every technique has to be applied as a function of an esthetic goal, it seems much more important to me to articulate those goals than to reengineer the material. Composers who are fond of analyzing their own music risk becoming prisoners of their own theoretical obsessions. But, in global terms, I can say, that all the ingredients of opera are present in my *Doktor Faustus*, be it in a quite ironic or perverted form. It has a real "ouverture" and two male protagonists. Even worse, a real miracle happens: the holy virgin Maria appears as a deus ex machina, though this appearance leads to the contrary of that which miracles in general achieve: no healing or redemption, but a cruel murder committed by three monks, faithful sons of their church. That Faust's opponent, Mephistopheles, is an abbot, makes the confusion complete, though all these events are adapted from historical documents.

The Dramatis Personae

Only a small number of documents concerning the historical figure of Faustus remain. A contemporary of Martin Luther, Pope Leo X, Calvin, Zwingli, Erasmus of Rotterdam, Jacob Fugger, Emperor Charles V, Machiavelli, Paracelsus, Michelangelo, and Raffael Sanzio, as well of lots of impressive German Humanists, Faustus lived in what is perhaps the most exciting period of our European history: the discovery of America, emergent modern science, the Reformation, peasant wars, and flourishing arts: the Renaissance as a breaking line between the Middle Ages and modern times hosted the most exiting figures of cultural and intellectual life—from extreme conservatives to revolutionaries, from scientists to swindlers or quacks.

A look at the few Faustus documents places our protagonist between all extremes: at one moment a quack in the marketplaces, we see him in another disguise as councilor of high-ranked secular or ecclesiastic persons. Among all historical documents, there is one that has influenced the Faust mythology in a decisive way. A letter, written in 1507 by abbot Trithemius (Johannes von Heidenberg, 1462–1516) to Johannes Virdung, is not only the most extensive but also the most vindictive document of all. In this letter, Trithemius accuses Faustus of all the crimes, villainies, and sins one can imagine. As this letter would become my key to the story, I took a more precise look into the personality of that abbot. His writings are a strange mixture of (European) Talmudism, "Rosenkreutz" hermetism (Trithemius was a member of the Rosicrucian sect), and medieval scholasticism. If one adds the abbot's alchemistic interests to his writings, Trithemius appears as a backward, medieval mirror of everything of which he accuses Faust. As it would have been impossible for me (I am not a Christian) to introduce a Mephistopheles devil as a counterpart to Faust, Trithemius seemed to me the ideal opponent to the protagonist.

Looking at the interaction between these two characters, I needed a third person, the incarnation of their most secret dreams. I found it in the young boy Hans Böhm (c. 1450–76), a historic figure better known under the name "Pfeifferhänsle of Niklashausen." During the spring of 1476 he started preaching to the peasants: he had had apparitions from the Holy Virgin Maria asking him to tell everybody to do penance to avert their own misery. After up to forty thousand people had begun assembling around little Hans Böhm, the bishop of the nearby Würzburg intervened and removed him to a prison. On July 19, 1476 he was burned in a backyard of the same Saint Jacob Monastery where Trithemius was appointed abbot on October 15, 1506. What a coincidence . . .

Hans's and Mary's agitations fit perfectly into the ideological motives of the peasant wars. These wars had started in Flanders, France, and England during the fourteenth century and later on extended to several German regions, especially Francony, Faust's homeland. Their main incentive was a mixture of religious and political proto-communism. One could compare them to the actual Occupy movement, though their struggle was much more violent and their defeat incomparably more traumatic. For me, integrating the Hans episode into the psychodrama Faust-Trithemius had a double purpose: on the one hand, this young boy represented the peak of Faust's erotic dreams and, on the other hand, he was the intrusion of political reality into that psychodrama. Hans is created by the two protagonists as a "homunculus," but quickly this alchemical creature unveils himself as the representative of reality.

The Development of the Plot

Before dealing with the plot, I should start by divulging its dramatic purpose. As Faust has become (thanks to Trithemius and the 1587 Spies Faust Book, one of the first bestsellers) a figure of mythology and as his entrance into the world of literature has been the result of this mythologization, my central purpose was to describe that strange process: how could it happen that a quite adventurous being could be distilled into a "category" of "literature," whose real life is treated in thousands of very learned books and dissertations? The cause of this is the culture of an upcoming middle class which conceives of the disorder of real life within the framework of an organized culture, wherein everybody, everything has its recognizable place. Think of the fate of Robin Hood, Kaspar Hauser, or even Che Guevara. Faust and his treaty with the devil is such a place too. My "drama in music" describes exactly this historic development. This is the reason why I had to "deconstruct" Faust. The most suitable form in which to do this was the most "middle-class" genre of music history, the "opera." That was my own dialectical choice. Whatever appears in my *Faust* as mythology or literature must be considered as "irony" (in the Romantic sense of the term). The plot is a simple mixture of historical elements and imagination:

1. Faust, in his alchemist laboratory, is busy trying to create the ideal homunculus, using formulas derived from Paracelsus. His mind is disturbed by the voices of young boys singing a chant to welcome spring. They enter his little room, disturbing him more and more. He bewitches them. When the furious parents assault Faust's cottage and threaten to kill him, Trithemius appears and saves Faust. In a long dialogue he proves to be Faust's master in every respect.

2. Trithemius offers to free Faust from his boring, provincial existence and to show him the world (a motiv in most Faust legends). These four travel episodes are—in a musical perspective—the concentration of historic colors. The first trip leads Faust to the center of secular power, at exactly the moment when the young, stuttering, and quite infantile Charles V receives the crown and the insignia of the Holy Roman Empire (in 1516). A motet composed by Thomas de Crequillon for that occasion is the historic color of that quite sarcastic scene. Disgusted by this shameless "ceremony," Faust longs for higher, spiritual values and travels to the court of Pope Leo X, who sits for Raffael Sanzio. The indications given by the pope to the painter testify a degree of frivolousness which terrifies our poor villager. When traveling to the Tibetan mountains, Faust discovers a Buddhist monk deeply lost in his meditations. To a mother next to him, with a starving baby in her arms, the monk can only mutter about an "eternal light." Faust objects that this child needs bread, not litanies. After all these deceptions, Faust choses the last escape left, a journey into the future. The landing ground is a dirty garage, where a gang of punks croaks a totally nihilistic song ("Nothing times nothing is nothing"). As none of the four journeys has suggested a "better" world, Faust returns to his cottage.

3. Trithemius offers him a last, ultimate achievement. Together they would succeed in realizing the alchemist's supreme dream, the creation of a homunculus. After gigantic efforts they finally succeed. The young boy who emerges from the phial is Hans Böhm. Let us be clear about this "miracle": the composer has not reverted to mysticism or metaphysics, but this scene is a dramaturgical move within an opera, which is not a scientific treatise but a tale, following its own logic.

4. More and more frequently Hans escapes Faust's cottage, preaching to the villagers about the increasingly revolutionary messages of the Holy Virgin. As some bystanders do not believe him, our "metaphysical" creature effects a second metaphysical act: he calls to earth the Holy Virgin herself which—in a long aria—confirms all the revolutionary messages formerly asserted by Hans.

5. During the night, three monks enter Faust's home and strangle Hans.

6. Faust, totally desperate, locks himself up in his little laboratory and nearly drowns in seas of alcohol. Once again the schoolboys (from the beginning of the piece) penetrate his hermitage and provoke the fat and ugly drunkard. In a last attempt to prove his genius, Faust enumerates all the utopian inventions he has achieved. Not impressed, the boys want to know where he has hidden the bottles of wine. In an outbreak of delirium tremens Faust seizes the wrong bottle, a test-tube full of poison. After a first, enormous gulp, Faust falls dead. The boys disappear after having searched Faust's pockets for money.

7. In the final scene, Faust's statue is already erected. Trithemius celebrates his ultimate triumph. In a long funeral oration, as much pathetic as mendacious, he catapults the "far seeing genius" Faust into the brains and memories of the surrounding middle-class bystanders and thus into the canon of literature. By being absorbed by culture, Faust, the complete outsider of middle-class norms, is finally neutralized. This is the aspect of repressive tolerance inherent to all culture.

Hugo Claus

Once I had decided on the outline of my quite ambiguous plot, I was approached by Dutch writers longing to write the libretto. (In the Netherlands it is impossible to keep anything secret.) As Dutch artists are great in spatial arts but not in dramatic ("temporal") arts, I finally approached the great Flemish playwright and novelist Hugo Claus. For American readers the difference between "Dutch" and "Flemish" might be minimal: neighboring small countries, (nearly) the same language. For us the difference is gigantic: the Dutch are Calvinists, the Flemish are Catholics. Hugo Claus was a complete atheist, but a Catholic one. Those who know his novels and plays have witnessed a truly baroque phantasy. That is exactly what I needed. When I met Hugo in Gent, confessing to him what I was doing, he reacted, somewhat surprised: "I thought that you were a specialist in killing operas instead of composing them." He understood very quickly that this was exactly the reason why I approached him. I needed an anti-opera in the disguise of a real opera. After I had exposed my plot to Hugo, he immediately agreed to write the book. During numerous meetings, we went through every detail of the scenes, spending long nights with strong Belgian Trappist beer in the pub owned by one of Hugo's brothers. Though my writer proceeded in an extremely professional way, he modestly accepted every wish for alterations to his text which were merely caused by musical necessities. One of the advantages of having Claus as writer was that he had a tremendous experience as a playwright and author for the cinema. As he has been the director of many of his own dramas and scripts, he had an excellent feeling for timing. Whenever I asked him to make a scene a little bit shorter, he did not just cut the existing text but rewrote it. As his own theater plays cover the period from the Middle Ages until our time, Claus was perfectly able to get into the spirit of the quite contrasting (historical or social) situations of the plot.

Again: An Opera?

Those who conceive musical production in terms of linear progress have a strange—and quiet old-fashioned—image of history, which they reduce to the ideologies of industrial progress from previous centuries. Defending progress by resorting to outdated philosophies of history seems quite inconsistent to me. We all know that this outdated ideological model has had a devastating influence on the ideas about musical "progress" during the second part of the twentieth century. Having been the only "pupil" of the legendary "Cologne School" (which in reality never existed), I recall that talking about music of previous periods there was completely taboo. When I told Luigi Nono (in 1962) that "Cologne" was horrified by the idea of even mentioning Tchaikovsky, Nono drew my attention to his Trio in a minor that he considered an absolute masterpiece. Around that same time, Bruno Maderna, whom I assisted during the preparations of the German premiere of Nono's "Intolleranza," introduced me to the extreme adventures of Italian Renaissance music. As Maderna was an incredibly sophisticated thinker, he convinced me that pure material progress in music was just a fiction and that all music—whether "popular" or "serious"—was related to the emotional dimensions of its own time, or it would not be relevant at all. No "progress" but "evolution" would be a better aesthetic option for contemporary composers. Where "Cologne" (or even worse, "Darmstadt") ideologists had banned "opera" (mostly referring to the quite uninteresting operas by Hans Werner Henze), I was convinced that no compositional "system" or genre was outdated but that one had to reinterpret it in one's own way. That is what Orlando di Lasso did with the "old" style, what Bach did (in his E-major fugue of the well-tempered piano) with Palestrina, and what Mozart, Beethoven, or Schumann did with Bach's "fugue" processings. It is also what Schoenberg or Webern did with the basic principles of "counterpoint." It is, by the way, what B. A. Zimmermann or Henri Pousseur did with the starting points of "harmony"; one may even consider Xenakis's "Jonchaies" (1977) to follow this line.

My Faust was not a continuation of the opera tradition but a complete reinterpretation of it. Let us remember the purpose: a plot that catapults Faust into the canon of the arts could not be more dialectic than through the use of one of the most established genres of "bourgeois" music. Creating my quite "materialist" plot with the help of dialectic-metaphysical tricks calls for a form which in itself has dialectic implications. From Monteverdi's *Orfeo* to Zimmermann's *Soldaten*, opera has always had a double ground: it is theater, drama, and at the same time it is nonverbal, music. Classical opera has tried to solve the tensions between the two spheres by leaving the development of the action to the recitative and the emotional reflections to the arias. This solution was already questioned by Wagner and it cannot work anymore when action and (emotional) reflection merge. For this reason I reduced structural categories to types of treatment of the (verbal) material, from crying and speaking to (monophonic, homophonic, and polyphonic) singing. I organized the orchestral material in different levels: from the (most passive) accompaniment to passages where the orchestra intervenes as an active partner of the action. Within the instrumental layer I applied different degrees of complexity: as my initial material is extremely reduced (four pitches only) I could develop and vary it in all imaginable directions. As I kept (at least in *Doktor Faustus*) to (Schoenberg's) "logic of representation," I made all my decisions in relation to the (dramatic) context. This means that there exists no all-encompassing abstract serial plan, although my roots in the traditions of serial music may have helped to articulate larger connections. My decision was not for (pre-established) organization but for composition (as a process which allows one to take decisions "on the spot"). Only this attitude enables a composer to develop a "drama in music." I borrow this term from Monteverdi, who used it for the first "real" opera, his *Orfeo*. The term applies perfectly to what is perhaps the last opera, my *Faust*.

When *Doktor Faustus* was prepared and rehearsed for its premiere in the Paris Grand Opera (February 1985), I experienced some bitter lessons. The opera house of that time was still the "Palais Garnier" (inaugurated in 1875) with its important auditorium (2131 seats) and that lustre which we all know from the *Phantom of the Opera*. As neither the technical installations of that building seemingly had not been replaced since the day of its opening nor the organizational structures updated, the entire rehearsal process became a nightmare comparable to that of the victims of the *Phantom*. In response, I started writing a diary for the first time in my life. I will never forget the first stage rehearsal. In the middle of the stage there stood a chair, which hindered everybody. The stage director just wanted to move it aside. The chief of the properties department intervened immediately, explaining that it first had to be decided under whose responsibility the chair fell. Was it a requisite, was it just part of a decoration, or might it be just a chair? In every case, another department was responsible. After forty-five minutes of discussions, I climbed up and took the chair, putting it aside. I explained to that important manager of furniture, "Sir, I am from a civilized country, and in my country we do what I have done." After the rehearsal, an even more important manager of that opera approached me and told me that I should be very happy that my action had not led to a general strike. Later, at the general rehearsal, a video was going to be made. A camera was put in position, and since the work begins with an overture, the camera was pointed toward the orchestra pit. During the entire general rehearsal, nobody thought of focusing the camera on the stage. The result was that for hours the video only shows the feet of some actors. The lesson I had to learn very quickly was that even if you confide an opera against

the opera to such an established institute, the organization will do its utmost to sub-
jugate your work to the old jogtrot of four centuries of "tradition." It became Doctor
Faustus against Kafka. And the main lesson for me was the understanding that if you
compose whatever piece of music, you have to consider in an extremely critical way
the structure and ideology of the institution to which you do entrust it. Most of them
cannibalize art instead of serving it.

Faust after Faust

Shortly after having finished *Doktor Faustus* (in 1983), a commission by the Dutch
National Radio seduced me to approach the "Faust" problem from a different perspective. The title of the work (*Apocalipsis cum figuris*) refers to one of the two major
compositions by Adrian Leverkühn, the fictitious composer of Thomas Mann's novel
Doctor Faustus. The particular characteristic of Mann-Leverkühn's *Apocalipsis* is
that it stands all traditional concepts of music aesthetics on their heads: the "beautiful" becomes the banal and the "ugly" becomes the beautiful. Leverkühn's "howling
and crying" could best be realized with recorded and further elaborated sounds. At
the end of the piece a group of pop singers intones a kind of Elton John mainstream
song in the purest C major before the background of steadily increasing "apocalyptic"
noises. The piece is conceived for a six-track tape ("electronic" music without a single
synthetic sound in it), percussion, pianos, and three or four pop singers. In any case,
the rehearsals for this piece were much more effective and pleasant, because the production modes were much more in accordance with the spirit of the piece.

In 2005 Faust caught up with me for a third time. For the organization of a
Faust week, the Philharmonic Orchestra of Würzburg (Trithemius's town) wanted
a purely instrumental composition closely linked to the Faust figure. The only option was to write a kind of program music (I am ashamed of nothing). This time I
transformed into music two scenes from Goethe's *Faust* and an additional one: the
"Contract" (with Mephisto), the "Easter Walk" and, finally, the "Ride to Hell." With
this orchestra piece I turned back to my early youth, when I had to write a composition for German language lessons. Its title was "Faust aufs Auge" ("Fist in Your Eye"
= like a square peg in a round hole). In this little text I had already adopted quite a
critical attitude towards Goethe's *Faust*. After having encircled this figure from all
sides, I wonder what will be next?

Author's Profile

Konrad Boehmer was a composer and music scholar. He taught music history and
theory at the Royal Conservatory in the Hague. His opera *Doktor Faustus* received
the Rolf-Liebermann prize. His other works include *Apocalipsis cum figuris* (1984)
and *Dokor Fausti Höllenfahrt* (2005).

Chapter 8

Faust's Dreams (أحلام فاوست)
and Egyptian Identity

David G. John

Abstract

In his article, "Faust's Dreams (أحلام فاوست) and Egyptian Identity," David
G. John analyzes an unusual Egyptian adaptation of the Faust legend, performed by the Alternative Theatre Group in Alexandria, Egypt in 2002, and
written and directed by Dr. Mahmoud Aboudoma. The adaptation draws from
the *Faust*s of Marlowe, Goethe, and Valéry, *One Thousand and One Nights,*
the Egyptian *Book of the Dead,* the Koran, and the Bible. With the assistance
of a team of native Egyptians, John engages with the tangle of symbols, archetypes, and myths represented in the dreamlike action on stage. The production, he concludes, is a pessimistic depiction of the state of political affairs
and mood of the Egyptian nation in light of their recent losses in the Six-Day
War with Israel, the effects of globalization in the Mediterranean area, Egypt's
loss of the power it traditionally held there, and its resulting crisis of self-
confidence and identity. The article includes a review of the history of *Faust*
adaptations in Egypt and the scholarly literature pertaining thereto.

The Egyptian playwright, director, scholar, and social critic Dr. Mahmoud Aboudo-
ma authored and staged the play أحلام فاوست (Faust's Dreams) in Arabic, in 2002. It
was performed by the Alternative Theatre Group in The Garage theater of the Jesuit
Cultural Centre in Alexandria, in Studio Oscura in Göteburg in 2004, and Thron
Theatre in Glasgow in 2006, directed by Simon Sharkey and Mahmoud Aboudoma
("*Faust's Dreams*"; McCleod). *Faust's Dreams* is a surrealistic exploration of Faust's
central problem of finding personal meaning in the modern world and especially the
Eastern Mediterranean context. By his own explanation, director Aboudoma derived

his drama from the thematics of the Faust works of Goethe (1808, 1832), Marlowe (1604), and Paul Valéry (1946), supplemented by *One Thousand and One Nights*, the Egyptian *Book of the Dead*, the Koran, and the Bible. His play operates within the realm of symbols, archetypes, and myths, but its theme is the disorientation of individuals within the contexts of globalization and contemporary Egyptian history, politics, and society. It maintains Goethe's references to Christian symbolism by connecting the adaptation to Egypt's Coptic Christian foundations, but more emphatically, it explores Egypt's loss of self-confidence, sense of identity, place in Africa, and status as an Islamic power. Aboudoma considered the trigger for this loss to have been the humiliation of the Arab states in the Six-Day War with Israel (June, 1967), but that shock was exacerbated by the process of globalization during which Egypt also lost its position as a Mediterranean power with primary links to Europe. Of course, director Aboudoma could not have imagined the more recent political and social events in Egypt since 2002 which make his adaptation even more meaningful. The first part of this chapter outlines the literary, performance, and scholarly history of *Faust* in Egypt and the Arab world, the second offers a descriptive analysis of *Faust's Dreams*, the third a sociohistorical interpretation, and the fourth, observations on the production within the broader context of Egyptian, Arabic, and Eastern Mediterranean society.

Faust in Egypt and the Arab World

In a short booklet, published in both German and Arabic in 1982, Kamal Radwan became one of the first scholars to write about Goethe's reception in Egypt (*Fauststoff seit Goethe*). In the following year he refined this material in an essay for the *Goethe-Jahrbuch*, pointing out that it was not until the first third of the twentieth century that Goethe became known in that country, beginning with the earliest translation of *Werther* into Arabic, in 1919, which soon spawned imitations. The centenary of Goethe's death in 1932 sparked interest for translators, brought tributes by numerous Egyptian writers and scholars, and the first translation into Arabic of his *Faust I* (Radwan, "Goethe-Rezeption" 72 and "Rezeption der Faustgestalt" 309; contrary to Radwan, this first Arabic translation of Goethe's *Faust* in fact occurred in 1911, and a second, the one to which he refers, in 1919). Other translations of Goethe works appeared in the 1950s and 1960s, including a *Faust I* in 1959 and an *Urfaust* in 1964, with tens of thousands of copies going to print. At the same time, three major Egyptian universities, Cairo, Al-Azhar, and Ain-Shams, opened departments of German studies and began to cultivate academic and intellectual relations with Germany and publish scholarship on Goethe as well as other outstanding German authors (Radwan, "Goethe-Rezeption" 73).

In light of the fact that Goethe's *Faust* has been translated into at least fifty-four languages (*Goethe-Bibliographie Online*) it is not surprising that Arabic is among them, nor that it has reached Egyptian scholars, readers, and audiences in various forms. Aladin Hilmi was the first to attempt to catalogue all Arabic and

Egyptian translations and adaptations until 1986, when his book on Goethe reception in Egypt appeared. In the bibliography he lists five translations of *Faust* (three of part 1, one of part 2, one undetermined), the first of which was published in 1911, the last in 1971 (219). In this very broad and detailed study, Hilmi provides commentary on each of Goethe's works that found a readership in Arabic in Egypt, and in the sections on *Faust* he lists by author and evaluates briefly each of the translations or adaptations into Arabic to date, with varied amounts of detail (54). They are:

- Salih Hamdi Hamad, *Faust I*, 1911.

- Muhammad Awad Muhammad, *Faust I*, 1929, which became the best known Arabic rendering and by 1971was republished five times. Muhammad's translation enjoyed an introduction by the prominent Egyptian scholar Taha Hussein (1889–1973), who praised his linguistic knowledge and sensitivity to Goethe's poetry. Muhammad appended a useful summary of *Faust II* as well.

- Ismail Kamil, *Faust*, undated, in ten prose chapters, in a widely popular and inexpensive penny novel press, emphasizing the confrontation between the devil and the Lord.

- Mahammad Badr Khalil, *Mephisto*, undated, in prose chapters, published with the same press and similar to Kamil's above.

- Muhammad Abdel Halim Karara, *Faust I*, 1959, in verse, including a sophisticated transition to Arabic verse forms and a substantial introduction on Goethe and the history of the Faust legend.

- Muhammad Abdel Halim Karara, *Faust I*, republished in 1969 and, remarkably, supplemented by a translation into Arabic of *Faust II*.

- Mustafa Maher, *Urfaust,* 1975, with an introduction about Goethe and *Faust*.

In other sections of his book, Hilmi provides publication details in his footnotes as well as further information and commentaries on some of these translators and adaptors and the translations' reception (67, 92–95, 150, 219). The details of some of these can also be found in the Weimar *Goethe-Bibliographie*, but it is not as complete as Hilmi's list; for example, it does not include the 1929 translation's first edition, nor the second, or fourth, including only the third and fifth (1958, 1971). Other titles are missing as well.

Katharina Mommsen established herself as the leading German expert on Goethe and Arabia in 1988 when she published her lengthy volume, *Goethe und die arabische Welt*. Its references are overwhelmingly to the *West-östlicher Divan*, with only scattered comments on other Goethe works, among them *Faust*. She also wrote the article on "Arabien" for the *Goethe-Handbuch*, three dense columns which stand as a useful summary of Goethe's relationship to Arabic language and culture, as well as a tightly informative description of his adaptation of Arabic models in some of his own works (72–73). In his writings, Goethe spoke highly of the Arabic language and culture, learning sufficient Arabic to read many works in the original, especially lyrics and short tales, some of which he translated and used as models for his own works (see especially *One Thousand and One Nights*. Parts of his *Unterhaltungen deutscher Ausgewanderten, Wilhelm Meisters Wanderjahre*, the *West-östlicher Divan*, and part 2 of *Faust* [*Mummenschanz*, act 3] particularly show Arabic influence). Strangely, although Hilmi's book on Goethe reception in Egypt appeared two years before Mommsen's grand study and twelve years before her article in the *Goethe-Handbuch*, in neither of these is he mentioned. The second volume of the *Handbuch*, on Goethe's dramatic productions, contains an enormous section on *Faust*, including a lengthy one on its reception (Anglet and Fusenig), but there is no consideration of that reception abroad, let alone in Africa, Arab countries, or Egypt. Even encyclopedic works of that kind are forced to limitations given the enormous influence of the writer they consider.

In 1992 Moustafa Maher published a valuable and extensive, though admittedly selective and incomplete, scholarly account of Faust reception in Egypt, Goethe's rendition being the most important. He argued that the reception and integration of the Faust theme in Egypt was driven primarily by dramatists and the theater, having major impact beginning only in the twentieth century. The reasons for this late reception, he summarizes from the work of other scholars, were several: the Arabic mentality was indisposed to tragedy; the nature of Arabic theater was traditionally itinerant, whereas tragedy requires more stability; and the Islamic emphasis on forgiveness, brotherhood, the acquiescence to God's will, and His admonition to accept one's fate, all of which contradicted some of the fundamental thematics of the Faust legend (Maher 437). At the end of the eighteenth and beginning of the nineteenth centuries, Egyptian cultural historians Hassan el-'Attar and Rifa'a at-Tahtawi advocated that Egypt and the Arab world draw closer to Europe (439). As a result, from the early nineteenth century Egypt opened itself to European thought, style, and artistic expression. Translations of European works into Arabic began to appear, including new literary forms such as the novel, tragedy, comedy, and the libretto (439). There followed a spate of newly constructed theaters in Egypt: in 1860 the Masrah el-Komedi theater, in 1868 the Azbakeya Theater, in 1869—the year of the Suez canal's construction—the opera house, and in 1870 the El-Tetro el-Wani theater, with European works appearing in Arabic, as well as operatic, Broadway, and vaudeville-like plays. Egyptian society was becoming more diversified, with not just the upper class but a broader spectrum attending (439). In 1903 a French guest ensemble performed Gounod's *Faust*, and between then and 1924 the opera house played it, among other European works, eight times. They also performed Mozart's *Don Juan*, and the German *Die Afrikanerin*, *Werther*, and *Lohengrin* as well as French and Italian works (441). These were gradually translated and performed in Arabic. Sheikh Salama Hegazi began to compose an original libretto of the Faust legend in 1916–17, but died before finishing it and the fragment has disappeared (441). Yet Maher quotes excerpts from it recorded in the writings of Muhammad Fadil, which indicate that Hegazi was consciously rendering an adaptation of Goethe's *Faust*, as, for example, in his introductory lines for the chorus, in keeping with the opening of Goethe's "Prolog im Himmel" ("Prologue in Heaven") in *Faust I* (lines 243–70). Hegazi has the angels, the devils, along with holy men, sing, each with their own melody. Translations of Marlowe's and Goethe's *Faust*s into Arabic were not far behind, as we have seen above from Hilmi's work. Maher refers as well to the many adaptations of the Faust legend in dramatic, prosaic, and even cinematic form by Egyptian writers which go beyond Hilmi's scope, providing a selected list of thirteen titles (Maher 443). In general they focus on the Mephisophelean element and how individuals confront it.

Maher further investigates the commonalities between Arabic treatments of the Faust legend, characters, and themes in Goethe's *Faust*, such as, for example, the Satan figure Dschinn or Shaitan, Iblis, the leader of the angels, as well as connections to the Christian Adam at creation and Paradise (Maher 445–47). He further links many Goethean *Faust* motifs to the writings in ancient Egyptian sagas and folklore, as well as the Koran and several particular works in some detail, specifically, Taufik el-Hakim's story *'Ahd esch-Schaitan* (Satan's Pact, 1930), Muhammad Farid Abu-Hadid's drama *'Abd esch-Schaitan* (Satan's Servant, 1929), and Ali Ahmad Bakathir's drama *Faust al-Gadid* (or *Faust al-jadid*, The New Faust) which he dates as 1987 when it was produced as a radio play (445, 449). In fact, Bakathir wrote the work around 1967, two years before his death. It is set in Europe, though Germany is not specified, nor is the place and time. It addresses Goethe's *Faust* and closely depicts the essence of its model and general themes of the human predicament while integrating aspects of Egyptian social, political, and religious life (446–48). Christian Szyska has more recently treated Bakathir's rendition extensively (see also Chelkowski 63; Hilmi 154; Shaikh).

In 1993 Kamal Radwan refined his research of 1983 to focus specifically on the reception of *Faust* in Arabic literature ("Rezeption der Faustgestalt"). Here he reviews the adaptations and translations treated in his first article of 1983, but, more importantly, he expands Maher's examination of Faustian thematics as parallels to figures, incidents, struggles, and conflicts depicted in Islamic folklore and the Koran (304). He further discusses the new stream of Egyptian scholarship on *Faust*, interpreted from an Egyptian and Islamic point of view, and new adaptations of the Faust legend by Egyptian writers. Among these, Farid Abu Hadied and the aforementioned Aly Ahmed Bakassier stand out as writing under the influence of Goethe's *Faust* and setting its characters and themes into an Islamic context. His list of numerous works in Egypt and other Arabic countries is a valuable addition to the scholarship. The broader academic discussion of the Faust theme continued in Arabia through the 1990s, as, for example, in Sharif S. Elmusa's "Faust without the Devil" which examined the motif within the context of technology and culture in Saudi Arabia, but with only casual reference to Goethe's version (350).

More recent scholarship indicates a continuing interest in Arabic *Faust*s internationally. A conference held at McGill University, Montreal, in 2008 with the theme "Orient und Okzident. Zur Faust-Rezeption in nicht-christlichen Kulturen" resulted in a book with two chapters on *Faust* in Arabic countries, by Lale Behzadi, "Ausblick und Spiegelung: Goethes *Faust* in der arabischen Literatur," and Aleya Khattab, "Die faustische Frau in der arabischen Literatur: *Die Frau, die über den Teufel triumphierte* von Taufik Al-Hakim." Conference organizer Adrian Hsia's essay, "On the Reception of *Faust* in Asia," links his commentary with recent scholarship on Islamic *Faust*s as well. Overall, the most current and complete bibliography on the subject of Faust adaptations in Arabic is appended to Iyad Shraim's master's thesis of 2008 at the Westfälische Wilhelms-Universität Münster on "Goethes *Faust* und der neue arabische Faust. Die Rezeption eines Stoffes der Weltliteratur bei Ali Ahmad Bakathir und Hamid Ibrahim." Shraim provides a list of twenty-eight works in Arabic based on Faust thematics as well as an extensive bibliography of secondary works on this subject in Arabic and European languages.

Faust's Dreams: A Descriptive Analysis

The author's knowledge of the play stems from a personal interview conducted with Mahmoud Aboudoma in Alexandria in April, 2006, a DVD recording of one performance, and print materials, both of which Aboudoma generously provided, as well as some dialogues from the play translated into English. A detailed review of the performance by theater and culture critic Nehad Selaiha was also extremely instructive. Since the author does not read or understand Arabic, he engaged four graduate student assistants at the University of Waterloo, Canada, all native Egyptians, a mix of males and females, Christians and Muslims, to assist him in understanding the performance and interpreting the play. They were not identified to each other at the time. Each was given a copy of the DVD of the performance and a set of questions about the action, which they answered and submitted to the author. From these replies, further individual interviews with them, and other materials, he compiled his description and performance analysis.

Structurally, *Faust's Dreams* consists of seven scenes depicting dreams, more accurately, hallucinations of Faust, which provoke him to enter into a contract with Mephisto. The action lies metaphorically between heaven and earth. In these dreams, the actors reenact grotesquely the stories of the fall, Adam and Eve, and the snake giving birth to the apple of sin, beneath what is now the lifeless tree of knowledge; the great flood; the coming of Christ, the last supper, His death and resurrection, and His failure to save the world from despair and futility; and Faust's own degradation to the status of lifeless puppet. God himself reverts from a puppet master to such a puppet as well. The spirit of Nature attempts to move between heaven and earth, giving momentary solace to Faust, but is ultimately helpless. Her symbolic attempt to eradicate the original sin is futile and laughable, and at the end there remains only the slightest ray of hope. Some of the scenes suggest that they were modelled on Goethe's *Faust I*, the "Prologue in Heaven" ("Prolog im Himmel"), "Night" ("Nacht"), "Before the City Gate" ("Vom dem Tor"), "Study" ("Studierzimmer"), the Gretchen scenes, and "Walpurgis Night" ("Walpurgisnacht"), but the overall mood is reminiscent more of *Faust II*, particularly the phantasmagoria of the "Classical Walpurgisnight" ("Klassische Walpurgisnacht") the theme of the mothers, the classical legend and mythology surrounding Helena, and the concluding metaphysics. The dramatis personae includes seven actors, five males, one of whom represents Faust, one the Lord God, and three Mephisto figures, or his assistants, Gogo, Shamoorish, and Azeil. For Egyptians, Mephisto is a comic character enjoyed by Muslims and Christians alike—in Aboudoma's words, they say he is "the person who carries our sins." The same is true in many cultures, as, for example, in Hindu India and the Christian Philippines. There are two females, vaguely suggestive of Gretchen and Helena. The actors also represent at various times the crippled mock savior Jesus and the prophet Mohammed. Finally, there are four life-size dummies (or puppets) and one baby one. All of the characters, including the dummies, wear black suits or cloaks, with black gloves and flashes of white beneath, the white representing original innocence, and black the sin that has covered and almost hidden it in the course of life. Black also indicates the constant presence of the afterlife, which is glimpsed during the action, and rooted in the symbolism of Egyptian mythology and the gods Horus and Osiris. Single and choral voices are heard frequently from the OFF and there is a variety of instrumental music. A solitary violin and recorded excerpts from the Japanese composer Kitaro, the Greek composer Spanoudakis, sound tracks of *The Temptation of Christ*, *Pearl Harbor*, and *Jesus of Montreal*, and traditional Sufi dances and songs, accompany many scenes. Little dialogue occurs, most of the text being spoken or chanted as commentary from the OFF by voices related or unrelated to specific characters, and at times in a language other than Arabic, muffled, but likely Azarian of the Tukic family. There is much symbolic posing, movement, and dance, and all takes place in a dimly lighted, confining yellow box on the stage, with only one small high window linking it to the outside world. The pervading mood is one of lament, depression, and pessimism.

The following dialogue outline, which Aboudoma provided, is divided into seven scenes, as he intended it. These scenic divisions, however, are extremely difficult to discern from the video recording. The Egyptian assistants employed to record the structure of the play and its dialogue differed widely in their understanding of this, dividing the play into up to thirty individual scenes.

Scene One

Eva: O Lord, do not return.
All: O Lord, do not return.
The sounds here have grown terrifying, the perfumes have faded;
Even our crops, they burned on rainy nights,
And the tales we told each other a hundred times have fallen silent.
Nothing is left here but cold, and sand, and tedium; nothing left but

desolate nights,
Nothing but resentment.
Do not trouble yourself any more with the people, Lord,
For they shall soon forget you, even before the autumn season comes.

(The above is repeated by merging voices and then by the Faust figure himself.)

Scene Two

Gogo: The Earth keeps its old promise.
Each day the sun plays a hymn;
Each day the Earth weaves a new garment.
But all the hymns it plays,
All the garments it weaves are not enough to
Stop me hearing the voice of misery.
Its color is cold, pale as death.

Faust: I am Faust. Many have written about me, but no one truly knows me.

Mephisto: I am Faust. I am innocent of all that has been written.

Shamoorish: I am Faust. Here I am, as you see me, no blood on my hands,
No blood on my papers, no blood on my clothes.

Azeil: I am Faust. I am a criminal, no victim I.

Faust: I am Faust. I am a criminal, no victim I, but my heart is full of wounds.

Mephisto (seductively): I never dreamt of a rose.

All (mingling): I never dreamt of a rose nor a girl to love;
In my dreams I never saw the sea, nor did I see a green forest.
It was autumn. I always dreamt of grey skies, bare pale trees;
It was people who had come and gone in my life that I dreamt of.
Sometimes I talked to them; sometimes in the daytime I would see them.

Mephisto: Magic.

Faust: Magic is imagination and control.

Shamoorish: Magic is unlimited knowledge.

Faust: Magic is hidden treasures.

Azeil: Love affairs with beautiful women.

Faust: Magic is license.

Mephisto: Boundless freedom.

Faust: You can meet all those who have expired—

Shamoorish: And see cities buried beneath the dust.

Faust: Magic is the true Deity.

Gogo: Afraid to wear the same garment every day.

Faust: Eternal, that is.

Gogo: And put the same wrinkles on your face.

Faust: Command the cold, the wind, the thunder.

Gogo: A sad instrument—

Faust: Dry up the sea—

Gogo: That plays the same tune every day.

Faust: Two lifetimes in one.

Gogo: The wages of sin is death.

Faust: I am not a tale of good and evil.

Gogo: Who made the world?

Faust: I am shades of grey.

Gogo: We shall all be struck down with the same plague.

Faust: I am every man.

Gogo: Who made the world?

Faust: I am every man who refuses death. I am every man who refuses death.

(Mephisto hands him a cup. He drinks, and a certain change comes over him.)

Gogo: I'm the only witness to defilement.
I'm the only witness to hypocrisy, injustice, betrayal.
I'm the only witness to fear, sadness and hatred, to wounds and tears, to dignity and beauty.
I'm the only witness to silence, to words, to dreams, to the story's end.

Faust: There's something in my heart, it's got to get out.

Gogo: I'm the only witness to the death of sin.

Faust: There's something in my heart, it's got to get out. There's something in my heart, it's got to get out. (Falls to his knees.) There's something in my heart (in a whisper. Lies down) in my heart . . . (a whisper).

Scene Four

Letters of Eva (the Spirit Woman)

Why is it that we forget many things when we become taken with our own image?

Why is it that we forget so many things when we say goodbye; why do we hold back our tears when we part; why do we not come together when we're afraid?

Why are we afraid to touch one another?

Why are we afraid of admitting our pain?

Rise! Don't pretend to be dead. I know you hear me; I know you don't want to speak.

What I don't know is how you managed to soar so high, like a migrating bird, parting and hurried, not knowing where to go.

When I read your notes I knew that you had read from the book of confusion, dreamt the dreams of the defeated, and given your heart for them. I knew that when you yourself lusted after glory, you slapped it down with savage cruelty.

That is how I knew you were coming back, only no one believes me. Even those who knew you, those who drank water from your cupped palms and touched your heart with their hands assured me you were dead; but because I believe in you I know you are coming back. So I wait for you to heal your wounds and draw your portrait in the eyes of many who await you; when that happens, painful memories and days of sadness will vanish, leaving nothing behind but fragments of stories long gone.

Yesterday I saw your image in my heart, and when I tried to touch your features as I was wont to do, a habit you taught me, you escaped.

I wished you would announce the date of your return to everyone, to do away with injustice, to place a rose of kindness in every heart that has hardened since you went away.

I wish you would send them a breeze, fragrant with your perfume, to make them feel that you're on your way; so that I, too, won't lose my faith in you.

The thing that baffles me is that you always dreamed the dream of the defeated, that you gave your heart for them, that when you yourself lusted after glory you slapped it down with savage cruelty; why, then, did you chase after worldly things when they called out to you?

Why did you become so attached to the world that you died, painfully, lying upon its breast?

Gogo: Absent like an unknown promise,
Waiting for the journey,
Believing in your life-like flame;
True glory is not here. (Lowers his voice.) True glory is not here.

Gogo: Every time I'm tempted to cry.
I can't forget my old pain.
At night, when darkness falls, my tears escape like words with silent letters. (He repeats this phrase while the other characters move around chaotically.)

Gogo: When darkness is born, it comes to the world in secret.

Faust: Who am I? I want to find out what I am.

Gogo: I must give the scene a definite ending.

Faust: I want to know what I really am. Am I alive or dead?

Gogo: Who made the world?

Mephisto: What am I? A mirror, or a corpse?

Gogo: I'm not going to die. It might be a lie.

Faust: I'm a criminal, not a victim.

Gogo: Who made the world?

Azeil: A beautiful tale, and a sad one.

Gogo: Do you want to spread evil on the way?

Shamoorish: Beyond the wall something beckons.

Gogo: I must give the scene a definite ending.

Merging voices: I want to know what I really am.
Who made the world?
Beyond the wall, something beckons.
I must give the scene a definite ending.
I want to know what I really am.
Who made the world?
Something's dragging me down.
I must give the scene a definite ending.
I want to know what I really am.

(The merging of voices degenerates into chaos. All fall to the ground.)

Gogo: All roads are the same. Seven pains, seven sins, seven dreams.
All that's written in your heart has been taken down here.
Violence.
All roads are the same. Seven pains, seven sins, seven dreams.
All that is written in your heart has been taken down here.

The play begins with a visual link with pharaonic times through the symbolism of the pyramid, a shape and structure in its ancient form that is still part of daily life in Egypt, where pyramids today dot the landscape in many areas, some of which can still be entered. The nine actors, including dummies, are grouped downstage forming from the bottom row a triangle constructed of four characters, then above them three, then two, then one, the last represented by a bright light symbolizing the deity. The bottom row represents living beings, the left corner birth, the right corner death. One figure holds an effigy of the pyramid and its inhabitants, which she later carries with her, evoking the memory of ancient Egypt's constant presence. The second row is inhabited by the dummies, representing the dead, who have experienced life and made the mistakes that we, the living, are making now; the third row, two figures, the son of God, the new savior or the prophet, Jesus or Mohammed, beside his father, the old God, who is dying. The fourth row, the light from above, represents the true God, as the perfect being. He is invisible, by Islamic law never depicted, as usually in Christian practice. There is a slow wordless chorus of female voices, suggesting praise to the heavens and the spiritual world.

The light from above is extinguished and the figures on stage almost completely darkened. A woman's voice is heard: "O master, please do not return." The chorus continues,

> O Lord, do not return. The voices and scents that were present are gone. Your grasses were burnt on rainy nights and their scents have vanished. The stories we told a hundred times have vanished and we are left only with cold, and the sand, and boredom. There is nothing here but lonely nights and anxiousness. Do not bother with the people for they shall soon forget you, even before the autumn leaves fall.

A foreboding male voice is heard from the OFF: "Dreams, dreams, I cannot sleep." The chorus repeats its initial lines, "O Lord, do not return."

There is a dominant male voice from the OFF, which sings "menem misafirem menem vücud- u şehrimde misafirem" to a haunting melody. This song is a Sufism, that is, a melody sung by meditating Sufi dancers as they twirl. The same line occurs in a song recorded and probably written by Omar Faruk Tekbilek. Unlike the play's Arabic text, this song is in an older variety of Turkish, and the first word "menem" (I am) is in the Azeri variant. The song is the voice of a soul saying, "It is I, a guest in my own body, a guest I am," which is still quoted frequently by people and used in personal exchanges. The video has a haunting melody, which is also a musical leitmotif throughout Aboudoma's play. Its visual content consists of a series of still images, sunset scenes of idyllic tropical nature, beautiful mosques, Arabic murals, and still shots of white-clad Sufi dervishes in twirling dance meditation. All of this suggests ancient links and the pan-Arabic relations of Egypt.

The somber sounds of a flute waft through the air, the figures of the pyramid move slowly apart and dissolve the structure. The bright light at the top of the pyramid is extinguished. The figures wander aimlessly about the stage and move the puppets who sit in wheelchairs, one carrying in her hand the miniature model of the pyramid with tiny figures. A male voice sings loudly and emotionally in Arabic the same lament as above. There is silence, the group divides stage left and right. A bright light above illuminates the head of one of the puppets in the group stage right who speaks:

Fire on the enemies of the old! Every day the sun plays a new song and every day it dresses the earth with a new dress, but every song it sang or dress it has sewn could not prevent the voice of misery from me. It is a voice whose color is dark, whose color is pale like death (repeated). Much has been written about me, but nobody has understood the sense behind me.

Both groups talk excitedly among themselves, then stop. A male figure (Faust) speaks: "I am free from the guilt of anything written about me. Here I stand in front of you, neither my hands nor my papers are stained with blood, nor is there blood on my garments." Several figures begin a chant, a parody of the Easter song "Christ is risen! Joy to all men!" repeating, instead, "O Lord, do not return."

A further scene shows through symbolic dance and narration the myth of original sin, Adam and Eve, the apple, and the tree of knowledge. The dying God and his son sit in the background, and again through symbolic dance, Mephisto's entrance, his self-introduction, and new control over Faust. With a clap of his hands, Mephisto changes the music from Western to Eastern, showing his absolute control and the departure of the Faust legend from Western Europe to Egypt and Arabia. He divides into his multiple identities and introduces himself to Faust as Diablo, Azeil, Gogo, Shamoorish.

In the final scene, Faust dies; the son of God has now taken the old God's place, himself, in the old God's wheelchair, infirm and dying. The people attack him, tear open his chest, and while he dies seize from his chest a carnation, the last ray of hope in an otherwise thoroughly pessimistic world.

Sociohistorical Interpretation

Just as the play is acoustically, visually, and textually difficult to understand, so is it historically multilayered and thematically multivalent, its author deliberately confusing the audience and forcing them to operate on a mystical, subconscious level. Yet the tone is consistent: funereal and pessimistic. The initial image of the pyramid is the play's visual anchor and suggests the pharaonic age, which lasted some three thousand years until Alexander the Great's conquest of the land in 323 BCE, marking the beginning of the Hellenization of the country and its domination first by the Greeks and Ptolemaic rule, then the Romans from 30 BCE. It remained part of the Roman Republic and Empire and then part of Rome's successor state, the Byzantine Empire, until it was conquered by Arab Muslim armies in 639–42 CE. Within that Byzantine Empire the Egyptian Coptic Christian Orthodox Church of Alexandria flourished and until today remains relatively strong, if oppressed by Muslim rulers. It was estimated in 2011 that ten percent of the Egyptian population is made up of Coptic Christians, though because of the recent suppression of their numbers by Muslim radicals they have been fleeing the land in droves for safe haven abroad.

In the past millennium and a half, the country has been invaded and ruled by a number of foreign powers, including Kurdish, Circassian, Turkish, and French, when Napoleon I occupied the country for three years from 1798–1801, which also marked the turn of Egypt towards Western Europe. We have seen above in some of the scholarship on the development of theater in Egypt the acceptance, adaptation, and popularity of the Faust legend on Egyptian stages and in scholarly studies. Since the Napoleonic era, Egyptian trade has become increasingly entwined with that of Europe as opposed to Africa and Asia. Its strategic location at the end of the Mediterranean Sea, connecting it to the Red Sea, was made possible by the opening of the Suez Canal in 1869, to which Western powers contributed economically, making it an intercontinental hub. The protection of this hub was also in the interest of Western European trading powers, and hence Egypt's relations with these countries strengthened well into the mid-twentieth century. But a military coup and a new revolutionary regime nationalized the Suez Canal Company in 1952, leading to the Suez Crisis of 1956 which was resolved by the intervention of the United States and Soviet Union. Egypt played a central role for Arabic countries during the Cold War (approx. 1945–91) between Eastern European and Western powers, giving it an increased sense of importance which resulted in its leading Arab states in a series of wars against Israel, though they also led in making peace with Israel in 1979. Its relations with Western Europe continued to strengthen. As a relevant case in point for the focus of the current chapter, anyone who has been associated with Germanists in Egypt in recent years will be aware of how strong this discipline is in Egyptian universities today, and how strong the academic ties are between the two countries, as evidenced by scholarly and student exchanges and German institutional financial support. Many intellectuals in Egypt look to Europe for their scholarly sustenance. Egyptians' ongoing fascination for Goethe and *Faust* is one of the principal focal points of this interest.

This historical overview demonstrates two important points for our understanding of Aboudoma's *Faust's Dreams*. Although the Faust figure himself is correctly understood to be first and foremost quintessentially German, through centuries of reception and adaptation he has come to represent the struggling human in many lands and cultures. Aboudoma's Faust is quintessentially Egyptian, both a Muslim and a Coptic Christian figure. He is torn between Islam and Christianity, torn between his ancient roots and Egypt's modern history of foreign domination, a figure desperately suffering from compromising his own identity. That is indeed what Aboudoma's *Faust's Dreams* is about: identity, Egyptian identity, and the crisis in which it has found itself in the early twenty-first century.

Aboudoma claims that Egypt has lost its sense of identity as an Arabic, Mediterranean, and world power. He considers the triggers for this sense of loss to have been the humiliation of the Arab states by Israel in the Seven-Day war of 1948 and the Six-Day War of 1967, combined with the social, political, and economic problems and restrictions of the modern Egyptian state. But what was Egypt's identity? Better said, what were its *identities*? One must distinguish first between the ancient and the modern. Ancient Egyptian culture, dating back five millennia to the age of the pharaohs, is one of the most prevalent in the cultural awareness of most of the rest of the world because of its remarkable role in the development of both Eastern and Western civilizations, especially in learning and scholarship, symbolized by ancient Egypt's great library of Alexandria and the country's remarkable advancements in medical practice, which can still be witnessed today in the hieroglyphics on pyramid and temple walls. A second identity is associated with Egypt's Coptic Christianity, at about two millennia only half the age of its pharaonic predecessor, but a mighty influence on both the history and culture of Egypt from that time. The third identity, introduced to Egypt by Arab Muslims in 642 CE, is the religion of Islam, which since the seventh century gained many followers in Arabia, the Eastern and southern Mediterranean, most of Africa, and now many other parts of the world. Finally, there is Egypt's modern identity, beginning about a thousand years ago as it became increasingly linked with northern Mediterranean countries and hence all of Europe.

It is striking to any visitor to Egypt today, how all four identities, the ancient pharaonic, the Coptic Christian, the Arabic Islamic, and the modern, increasingly global, Mediterranean, are simultaneously evident, particularly in the capital of Cairo. Modern Egyptians live daily with a constant awareness of, and appreciation for, all four identities. As the Egyptian cultural scholar Abdul Aziz Hammouda puts it, "Culturally, Egypt [today] is a synthesis of its ancient history, its strong Islamic traditions, its colonial influences and its modern pan-Arab political and intellectual movements" (Hammouda, Zaki, Awad, Kamis, Hameed, and Khashaba 71).The Seven-Day War in October 1948 saw fighting between the armies of Israel and Egypt, in which the Egyptians represented all Arab states. The Egyptians took an unexpected loss. Despite the course of this war, Abdul Rahman Azzam Pasha, Secretary-General of the Arab League, reported in a message to Arab delegations at the United Nations, "After a battle of seven days the Egyptian Army has emerged victorious. . . . We are looking to future battles with more confidence . . . It has now become clear that the Egyptian army alone can repulse all Jewish forces" (Observer). But the reporter of that speech entitled his piece "The Egyptians are Weak with the Sword but Strong with their Mouths," for the truth was precisely the reverse of the Arab leader's claim. In 1956 Israel overran Egypt in the Suez-Sinai War. Egyptian president Gamal Abdel Nasser vowed to avenge Arab losses and organized an alliance of Arab states surrounding Israel. Israel countered with its own attack on June 5, 1967 and in six days drove the Arab armies from the Sinai peninsula, all of which it occupied and has held ever since, to the bitter protest of Arab nations. Israel's military supremacy and seizure of their lands left the Arab allies in a shock from which they have never recovered. As the traditional leader of the Arab world, Egypt has felt the humiliation more than any other Arab nation, and the international peace process from the 1970s into our own millennium has failed to reconcile the opponents. Egypt's repeated humiliation in ancient and modern times has overshadowed the glory of its pharaonic past. Its leadership among Arab nations is in question. Its Christian base has been dwarfed by Islamic influence—approximately 90% of Egyptians are now Muslims, and only approximately 10% Coptic and other Christian, the latter slightly larger at the time the play was produced ("Egypt Demographics").

Unlike Goethe's Faust, who strives for knowledge and experience, and is a positive, if problematic, symbol of human endeavor, Faust for Aboudoma is a victim who represents Egypt's everyman. In the end, he disappears into oblivion and meaninglessness, he has lost his sense of identity in the modern world. Abouduma's adaptation incorporated Egyptian identities over five millennia to deliver a pessimistic message about Egyptian identity today with only a slim ray of hope for the future.

The Broader Context

In 2003, Robert Springborg, Director of the London Middle East Institute at the School of Oriental and African Studies, London, explained, in an article on the crisis of Egyptian identity, that fragmented national identities indicate competitive social formations and immobilized governmental institutions, which lead to political contestation and change. The rise of Arab nationalism had failed to take into account this fragmentation and integrate its pluralism into political governance (18). This situation, Springborg argued, was not sustainable as it denied the reality of the social fabric, and in Egypt's case particularly because it was failing to adjust to the new political and social realities of an increasingly globalized world. Egypt had been resisting such change, he suggested in 2003, and the resistance subsequently intensified. From his perspective at that time, Springborg made this striking statement:

> Radical Arab nationalism is dead, but is yet to be buried. Its corpse is retained, like an El Cid, as a symbol of the earlier phase, the linkage to which serves as a justification of claims to present incumbency. The rotting corpse cannot be interred until a new source of legitimacy is produced, a legitimacy which must rest on the recognition of three separate realities and accommodation to them, tasks to which the Egyptian leadership as well as that of most other Arab states, have thus far proven unequal. (19)

Springborg's opening sentence is shocking from today's perspective, but we have the advantage of hindsight. The "three separate realities" for which he calls include subnational groups with distinct political entities. Especially important are the Coptic and other Christians, the Islamist-modernists, and the "haves" as opposed to the "have-nots," that is, those who have become part of the international business world and whose wealth is generated by external economic relations and foreign links, versus those who have not and remain poor. Such heterogeneity, argues Springborg, had not been acknowledged or accommodated by the prevailing powers in Egypt who wish to propagate an identity of homogeneity (20). His historical perspective in 2003 was the same as Abouduma's when *Faust's Dreams* was produced, though the playwright wished to emphasize the struggle of the Christian minority within the context of Egyptian historical memory, and the pessimistic gloom of his play pointed to today's reality. Furthermore, it does not include Springborg's elevating possibility of change in society to include the politically disenfranchised minorities, and especially not the "McWorld" minority who was ready to embrace Western capitalism and exploit Egypt's traditional location as a geographically pivotal trading nation.

What of Goethe's *Faust II*? What of the spirit of the Faust character who drank deeply of the waters of classical Greece, who dove into the fray of European power politics and commercial intrigue in the Middle Ages, who fathered a son with the epitome of classical female beauty, who challenged the forces of Nature herself to create new living space for his humankind, who faced the devil to his death in the court of the heavens, and who *never* abandoned his vision and goal for a new world? Goethe's *Faust* is a hymn of praise to the human spirit. Aboudoma's *Faust's Dreams* is a fascinating metaphysical exploration, but in the end a dirge of pessimism over the loss of Egyptian identity. But the history of Egypt is long and deep, five or six millennia at least, and the timespan represented in Goethe's *Faust* even greater. Both are epic, both have their magnificent triumphs and highlights, both their valleys of despair. Perhaps director Aboudoma will have occasion to write a different *Faust* for his countrymen and women at a future stage of Egypt's evolution. Let us hope so.

Acknowledgments

I wish to express my sincere thanks to Mahmoud Aboudoma for his openness and generosity; graduate student Mahsa Kalatehseifary, who initially discovered and re-searched the adaptation; my four assistants, Mohammed Rahman, Christen Salib, Iman Thabet, and Rosemary Victor, who helped me understand the Arabic text of the performance; and doctoral candidate Sara Ghaffarian, who also assisted.

Works Cited

Aboudoma, Mahmoud. Playwright and director of *Faust's Dreams*. Interview with the author. Alexandria, Egypt. April, 2006.

Anglet, Andreas. "*Faust*-Rezeption." *Goethe Handbuch*. Band II. Ed. Theodor Buck. Vol. 2. Stuttgart: Metzler, 1996. 478–513.

Behzadi, Lale. "Ausblick und Spiegelung: Goethes *Faust* in der arabischen Literatur." *Orient und Okzident. Zur Faustrezeption in nicht-christlichen Kulturen*. Ed. Jochen Golz and Adrian Hsia. Köln: Böhlau, 2008. 67–76.

Chelkowski, Peter. "Islam in Modern Drama and Theatre." *Die Welt des Islams* 23.1 (1984): 45–69.

"Egypt Demographics Profile 2014." *Index Mundi*. Last updated June 30, 2015. <http://www.indexmundi.com/egypt/demographics_profile.html>.

Elmusa, Sharif, S. "Faust without the Devil? The Interplay of Technology and Culture in Saudi Arabia." *The Middle East Journal* 51.3 (1997): 345–57.

Faust's Dreams. An adaptation of Goethe's *Faust* performed in Arabic (2002). Private DVD of playwright and director Mahmoud Aboudoma, copy in posses-sion of David G. John.

"*Faust's Dreams*." *UK Theatre Web*. <http://www.uktw.co.uk/archive/play/fausts -dreams/L01015097089/>.

Goethe-Bibliographie Online / Faust / Übersetzungen. <http://opac.ub.uni-weimar.de>.

Hammouda, Abdul Aziz, Ahmed Zaki, Samir Awad, Shawky Kamis, Ahmed Abdel Hameed, and Sami Khashaba. "Egypt." *The World Encyclopedia of Contemporary Theatre*. Vol. 4. Ed. Don Rubin. London: Routledge, 1999. 70–100.

Hilmi, Aladin. *Die Rezeption Goethes in Ägypten*. Stuttgart: Hans -Dieter Heinz, 1986.

Hsia, Adrian. "On the Reception of *Faust* in Asia." *International Faust Studies: Adaptation, Reception, Translation*. Ed. Lorna Fitzsimmons. London: Continuum, 2008. 149–60.

Khattab, Aleya. "Die faustische Frau in der arabischen Literatur: *Die Frau, die über den Teufel triumphierte* von Taufik Al-Hakim." *Orient und Okzident. Zur Faustrezeption in nicht-christlichen Kulturen*. Ed. Jochen Golz and Adrian Hsia. Köln: Böhlau, 2008. 77–90.

Maher, Moustafa. "Die Rezeption des Faust-Stoffes in Ägypten und die vermittelnde Rolle des Theaters." *Europäische Mythen der Neuzeit: Faust und Don Juan: gesammelte Vorträge des Salzburger Symposions, 1992*. Ed. Peter Csobádi. Anif: Verlag K. Müller-Speiser, 1993. 437–50.

McCleod, Alec. "Diaspora." *The Skinny*. <http://www.theskinny.co.uk/theatre /features/36016-diaspora>. July 15, 2006.

Mommsen, Katharina. "Arabien." *Goethe Handbuch*. Band 4/1. Ed. Hans-Dietrich Dahnke and Regine Otto. Stuttgart: Metzler, 1998. 72–73.

Mommsen, Katharina. *Goethe und die arabische Welt*. Frankfurt: Insel, 1988.

Nasched, Shahir. "Faust—erstmals 1929 in arabischer Sprache." *Goethe-Spuren in Literatur, Kunst, Philosophie, Politik, Pädagogik und Übersetzung*. Ed. Detlef Ignasiak and Frank Lindner. Bucha bei Jena: Quantus, 2009. 40–42.

Observer. "The Seven-Day War." *New York Post*, October 31, 1948, 1. <www .varchive.org/obs/481031.htm>.

Radwan, Kamil. *Der Fauststoff seit Goethe*. Hamburg: Borg, 1982.

Radwan, Kamil. "Die Rezeption der Faustgestalt in der arabischen Literatur." *Im Dialog mit der interkulturellen Germanistik*. Ed. Hans-Christoph Nayhauss and Krysztof A. Kuczynski. Wroclaw: Wydawn, 1993. 303–12.

Radwan, Kamil. "Zur Goethe-Rezeption in Ägypten." *Goethe-Jahrbuch* 100 (1983): 71–76.

Selaiha, Nehad. "A Faustian End-game." *Al-Ahram Weekly Online*, 581, April 2002, 11–17. <http://weekly.ahram.org.eg/2002/581/cu2.htm>.

Shaikh, Khalil. *Der Teufel in der modernen arabischen Literatur. Die Rezeption eines europäischen Motivs in der arabischen Belletristik, Dramatik und Poesie des 19. und 20. Jahrunderts*. Berlin: Klaus Schwarz, 1986.

Shraim, Iyad. "Goethes *Faust* und der neue arabische Faust. Die Rezeption eines Stoffes der Weltliteratur bei Ali Ahmad Bakathir und Hamid Ibrahim." MA thesis,Westfälische Wilhelms-Universität Münster, Westfalen, 2008. <http://www .db-thueringen.de/servlets/DerivateServlet/Derivate-18276/sharimMA.pdf>.

Springborg, Robert. "Identity in Crisis: Egyptian Political Identity in the Face of Globalization." *Harvard International Review* 25.3 (2003): 18–23.

Szyska, Christian. "Rewriting the European Canon: Ali Ahmad Bakathir's 'New Faust.'" *Encounters of Words and Texts. Intercultural Studies in Honor of Stefan Wild on the Occasion of His 60ᵗʰ Birthday, March 2, 1997, Presented by His Pupils in Bonn.* Ed. Lutz Edzard and Christian Szyska. Hildesheim: Olms, 1997. 131–45.

Author's Profile

David G. John is a member of the Germanic Studies faculty at the University of Waterloo, Ontario, Canada. His interests include modern German literature in the broad sense, from 1750 to the present, with specializations in the classical period, Goethe, Schiller, and German drama. In addition to many articles, he has published books on Johann Christian Krüger (1986), the German *Nachspiel* (1991), Goethe and Schiller (1998), and Goethe's *Faust* in intercultural stagings (2012), and has coauthored or edited several others.

Chapter 9

Repackaging Goethe's *Faust* in Bridge Markland's *Faust in the Box*

Lynn Marie Kutch

Abstract

In her article, "Repackaging Goethe's *Faust* in Bridge Markland's *Faust in the Box*," Lynn Marie Kutch examines Berlin-based German perform-er Bridge Markland's one-woman puppet show, *Faust in the Box* (2006). Markland's version of Goethe's *Faust* uses a distinctive assemblage of mu-sic and props, through which the actress brings an ironic difference to the puppet play tradition. Through a detailed analysis of the visual and aural elements that contribute to the work, Kutch describes ways that Markland's performance challenges the core themes and assumptions that audiences have associated with Faust over the centuries. The investigation indicates that Markland's bold and innovative style of storytelling results less from fidelity to the expectations of performing a classic text than from loyalty to the creative process.

Since the publication of part 1 in 1808, Goethe's *Faust* has been widely revered for its form and style, and also respected for the frequency with which it has been adapted. Viewing adaptations as culturally influenced renderings that emerge at sig-nificant historical turning points provides one sound method for indexing the diverse treatments of the Faust theme through the ages and across borders (Fitzsimmons, *Lives*; *International*). In addition to a sociohistorical approach to classifying and evaluating adaptations, however, many Faust variations, including cinematic and multimedia interpretations, could also represent entries in a catalogued history of diverse approaches to storytelling. A review of adaptations reveals, however, nearly equal amounts of innovation and recurrent patterns. For example, the puppet plays from the 1700s, which "became a great, lasting influence" on Goethe and motivated him to create *Faust* (Goethe, *Poetry* 24), have also inspired newer approaches that fuse live performance with puppets and audio as well as digital media. In her one-woman show, *Faust in the Box*, which premiered in German at the Saalbau in Berlin in 2006 and in English at the English Theatre Berlin in 2008, Berlin-based German performance artist Bridge Markland renegotiates storytelling patterns with her extensive use of puppets and a prerecorded acoustic layer—made up in part of pop music clips and an original audio book version recorded by German or British actors. *Faust in the Box* combines pop culture props and sound bites in the form of intercut music, ranging from classical to modern-day, to which the performer and the puppets lip-sync. In this article, I will describe and assess *Faust in the Box*'s ironic aesthetics of storytelling, which involves packing and unpacking a classic legend in and out of a cardboard box—the complete performance space of the piece.

In general, adaptations are concerned with an intentional and original packaging of the classic material, but Markland does this in a literal sense: the entirety of the storytelling equipment, including the performance artist herself and props, fits inside an oversized box. This unusual approach invites the audience to look beyond the well-known elements of the legend and to scrutinize instead the imaginative process that culminates in Markland's performance. Innovative modes of storytelling, particularly ones found in *Faust in the Box*, have the potential to provoke a critical spirit of confrontation because they reconceptualize canonical material. As Christina Wegel explains, readers and audiences often think of classic texts as "firm and static," but they are actually "adjustable, moveable cultural objects" (219–20). Markland's choice to adjust the source material by drastically reducing its performance space, cast, and visual aesthetics could conflict with rigid expectations that audience members and critics maintain for well-known cultural pillars such as Goethe's *Faust*. In a summary that Markland provides on her website, she seems to close the gap between the source and its adaptation by using descriptors that Goethe himself might have used to characterize his own work. Not hinting at much radicalism beyond that found in the original play, Markland states, "The piece carries audiences to laughter and to tears as the storyline unfolds before them with humor, emotion, great sensibility and much grotesqueness" (Markland). Her unusual enactment of Goethe's material has nonetheless on occasion provoked criticism and discord, as is often the case with adaptations, as this Fringe Festival critic demonstrates: "Markland mimes along to an audio-book reading of Goethe's *Faust*— gurning inanely and employing the most rudimentary of puppetry skills—while irritating snippets of modern pop music are cut . . . into the soundtrack" (Judge). As this spirited reaction strongly suggests, *Faust in the Box* provides a compelling example of the creative tension that can develop between a canonical text, its mutable relevance, and an inventive approach to its adaptation.

Since Goethe published *Faust* more than 200 years ago, it would seem that any recent adaptation would have to prioritize the artistic process over the storyline and its common themes, considering the question of whether "such motifs still have any relevance in an age of mass entertainment" (Erlin 170). In an interview I conducted with Markland in 2012 (see also Kallin), the artist explained her process of accessorizing her artistic interpretation with pop culture-inspired auditory and visual elements and with props that facilitate the hyperbolic mode of storytelling that David J. Baker deems requisite for today's audiences of *Faust* performance (37). For members of the "cast" who perform multiple functions as storytellers and interpreters of dialogue, Markland chose Barbie dolls and puppets that are available in German department stores or secondhand stores (Kutch). Just as they would a celebrity or a famous brand, audience members readily recognize these objects; but the "product placement" in this new context urges viewers to imagine different connections. Commenting on her use of audio devices, Markland also explains that she creates "collages from people's lives, enhancing facts from their life with music" (Kutch). Unlike a typical musical theater performance, in which full-length pieces or substantial musical selections supplement the text with song, *Faust in the Box* features short snippets that disrupt the prerecorded recitation of the excerpts from the Goethe text. Markland's inclusion of cuts by disparate artists who have mass celebrity appeal in common, such as Johnny Cash, Madonna, and Elvis, serves well to elevate the Faust legend to celebrity status. In contrast to a full-blown operatic or cinematic production, however, the one-woman show format and pre-recorded script impose certain limitations. While *Faust in the Box* cannot approach a cinematic level of spectacle, its accomplishments reside in Markland's multifaceted storytelling, which not only involves manipulating props and costumes, but also entails the live performer's careful coordination of the props and the piece's sound collage.

Typical of live performances, *Faust in the Box* features auditory and visual components as separate yet interlocking elements. In conceptualizing *Faust in the Box*, Markland blends image and sound, but in a way that emphasizes the form of each medium. First, I would like to examine the piece's carefully engineered soundscape and its vital role in the piece as a whole. The Faust legend as inspiration for composed musical pieces forms a long tradition of Faust adaptations. In her conceptualization of *Faust in the Box*, Markland does not, however, compose her own music; rather, she integrates the work of songwriters from various decades and of widely dissimilar musical genres to punctuate the original Goethe text, but more importantly to provide *Faust in the Box*'s aesthetic with a prominent aural narrative space. Although Markland's implementation of music has some things in common with operatic versions of Faust, the content and engineering of *Faust in the Box*'s musical montage points to important differences in aesthetics and purpose. In an assessment of operatic treatments of the legend, Marcia Green speaks of a "quest in opera to unify text and music within the confines of one integrative form" (34). Also emphasizing a sense of accord that corresponds to *Faust*'s theme of redemption, H. Wendell Howard argues, in reference to Gounod's *Faust*, "Faust is not a story that can be wedded to dissonances, and atonality, and the clashing chords of *Wozzeck*. Alienation and societal and psychic breakdown are not the substance of Faust" (90). In a sense, *Faust in the Box*'s musical landscape parallels that of opera in that both genres represent "musical modes of externalizing the inner spirit of *Faust*" (Howard 90). On the other hand, however, the ironic intercutting of music as perceptibly discordant as that by Metallica and Rammstein suggests bold subversion and a quest to reengineer the sounds of *Faust* for a contemporary audience. In so doing, *Faust in the Box* explores and emphasizes the acoustic level as an active aesthetic agent that can disrupt and disturb expectations.

In addition to a track based on Goethe's *Faust I* and recorded by contemporary actors and actresses in Berlin, *Faust in the Box*'s sound landscape consists of familiar musical selections from a range of time periods. As many contemporary theatergoers might agree, it is indeed much easier to register a performer's facial expressions and manipulation of props amid conspicuous lighting than to inventory and chronicle mentally the sound fragments that comprise a show's acoustic design. *Faust in the Box*'s design, however, strongly supports the legitimacy of acoustic space, even at a juncture in media development where the visual is often prioritized. Full appreciation of *Faust in the Box* requires the spectator to focus on the numerous audio clues amid the overwhelming visual stimulation. In his seminal work on acoustic environments and their appreciation, *The Tuning of the World: Toward a Theory of Soundscape Design*, in which he coined the term "soundscape," R. Murray Schafer calls for a deliberately heightened awareness of sound markers and their meanings in a world of predominant visual cues. Although Schafer implements "soundscape" to signify features of the natural and industrialized environment, aspects of his theory that call for interpreting audio cues just as readily as visual cues are pertinent to my interpretation of *Faust in the Box*. As Schafer acknowledges, however, "it is less easy to formulate an exact impression of a soundscape than a landscape. There is nothing in sonography corresponding to the instantaneous impression which photography can create" (7). Markland deliberately chooses well-known objects, whether visual or aural, with which audiences can relate. Schafer describes the "permanent record of past sounds" that music furnishes, or the "largely subconscious influence on our senses and memory that music can exert" (103). With its frenetic intermixing of songs, however, *Faust in the Box* reprograms that permanent record in order to arrive at a newly synthesized and original creation.

Markland uses brief but richly expressive musical segments to create an auditory plane that complements the visual plane of performance. Providing a theoretical framework for constructing the auditory experience, Schafer differentiates between "gesture," or the "name we can give to the unique event, the solo, the specific," and "texture," or the "generalized aggregate," the "imprecise" (159). Given the fact that the German version of *Faust in the Box* contains more than one hundred musical segments, the piece consists of at least that many "gestures." Schafer argues that the "generalized aggregate," or complete sound picture, is not "merely a simple sum of a lot of individualistic sounds—it is *something different*" (159). *Faust in the Box*'s complex combination of sound occurrences produces something other than a mere list of songs taken from the hit parades of various decades and from various continents. Instead, the musical gestures contribute to *Faust in the Box*'s "photography of sound" (Schafer 8). In his book *Aesthetics and Music*, Andy Hamilton alludes to this multisensory experience when he defines aesthetics as "an attitude of intensified or enriched experiences" (1). Clearly, Markland uses sound to intensify the visual experience as when, at the start of the performance, the spectator sees the solo actress in an almost mime-like state, with a shaven head, full white makeup, and wearing entirely black clothing. A single powerful spotlight illuminates the actress, but because of her clothing, her head and hands appear to float independently. Despite this striking visual impression (to which I will return below), however, the sound montage also commands attention and supplies an enriched experience because of the artist's inventive editing and juxtaposition of individual sound contributions. When the music interrupts the flow of the Goethe text, the original dialogue of *Faust I* essentially disappears for that moment, thereby giving the music not only narrative but also interpretative authority by both distancing the audience from the story and commanding their attention to the creative process.

Faust in the Box's first few minutes of musical moments, characterized by stylistic and temporal eclecticism, build an aggregate the heterogeneity of which characterizes the remainder of the show as Markland progresses through *Faust I*'s plot. Taken as individual gestures, the choices may seem haphazard, and only vaguely connected to the Faust plot. When viewed as individual parts of an aggregate, however, the songs form a much more coherent aesthetic pattern. Both the German and English versions begin with the Away Team's remix (1997) of Shirley Bassey's "Where Do I Begin?" from the soundtrack of *Love Story*. Opening with Bassey's version might serve to highlight the love story between Faust and Margarete—the core of Goethe's version. On the other hand, the song's altered musical profile draws more attention to the dance-mix acoustic frame and away from the lyrics, suggesting ambiguity through irony. The subsequent use of "Sympathy for the Devil" (1968) by the Rolling Stones, in which the devil as narrator recounts his mark on history, allows Markland to introduce the character of Mephistopheles. However, we must look beneath this rationale to see how this song impacts *Faust in the Box*'s soundscape. The stark change in musical style from a slow ballad to a penetrating rock song displays a mottled auditory landscape that speaks to a diversity of experience. The subsequent aesthetic texture, or incorporation of songs from vastly different genres, presents a soundscape no less ambiguous, and even hints at improvisation, or what Hamilton terms the "aesthetics of imperfection," which find "virtues in improvisation" (196). Although the prerecorded nature of *Faust in the Box*'s soundtrack precludes audience perception that the performer is improvising the audio selections, presenting drastically truncated pieces of songs calls to mind the dynamic and "unfinished state" of improvised performances (Hamilton 196).

In debates about improvisation, there are those who defend the "autonomy of the composer-genius . . . which requires the complete subservience of the performer," while others advocate "the arrangement of a composition for instrumental forces different from those for which it was originally composed" (Hamilton 195). The notion of musical interpretation as the transfer of an abstract idea seems to apply to free adaptations of other classic works as well as artistic appropriations, such as pop songs. As Hamilton emphasizes, the aesthetics of imperfection focuses on the "event or process of performance," implying the dichotomies of "process and product" and "spontaneity and deliberation" as well (196). Even though *Faust in the Box* does not include live musical performance, Markland's irony challenges the meanings and performative contexts of the chosen songs. For example, the juxtaposition of Metallica's "Some Kind of Monster" (2003) and Marius Müller-Westernhagen's "Sexy" (1989) has a satiric effect not only because of the perceived datedness of Westernhagen's 80s song, but also because of the glaring stylistic incompatibility of the two songs as they relate to each other and to the classic Faust legend.

Just as some of the opening songs draw attention to the aesthetic itself because of this incongruity, so the final sequence of songs has a similar effect. The length of the selections varies from more than one minute to a short yet significant three seconds. Margarete's sense of guilt and her imprisonment have driven her mad, which at first prevents her from recognizing Faust. When Faust witnesses the manifestations of her insanity, Markland inserts chords from Led Zeppelin's "In My Time of Dying" (1975). It's A Beautiful Day's "White Bird" (1969) accompanies Margarete's response. When she eventually recognizes Faust and he offers to help her escape, the sound landscape changes significantly with the transition to "Aufstehen" (Stand Up) (2004) by Seeed, a German reggae band. When Margarete refuses to leave with Faust, the sound backdrop features three extremely short selections from Rammstein songs: "Mutter" (Mother) (2001) and "Bestrafe mich" (Punish Me) (1997). Not only do these samples represent a completely different type of music, but their brief length (some only three seconds) also sets them apart while generating an ironic distance from the tensions of *Faust*'s plot. After this experience of intensified audio interference, the last few minutes of the scene, including the revelation of Margarete's redemption, draw on Soft Cell's "Tainted Love" (1981), the post-punk band Joy Division's "Love Will Tear Us Apart Again" (1980), and Müller-Westernhagen's "Nur ein Traum" (Just a Dream) (1989). Finally, in the absence of music, the audience hears Margarete's "Heinrich, Heinrich" as the last auditory fragment.

These last 7–10 minutes of *Faust in the Box* typify the show as a whole in its ironic soundscape and its compression of turbulent action into a limited physical and temporal frame. Especially significant for this last scene is the treatment of Margarete's transformation. Critics have interpreted the Goethean scene as emphasizing the female heroine's "tragic greatness" (Oergel 264), serving as a "masterpiece of psychological portrayal" (Brown 97) that evokes profound fear, pity, horror, or shock. Indeed, Goethe's text has moved audiences to experience a range of emotions as they witness the decline of the heroine. A related question for *Faust in the Box* concerns the role of the musical soundtrack in either reinforcing or complicating the audience's perception of emotions evoked by the original text.

In his study of theories about the connections between music and emotion, Malcolm Budd describes emotions as episodes or occurrences (1). Emotion as episode may have different states, from the onset of a feeling to its intensification and strengthening, brought about by circumstances or other emotions. In regard to the relationship between emotion and music, Budd contends that while music does not directly correspond to emotion, it does provide an expression of emotion (23). Music appears, therefore, as a symbol of emotional life and the "human vocal expression of emotion" (Budd 176). Such studies suggest the power of musical selections to influence emotions. The emotional impact of *Faust in the Box* is influenced not only by the selection of songs, but also their arrangement as abbreviated musical sound bites. In the final scene, the song snippets have the effect of constantly interrupting the portrayed emotion, which prevents any one emotion from enveloping the audience. Breaking up the gripping Dungeon scene with Rammstein and selections from German pop sensations of the 1980s and 1990s reminds the audience that *Faust* must constantly be interpreted anew.

The musical soundtrack and audio book version of *Faust* provide only one sensory aspect of *Faust in the Box's* total aesthetic. Another facet consists of the visual experience of one actress acting out the full story using not much more than a cardboard box, cheap accessories, and simple wigs and costumes. Even with the aural fabric as backdrop, the actress still has the large task of telling the story. By basing her script on Goethe's version of the Faust legend, but condensing that vast amount of material into a roughly ninety-minute production, Markland reduces the classic substance to correspond to her conceptual space, which distances the performer while nevertheless engaging the audience through its originality (Lei 55–59). Eliminating or admixing characters, events, and settings, Markland consolidates all characters in one performer and reduces all locales to one easily moveable set. With respect to the category of intrigue, the curiosity-provoking aspects of a play (Lei 56), the appeal of *Faust in the Box* seems to hinge less on the development and outcome of the plot, given that the majority of viewers are familiar with the Faust legend. To paraphrase Baker, for contemporary audiences *Faust* performance is less about the historical theme than staging (37). Hence, the intrigue of Markland's piece emerges from curiosity about how the performer will convey scenes of the classic legend "in the box."

The art of compression that *Faust in the Box* accomplishes has as much to do with a temporal time frame as it does with the use of limited performance space. Markland uses a very constricted space, not more than two to four feet around her cardboard box, to bring her version of *Faust I* to the audience. For most of the performance, the box acts as a miniature theater in and immediately around which Markland performs.

As the play opens, the audience sees the illuminated front surface of a cardboard box on an otherwise darkened stage. Markland appears from within the box dressed in black and wearing a top hat, establishing a persona as storyteller and creator. Viewed from a distance, the small shape of the box on the blackened stage not only reveals a utility and economy of space, but this very first visual impression also announces a strikingly unconventional approach to "telling" the material. One might think that a one-person recital of a classic text would count as the primary unconventional element. On the contrary, there is in fact a history of such performances for

Shakespearean actors, which can provide some parallels in the near absence of one-person recitations of the Faust legend, an exception being Calum MacAskill's 2012 single performer production of *Faust/us* based on Christopher Marlowe's version (Devaney). Determining characteristics on one end of the performance spectrum, John Gielgud's performance of *Ages of Man* takes a purist approach. With a very simple stage establishing the formality of the performance and the canonical text, Gielgud, as one reviewer commented, had "no need for gimmicks, such as the usual armload of prop books" (Gentile 155). By contrast, not all "compressed" Shake-spearean one-man performances convey this air of conventionality. Ian McKellen's *Acting Shakespeare* emphasizes a casualness that encourages contemporary dialogue with the audience about a classic piece (Gentile 158). Indeed, *Faust in the Box* employs a similar method of linking together or compressing different time frames and approaches to the material, but Markland's show is more about visual and aural exhibition, which, like cinema, uses light, props, and staging to organize the theatrical space. Although *Faust in the Box* is also limited to one performer, the performance aesthetic expands considerably upon other one-person renditions through the incorporation of props and pop music.

A striking example of the economy of the piece occurs at the beginning of the show when Markland transitions from portraying Mephistopheles to playing Faust. In the "Prolog im Himmel" ("Prologue in Heaven"), Markland takes on the role of the devil in conversation with the far-removed and pre-recorded voice of God. In addition to voice, or words only, Markland conveys her interpretation of the characters with exaggerated facial expressions as she moves around the limited stage area in darkness with a spotlight on her. Retreating behind the box for a quick change of costume and character, the actress reappears as Faust, standing inside the box and wearing a simple academician's tam. In contrast to the scene in which she portrays the devil and wildly gestures with her hands and distorts her face, now her arms rest on the front wall of the box and her hands face up, suggesting an air of humility or even desperation. In the opening monologue in Faust's study, the scholar is alternately portrayed in full stature behind the cardboard box and with the spotlight focusing directly on his face, which establishes a visual linkage between Faust and Mephistopheles. In addition to a tightly focused lighting design, Markland also uses simple and unlikely props, such as a cheap toy dog, which does back flips, to interpret and break up the lengthy monologues. In contrast to a traditionalist approach to presenting classic materials, such as those that might call for "no gimmicks," the production economically loads the cardboard box with a series of pop art devices that intensify the irony of performance and suggest that if the Faust legend resonates today, it does so within a hectic and subverted context.

The sense of intrigue grows when Markland portrays multiple characters in dialogue, which she accomplishes by incorporating puppets and dolls. Markland emphasizes that she is not a puppeteer, implying that her use of this medium is ironic and subversive. As a point of contrast, in his discussion of Svankmajer's 1994 film *Faust*, in which puppets and marionettes figure prominently, Pavel Drábek reads

Faust's existence in the context of the animate objects and provides a relatively conventional symbolic appraisal. For example, Drábek writes that the puppets accomplish a challenge to "corporeal integrity" and embody or dramatize the state of the human subject (531–32). While such readings might apply to *Faust in the Box*, a main aim of the puppets in Markland's piece is to enhance the visual impact, which she achieves by interacting with the puppets as if they were live cast members. In the scene when Faust sees Margarete for the first time, Markland portrays Faust while she also manipulates a Margarete hand puppet. In the subsequent scene when Faust and Mephistopheles speak about Margarete, Markland then steps into the role of the devil, while she manipulates a Faust puppet. Minutes later, when Margarete thinks about having met Faust, Markland appears in a wig and bonnet that match those worn by her puppet version.

The choice of interacting with and operating the puppets enhances the show's unpredictability and fascination. Using the puppets in a conventional puppet-show style would conceal the actress and relegate her to a role behind the scenes. The performer's choice not to use the puppets exclusively in a traditional manner allows her to show the audience how to engage in critical dialogue with the primary characters, as represented visually when Markland speaks directly to the puppets and responds to their dialogue with Goethe's scripted text. Her direct interaction with the props also underscores her creative participation in the show's aesthetic conceptualization. It is clear here how the actress takes on the role of the modern storytelling performer, as is common with one-person shows. Perhaps unique to *Faust in the Box*, however, the actress imbues the storyteller's role with a paradoxical elasticity that has the potential to test the boundaries of the medium, but also maintains those limitations as part of the boxed aesthetic.

Returning to the last scene of *Faust in the Box*, Markland's representation of Margarete is of particular interest. Countless critics have considered the significance of Margarete for the play as a whole, as a dramatic representative of moral complexity, and even as a "striving individual who engages in autonomous activity" (Oergel 45). In an aesthetic reading of Markland's staging of Goethe's "Kerker" ("Dungeon"), however, it is important to consider the scene's significance in relation to *Faust in the Box* as a whole. Unlike other performances of this scene, *Faust in the Box*'s visual effect forces the viewer to prioritize the staging rather than the content. Instead of performing from inside or behind the box, or having the puppets peer through a small door cut into the box's front, however, the actress and her accessories have now moved in front of the box. Here, as in previous scenes featuring Margarete, Markland takes on the role of the traditionally tragic heroine. For this last scene, the square cardboard box still relays the sense of restricted space and limitation that it had in previous scenes. The small door that framed much of the action has been taped shut, forcing Margarete in front of the box where she dominates and controls the scene with her central physical placement. Her immobility, conveyed through restricted blocking, continues to stress spatial limitations. In addition to the wig and the bonnet, the actress also wears a long brown tunic, which looks as if it has been spattered with blood. In her left hand, she holds the Faust puppet, while a plastic ball and chain figuratively immobilize her right hand. As I claimed above in speaking about the musical selections, these seemingly misplaced props amid one of Western drama's most revered scenes accomplish an aesthetic shattering of audience expectations.

Just as the sound provides an intensified and enriched experience of emotion, the props play a similar role not only in the intensification, but also in a corresponding de-escalation, of emotion. For example, the juvenile appearance of the costumes and props within this emotional scene accomplishes the same sort of alienation as that achieved by the intercut musical selections. In earlier scenes, Margarete appeared on stage as a simple hand puppet with a blue gingham dress, white apron, hair made of yellow yarn, and a bonnet. In the final scene, when Markland takes on the role of Margarete, she wears a wig made of the same type of yarn found on the puppet. The consistency of materials allows the audience to draw the artistic connection between the puppet and the performer; and Markland's portrayal of Margarete speaks to the female character's centrality and importance above Faust and Mephistopheles, who are both puppets in this scene. Markland lip-syncs to a recording of Margarete's lines that conveys the scene's changing spectrum of feelings. The recording evokes the states that audiences traditionally associate with this scene—despair, defiance, salvation; but the actress's appearance and her curious interaction with the puppets disturb the emotional continuity of the scene. In the context of the emotional episodes discussed above, the props also draw certain parallels to the music as symbolic of emotional life. For example, Margarete's words alone convey her insanity, but her lip-puckering and kissing the puppet emphasize that sense of madness even more by forcing the audience to attempt to process this aesthetic and artistic disruption. Similarly, the very final sequence, when Margarete manipulates the intertwined Mephistopheles and Faust puppets and makes them fly away, also draws attention to emotional responses that, without the benefit of hearing the text, might resemble those of a child sitting on the floor playing with toys. In this way, the props make a similar impression as the music when, to paraphrase Budd, we can make believe that music is the human vocal expression of emotion (133). Here, use of toys and juvenile props literally builds upon the notion of make-believe and figuratively extends the expression of emotion to include out-of-place and bizarre visual cues.

Compressing the emotionally intense Goethean material into performance in a limited physical area has the effect of intensifying and enriching the theater experience because audience members cannot rely on a traditional understanding of the drama to make sense of this interpretation. With its pop-culture audio and visual cues, *Faust in the Box*'s aesthetic system would seem to support Baker's assessment of current adaptations: "today the Faust myth seems to exist only as parody. But not parody based on firsthand knowledge of a familiar classic." Instead, he maintains, the "only association derives from the centrality of the Faust theme in pop culture" (37). The impression that *Faust in the Box* has less to do with the legend, and more to do with integration and assimilation of strands of pop culture, can help to bring us closer to a clearer assessment of its significance. Tony Jackson, in "The Dialogic and the Aesthetic: Some Reflections on Theatre as a Learning Medium," locates the quality of an aesthetic experience in the "liveness" of the event, "the emotional resonances it can offer, the dialogues that can be generated, and the complexity of texture that defies easy closure" (117). Jackson's three-pronged approach to "liveness" can offer a rubric of sorts by which to evaluate *Faust in the Box*'s aesthetics of storytelling. In the category of emotional resonances, *Faust in the Box* features attention-getting props and costumes and an intriguing layering of music onto the theatrical performance of the Goethean plot. As I have argued, these choices and their combination both highlight and adapt the range of emotions found in the source text by compelling the audience to view other perceptibly bizarre manifestations of those emotional spectra. *Faust in the Box* also has the power to generate debate and dialogue because of its iconoclastic treatment of the classic text. Finally, I would certainly maintain that *Faust in the Box* possesses a complexity of texture that defines its storytelling aesthetic and could, on the one hand, complicate its ready acceptance into a history of Faust adaptations, but, on the other hand, could confirm its value as innovative and subversive storytelling.

   Faust in the Box's complications and validity both stem in large part from its format as a one-woman show. In his book *Cast of One*, John S. Gentile observes that critics sometimes "disparage one-person shows by referring to them as 'stunts' or 'cabaret acts' and have thus diminished their contributions as theatre" (200). As one response to that, Arthur Peterson makes the important point that "since time immemorial we have had storytellers" (qtd. in Gentile 200). The connection of the one-person show to the ancient art of storytelling and the development of drama and literature underscores the aesthetic intricacy of one-person shows. The complexity of texture results not only from the dense and rich language of the classic text, but also from Markland's process of designing a performance space and incorporating accessories that show a contemporary audience one powerful method to call well-known literary passages into question. I would argue that *Faust in the Box* highlights the twentieth-first century storyteller delivering a performance for an audience that is accustomed to ironic and disruptive streams of information. Markland's hectic method of storytelling, in which she compresses frantic action and divides the labor of telling the morally complex Faust legend with a cast of puppets, seems to confirm Baker's view that the legend has become secondary to the need for new approaches. Baker writes, "what it cannot do—what none of the Faust merchants can manage anymore—is lure the genie out of the bottle to horrify or frighten us" (36). Perhaps Baker is correct in maintaining that "eternal damnation" and "blasphemy" do not instill fear in today's viewers. Yet Markland has shown that storytelling techniques implemented to convey adapted meanings of these concepts to today's audiences can in fact take over the legend's role to alarm and surprise.

   Many adaptations that could fall into the same category as *Faust in the Box* have been alternately lauded and subjected to lukewarm or even brutally negative reviews. In his treatment of Rudolf Volz's *Faust: Die Rockoper* (1999), which also features an elaborate, although composed, audio backdrop, Paul Malone extols the work for making the legend accessible and for implementing music as a powerful tool for characterization (224). In these respects, *Faust in the Box* is a comparable accomplishment. Speaking about another Faustian adaptation, *Phantom of the Paradise*, Malone concludes that while it "successfully satirizes both rock opera and theatrical rock of the era, . . . its mélange of elements from several sources finally devolved into chaos" (219). In the case of *Faust in the Box*'s mix of sound and visual elements from numerous different sources, perceived disorder or confusion in many instances makes a valuable contribution to the work's aesthetics of storytelling. In response to the question posed above about *Faust in the Box*'s suitability for inclusion in histories of adaptations of the Faust legend, it is my view that *Faust in the Box* contributes novelty through its daring storytelling. In an interview with Peter Hames, Svankmajer cleverly conflates the popularity of the Faust myth with the difficult process of adapting it by referring to the legend's core theme: "The myth of Faust is one of the key myths of this civilization, and its interpretations are numerous. . . . Sooner or later, everyone is faced with the same dilemma—either to live their life in conformity with the misty promises of institutionalized 'happiness,' or to rebel and take the path away from civilization, whatever the results" (qtd. in Drábek 525). As Markland indicated in my interview with her, she chose to prioritize her ingenuity, and therefore not bow to conformity: "I did not want to read Goethe's biography too much or too much subtext [so as] not to be too influenced within my own creative process" (Kutch).

Although many audiences may not understand that creative process as it relates to staging Faust, they might more readily comprehend ways that *Faust in the Box* represents a performance art form with subversive tendencies. In this vein, Lenora Champagne illuminates trends about female performance artists that could also apply to Markland: "Trying out personas, especially those of men or socially marginal women, was both a personal exploration and a taking or undermining of power by inhabiting images of it. . . . Artists were representing themselves in images created as alternatives to or comments upon the traditional images and roles they had inherited" (xi). By pressing herself as a female performer into roles from Goethe's complicated and canonical drama, Markland has indeed challenged the core themes and assumptions that audiences and critics have applied to *Faust* over the centuries. She has also, and perhaps more importantly, demonstrated the bold and innovative style of storytelling that can result from having more loyalty to the creative process than to the conventions and expectations of a classic text.

Works Cited

Andrews, Nigel. "Faust's Magic Is Accessible to All." *FT.Com,* September 11, 2011. http://www.ft.com/cms/s/2/440fcfda-daf4-11e0-bbf400144feabdc0.html #axzz2xmdfOXM5

Baker, David J. "Life in the *Faust* Lane." *Opera News* 76.5 (2011): 34–37.

Barricelli, Jean-Pierre. "Faust and the Music of Evil." *Journal of European Studies* 13.1–2 (1983): 1–26.

Berghahn, Klaus. "Transformations of the Faust Theme." *Lives of Faust: The Faust Theme in Literature and Music. A Reader.* Ed. Lorna Fitzsimmons. Berlin: De Gruyter, 2008. 160–69.

Brown, Jane K. *Goethe's Faust: The German Tragedy.* Ithaca: Cornell UP, 1986.

Budd, Malcolm. *Music and the Emotions: The Philosophical Theories.* London: Routledge, 1985.

Champagne, Lenora. "Out from Under: Women on Sex and Death and Other Things." *Out from Under: Texts by Women Performance Artists.* Ed. Lenora Champagne. New York: Theatre Communications Group, 1990. ix–xiv.

Christie, Ian. "Faust and Furious." *Sight and Sound* 21.12 (2011): 38–40.

Corness, Jeff. "*Faust*: A Theatre that Feels Like Music." *Canadian Theatre Review* 72 (1992): 16–20.

Drábek, Pavel, and Dan North. "What Governs Life: Svankmajer's *Faust* in Prague." *Shakespeare Bulletin* 29.4 (2011): 525–42.

Erlin, Matt. "Tradition as Intellectual Montage: F. W. Murnau's *Faust*." *Weimar Cinema: An Essential Guide to Classic Films of the Era.* Ed. Noah Isenberg. New York: Columbia UP, 2009. 155–72.

Feise, Ernst. "Goethes *Faust* als Hörspiel." *The German Quarterly* 32.3 (1959): 211–16.

Gentile, John S. *Cast of One: One-Person Shows from the Chautauqua Platform to the Broadway Stage.* Urbana: U of Illinois P, 1989.

Goethe, Johann Wolfgang von. *Faust: Der Tragödie erster Teil.* Tübingen: J. G. Cotta, 1808.

Goethe, Johann Wolfgang von. *Poetry and Truth Parts 1–3.* Trans. Robert E. Heitner. Ed. Thomas P. Saine and Jeffrey L. Sammons. Princeton: Princeton UP, 1994.

Green, Marcia. "The 'Demonic Pact': The Faust Myth in Music and Literature." *Lyrica: Society for Word-Music Relations* 6 (1992): 34.

Hames, Peter. *The Cinema of Jan Svankmajer.* New York: Wallflower Press, 2008.

Hamilton, Andy. *Aesthetics and Music.* London: Continuum, 2007.

Howard, H. Wendell. "Gounod's *Faust*: Opera of Redemption." *Logos: A Journal of Catholic Thought and Culture* 12.1 (2009): 79–92.

Jackson, Tony. "The Dialogic and the Aesthetic: Some Reflections on Theatre as a Learning Medium." *Journal of Aesthetic Education* 39.4 (2005): 104–18.

Judge, Ben. "*Faust in the Box*: Review." *Festmag*, August 19, 2009. <http://www.festmag.co.uk/archive/2009/96595-faust_in_box>.

Kallin, Britta. "In and Out of the Box: An Interview with Performance Artist Bridge Markland." *Women in German Yearbook* 30 (2014): 74–88.

Kutch, Lynn Marie. Interview with Bridge Markland. Email communication. September 1, 2012.

Lei, Zhu. "Aesthetic Quality in Theatre as a Genre of Performance." *International Journal of English Linguistics* 2.5 (2012): 55–59.

Malone, Paul. "They Sold their Soul for Rock'n'Roll: Faustian Rock Musicals." *International Faust Studies: Adaptation, Reception, Translation.* Ed. Lorna Fitzsimmons. London: Continuum, 2008. 216–30.

Markland, Bridge. *Bridge Markland.* <http://www.bridge-markland.de>.

Mason, Eudo Colecestra. *Goethe's* Faust: *Its Genesis and Purport.* Berkeley: U of California P, 1967.

Oergel, Maike. "The Faustian 'Gretchen': Overlooked Aspects of a Famous Male Fantasy." *German Life and Letters* 64.1 (2011): 43–55.

Pinney, A. "Between a Director and a Cast of One: A Beginning Aesthetic." *Theatre Topics* 16.2 (2006): 183–91.

Schafer, R. Murray. *The Tuning of the World: Toward a Theory of Soundscape Design.* Philadelphia: U of Pennsylvania P, 1980.

Seibert, Peter, and Sandra Nuy. "'In bunten Bildern wenig Klarheit'? *Faust* im Fernsehen." *LiLi: Zeitschrift für Literaturwissenschaft und Linguistik* 27.105 (1997): 125–36.

Semotschko, Svetlana. "Der Mustertext *Faust* als deutsches Kultursymbol." *Kalbų Studijos/Studies about Languages* 11 (2007): 51–60.

Sidnell, Michael J. "Semiotic Arts of Theatre." *Semiotica* 168 (2008): 11–43.

Wegel, Christina J. "Analyzing Dramatics Texts on the Big Screen: Teaching Theater through Cinematic Adaptations." *Dramatic Interactions: Teaching Languages, Literatures, and Cultures through Theater: Theoretical Approaches and Classroom Practices.* Ed. Colleen Ryan-Scheutz and Nicoletta Marini-Maio. Newcastle upon Tyne: Cambridge Scholars Press, 2011. 219–41.

Young, Jordan R. *Acting Solo: The Art of One-Man Shows.* Beverly Hills: Moonstone P, 1989.

Author's Profile

Lynn Marie Kutch teaches German language and literature at Kutztown University of Pennsylvania. Her areas of interest include German crime fiction, teaching language and culture with graphic novels, and translation studies. She has recently published "From Visual Literacy to Literary Proficiency: An Instructional and Assessment Model for the Graphic Novel Version of Kafka's *Die Verwandlung*" (2014) and *Tatort Germany: The Curious Case of German-Language Crime Fiction*, co-edited with Todd Herzog (2014).

Chapter 10

Imagining Faust in Recent German Historical Fiction

Waltraud Maierhofer

Abstract

In her article, "Imagining Faust in Recent German Historical Fiction," Waltraud Maierhofer examines the adaptation of the Faust legend in two recent German-language novels, *Faust, der Magier* (2007) by Andreas Gössling, and the children's story, *Hannah und der Schwarzkünstler Faust* (2004), by Uschi Flacke. Maierhofer argues that these retellings of the Faust legend for postmodern secular society have significantly changed its focus and tone. Their avoidance of the theme of the demonic pact, conventionally associated with the Faust character, introduces an open-endedness to the narrative. Ambivalence surrounds Faust's supernatural abilities, and his death is not given direct representation. Flacke's *Hannah und der Schwarzkünstler Faust* features a cross-dressed ten-year-old girl who goes on adventures with Faust, while Gössling's *Faust, der Magier* depicts a Faust sought by the Inquisition but helped by women.

Since the Faust Book *Historia von D. Johann Fausten* (*History of the Damnable Life and Deserved Death of Doctor John Faustus*), published in 1587, the story of the devil pacter Johann Faustus has exercised waves of fascination. This article investigates the adaptation of the Faust legend in two recent German-language works of popular fiction, *Faust, der Magier* (The Magician Faust) (2007) by Andreas Gössling and *Hannah und der Schwarzkünstler Faust* (Hannah and Faust, the Necromancer) (2004) by Uschi Flacke, both of which belong to the genre of historical fiction. Fantasy about magic and alchemy is evident in numerous bestsellers promoted globally in the last two decades. In the German-language market, fiction about magic and witchcraft and their persecution has been thriving, and it is not surprising that this interest has incorporated the legend of Faust. Such retelling is, of course, nothing new. When Johann Spies published the *Historia*, the Faust legend was already part of the vernacular culture of the time. Two examples from the eighteenth and nineteenth century will suffice here to indicate that prose adaptations of the Faust theme are not new at all, although they have received much less attention than drama. Friedrich Maximilian von Klinger wrote *Fausts Leben, Thaten und Höllenfahrt* (*Faust's Life, Deeds, and Journey to Hell*) (1791) as a satire of the Enlightenment. Gustav Schwab published *Doktor Faustus* within his popular and yet entertaining undertaking *Die deutschen Volksbücher für Jung und Alt wiedererzählt* (The German Chapbooks for Young and Old Retold) (1843) (562–630).

The novels examined in this article stand out among other recent retellings and modernizations such as Roman Möhlmann's 2006 self-published fantasy novel about Faust and Mephisto as time travelers, *Faust und die Tragödie der Menschheit* (Faust and the Tragedy of Humankind), or a historical mystery about Faust's persecution because of a mysterious book about magic, titled *Das Pergament des Teufels: Ein Faustroman* (The Devil's Parchment) (2010), by Christoph Andreas Marx, who holds a doctorate in theology and history. Bestselling author Kai Meyer, who writes historical fiction and fantasy in series, some of which are aimed at young adults, published a fantasy trilogy about Faust 1996–2000, bearing the titles *Der Engelspakt: Die neue Historia des Doktor Faustus* (Pact with the Angels: The New History of Doctor Faustus), *Der Traumvater* (Dream Father), and *Der Engelskrieger* (Angel Warrior), republished as a trilogy in 2007. The trilogy is marketed as "historical fiction" but shows little evidence of historical research about the Faust legend. In it, Doctor Johannes Faustus is a notorious magician, and his flights from the Inquisition catapult him and his assistant Christof Wagner from adventure to adventure, through libraries, prisons, and castles to a conspiracy in Rome and the Vatican that is believed to threaten all of Europe. A very free adaptation of the Faust theme is also found in the recent fantasy-occult thriller written in English *Faustus Resurrectus* (2012), by Thomas Morrissey, in which Faust is "resurrected" in order to assist another character to invoke Lucifer in contemporary New York. For more factually inclined readers, two biographies of Faust have been published in German (Mahal, *Faust. Und Faust*) and English (Ruickbie) within the last two decades.

All these narratives show that there is a market in Germany for light adaptations of the Faust theme; the Faust legend is once again popular with readers who might not be interested in reading the Faust chapbook, or one of the writings attributed to Faust, some of which are now available online. Today's readers may not even have read or liked Goethe's *Faust*. Although *Historia von D. Johann Fausten* is available in paperback, it is safe to assume that it is read exclusively for university studies.

This article does not apply fidelity criticism: it does not examine what is based on historical fact or trace how the writer adapts particular documents. Well-versed readers will enjoy recognizing these themselves. Instead, it inquires, what does the adaptation accomplish? How does it re-mediate the theme for today's historical context and audience? In Linda Hutcheon's terms, this article attempts a "temporal indigenization" (Foreword vii). Hutcheon's general questions in her seminal study *A Theory of Adaptation* (What? Why? For which audience? In which spatial and temporal context?) have guided my approach.

I will first briefly introduce both novels before investigating their portrayal of Faust. In my opinion, these retellings of the Faust legend for postmodern secular society have changed its focus and tone completely. In both selected works, Faust is not a devil-pacter, the major concept associated with Faust and the many literary adaptations of the theme. In these works, the demonic is above all an image for fears, especially related to sexuality. Faust's supernatural abilities are either greatly reduced or ambivalent. Both novels also convey knowledge about life in the early modern period and important changes around 1500, especially the role of magic and alchemy as well as individual identity. It is also interesting that both works do not describe Faust's death directly. Whereas in the chapbook, his horrible death is proof of his condemnation and the basis for religious exhortation, readers of today's novels are left with possibilities and appearances to interpret for themselves.

Hannah und der Schwarzkünstler Faust is aimed at girls between the ages of twelve to sixteen. Described through the eyes of Hannah, who is about ten years old at the beginning and a mature woman at the end, Faust remains mysterious. The setting is the early sixteenth century, and Faust is a traveling magician, fortune-teller, and alchemist—an inquisitive scholar and freethinker with strong opinions about the shortcomings of princes. Faust finds Hannah abandoned on the street and takes care of her. After her strength is restored she insists on joining him in his itinerant lifestyle, disguised as a boy. Faust "adopts" her, and they encounter adventures and dangers. Hannah has a modern mentality, wanting to learn from the necromancer as much as possible. A short romance involving Hannah takes place during her time at school. She has to go her own way, though, and leaves Faust. From a later episode that narrates Faust's death, we learn that she has become the owner of the Maulbronn monastery's apothecary. The end of the novel brings a new beginning for Hannah and the prospect of being reunited with a friend from her school days. A glossary for the historical terms used, as well as books consulted, emphasizes the pedagogical aspect of the novel.

Faust, der Magier, a voluminous novel for adult readers, narrates the fictional life of a man named Johann Georg Faust living in the sixteenth century. Drawing on both names, Johann and Georg, and other documents associated with the historical Faust, it has elements of adventure, romance, and erotic fiction. Its representation of the historical setting, demonology, alchemy, the Faust legend, the chapbook, and several additional characters seems well researched. Gössling claims that his main goal was "to make Faust as a likely historical person come alive for today's readers" ("Faust als mögliche historische Gestalt für eine heutige Leserschaft lebendig werden zu lassen" [*Faust* 605]). However, historical information is overshadowed by a pronounced emphasis on adventure and erotic or romance aspects. According to Jerome de Groot, female readers tend to prefer historical genre fiction with romance, while men prefer "adventure, authenticity, and heroism" (51–92). Gössling combines both and maximizes the appeal of his work for both genders.

Apart from some passages of dialogue and several sex scenes described in vulgar language, the novel is written in a fairly high linguistic style and has complex characters. Faust grows up abused by a foster father, said to be a child of the devil. His mentor, a monk and abbot, lets him study alchemy and presses him to make gold—which requires invoking a demon for a certain ingredient—but Faust stops before he encounters the demon. Repeatedly having to flee, he finds hideouts and a new lifestyle but is discovered, imprisoned, and returned to his mentor at the monastery. During his escapes he makes a modest living as an itinerant fortune-teller and healer with his de-facto wife, childhood friend Lena Siebenschöpf. It is left to the reader to believe whether Faust actually has magical skills or is just very clever, empathetic, and charismatic.

As Osman Durrani suggests, Faust is an "Icon of Modern Culture," and this includes not only "high" culture but extends to the popular imagination, claiming special connections to the historical or literary Faust in museums, memorials, festivals, merchandising, games, and other products (375–97). Günther Mahal has also examined Faust as an object of commercialism and kitsch (*Faust in Kommerz*). According to Durrani, there are "well over a dozen buildings in Germany that claim to have been lived in or visited" by Doctor Faust (385). It may be in connection with such encounters with the "lighter side" of the Faust tradition that readers may turn to one of the books I am discussing here.

Hannah und der Schwarzkünstler Faust

Uschi Flacke (born 1949 in Lippstadt) was a singer before she turned to writing fiction and television scripts for children and young adults, with historical (crime) fiction and sex education as two of her main areas. Her retelling of Faust was preceded by an historical novel about a group of children persecuted for witchcraft (*Hexenkinder*). *Hannah und der Schwarzkünstler Faust* was awarded the Austrian Award for Young Adult Fiction in 2005. The novel depicts the time period around 1500 as dangerous, due to rebellious peasants, robbers, and hired murderers, especially for a girl alone and without a home. It is also a time of political unrest under unjust princes and a powerful church. Flacke succeeds in evoking everyday life of the period, giving a lot of historical information, without sounding like a history lesson. A passionate magician, hand-reader, and healer, with homemade herbal remedies, Faust is also an alchemist seeking the philosopher's stone which is believed to turn mercury or stone to gold. When he finds Hannah, she can already read and write due to her mysterious mother, but she will learn from and with Faust. She masters a few magic tricks and hand-reading to earn a little money, and later she turns fully to herbal medicine. Hannah and Faust are often in danger because the magician publicly criticizes the church and boasts of his own powers. In addition, two odd beggar men, hired by his opponent alchemist, appear to be after one of his ingredients, a mysterious red powder. Although Hannah is nearly killed three times, she is very intuitive about escaping danger. In accordance with the few extant documents on the historical Faust, the magician and Hannah spend time in Gelnhausen, Würzburg, Kreuznach, Ebernburg, the university towns Erfurt and Heidelberg, and the monastery of Maulbronn. They encounter abbot Trithemius, Faust's opponent, and knight Franz von Sickingen, his benefactor, as well as the abbot of Maulbronn named Entenfuß who is in need of gold. After Sickingen employs Faust as a teacher in Kreuznach, even Hannah, still under disguise as the boy Hannes, learns Latin together with the town's boys while Faust turns more and more to alchemy. A tender romance develops between Hannah and the boy Sebastian, and she makes another good friend, Martin. However, Faust and Hannah have to leave Kreuznach because a jealous local alchemist spreads rumors that Faust molested a boy. Altogether, Hannah accompanies Faust many years. Faust dismisses Hannah because she does not share his excessive striving to learn. He becomes more and more self-destructive while she yearns for a life with Sebastian. At this point Faust is already being sought as an alleged devil-pacter.

A frame narrative of Hannah more than three decades later repeatedly interrupts the story of her time with Faust. Hannah is now an elderly woman who owns the apothecary at Maulbronn monastery. A monk named Martin, a childhood friend, brings her the news of Faust's death and the rumors that surround it. There is no attempt to find out what really happened. The Inquisition is seeking to destroy everything Faust touched, especially everything he wrote. In addition, earlier in the story, robbers took all his possessions, including his writings. Therefore, in the frame narrative, Hannah records her story and her memories of Faust. They make up the major part of the novel and are told in the third person. Longing earlier for the adventures and knowledge she lost by leaving Faust, she is, finally, content in her role as the one who carries the memory of Faust and preserves it for future generations. In addition, it is implied that she will be reunited with her childhood friend and love interest Sebastian, providing the novel with an optimistic ending which is customary for young adult historical fiction.

Two recurring mysteries are never solved, though: the identity and clients of two beggars who try to kill Hannah and Faust, and the story behind Hannah's amulet. We find out that Hannah's mother was executed for witchcraft and Hannah had also been suspect. Vagrant people rescued her just in time and brought her out of town. When Faust found her she wore an amulet depicting a lion eating the sun, which was important in Faust's decision to accept her as his companion. The amulet shows the symbol of the philosopher's stone and apparently predestines Hannah to alchemy. In her memory, there is also a sister named Theresa but she does not reappear. All these are ingredients for a possible sequel to the novel.

Since 2007, Uschi Flacke has turned readings from the novel into a performance, *Auf den Spuren des Dr. Faustus* (Tracing Dr. Faustus), which she conceptualizes as "Historical" ("Kabarett und Literatur"). She reads excerpts from the novel, performs cabaret and satirical scenes about the time period and its reception today, and also presents a lot of background information on posters. Her reading-turned-performance appears to be popular with schools and organizers of cultural events. One reviewer for the regional newspaper *Gießener Allgemeine* was full of praise for Flacke's success at stirring historical interest in children and young adults and recommended it especially to future teachers of history (Olz). This activity is a significant indicator of the predominance of the historical aspect in her fiction.

Hannah und der Schwarzkünstler Faust gives young readers an accessible introduction to the Faust theme and its cultural context around 1500, especially magic and alchemy, women and children, and the dangers of travel. The novel is marketed as about the "medieval" or "late medieval" period, although it thematizes issues characteristic of the transition to the early modern period. Above all, the systematic witchcraft persecutions which are hinted at in the novel peaked in the sixteenth century and are an early-modern phenomenon. Advertising for historical fiction often assigns it to the Middle Ages, reinforcing a popular misbelief, as Tatjana Bink confirms in her study of witchcraft beliefs (7–8).

Another market trend has certainly influenced the characterization of the protagonist Hannah. Many of today's young female readers crave strong, "modern" girl characters with whom they can identify—clever, skillful, intelligent, and self-confident role models. All these characteristics apply to Hannah. Flacke recognizes, though, that around 1500 a girl's possibilities were limited. For most of the novel, Hannah is dressed as a boy and only as such can she perform her magic in the marketplace or attend the Latin school. Hannah is a masculine heroine that Melanie Rossi in her study of historical fiction for young adults finds typical of the genre (103). Historically such young women and cross-dressers were certainly a minute minority, but the character allows today's girls to enter the unfamiliar world of the distant past through an intermediary of their own sex and approximate age.

There is no pact with the devil in this novel. Hannah learns that Faust is convinced the dark forces can be controlled by means of willpower, imagination, and concentration. Later Hannah witnesses Faust invoking spirits, and a "giant beast" ("riesiges Biest") appears whom he addresses as "Mephistophiel" (102–05); however, it is unclear if this is just her dream provoked by their earlier conversation about magic. Faust and she repeatedly discuss alchemy and the philosopher's stone. Making gold is Faust's obsession, and he becomes more and more driven by it. The only invocation of spirits that happens in the novel is a theatrical performance that Faust and Hannah stage for the students at the University of Erfurt: with the help of an optical trick, they make believe that the Cyclops Polyphemus appears.

In sum, the novel depicts Faust as human and sympathetic, but an outsider in society, literally without a home. He has radical views and increasingly loses touch with reality, bordering on the mad scientist cliché, a stock character in today's popular culture. Although Flacke has cast the story of Faust without a pact, she includes the pact in the rumors told during his lifetime and immediately following his death. Faust's pact with the devil is suggested to be an invention or myth. The life of Faust is here recast as witnessed by a person of the implied reader's age. It is transformed into an adventure story about a girl battling the same issues as Faust—questions of magic, knowledge, success, and the dangers of life in another, less comfortable age. Such an insight might be a good foundation upon which to build for an encounter with Goethe's *Faust*—or to visit Faust-related sites.

Faust, der Magier

Andreas Gössling (born 1958 in Gelnhausen) is a writer of historical, fantasy, and young adult fiction. He became familiar with the Faust legend during his child-hood, as his hometown was the place where Faust allegedly boasted he could repeat Christ's miracles (*Faust* 604). Having earned a doctorate in German, he is certainly familiar with the Faust theme through the centuries, and he also researched the cul-tural history and myths of supernatural beings such as dragons and fairies for nonfic-tion books. *Faust, der Magier* is not his only historical fantasy about alchemists and demons. Three more of his novels, two of them for young adults, vary the theme and time period. One of them, *Der Sohn des Alchimisten* (The Alchemist's Son) (2007), takes place during the time of the Inquisition and is marketed as a "Faust novel" ("Faust-Roman"), but Faust appears in only one episode.

Gössling's novel *Faust, der Magier* follows the literary tradition which claimed the small town of Knittlingen near Stuttgart in the southwestern province of Baden-Württemberg as the birthplace of Georg Faust, foster or illegitimate child of master cooper Jörg Gerlach (Mahal, *Faust. Und Faust* 13–30). Today, Knittlingen calls itself "Faust Town" ("Fauststadt"), with a Faust Museum (established in 1980) and a statue of Faust (1954) outside its Town Hall (Durrani 382–85). The novel also builds on the oral tradition which linked Faust with the monastery of Maulbronn in the same region, and especially one of the abbots. The monastery is today the best-preserved medieval Cistercian monastery complex in Europe and part of a Unesco World Heri-tage site. Since 1840, the monastery claims a "Faust Tower" where Faust is believed to have written several essays on alchemy—although the tower was not constructed until 1604, long after the time of the historical Faust (Durrani 385). The monastery also has two bloodstains said to be Faust's (Mahal, *Faust. Und Faust* 10). Gössling admits in the afterword that he manipulated and compressed historical events such as the time of the Swiss-Swabian war of 1499 and the late-Gothic additions to Maul-bronn Abbey. He also combined features of several historical abbots into the character he named Johannes Burrus, and was influenced in the depiction of his other monk and alchemist, Paulus Nigrethiuds, by the historical polymath and occultist Johannes Trithemius (1462–1516), abbot of Spanheim, and the philosopher Agrippa von Net-tesheim (1486–1535) (Gössling, *Faust* 606). The author explains further that in de-scribing Faust's studies, he relied heavily on sources in alchemy, and he also drew in-spiration for characters from figures such as Albertus Magnus and Lullus (607, 167).

I would like to suggest that Gössling succeeds in setting the alchemist Faust in an age of witchcraft persecutions and combining the two gendered narratives of magic—persecuting women's "witchcraft" while elevating the male alchemist and magician to a new type of scholar. My approach is comparable to that of Frank Baron, who, in *Faustus on Trial*, situates Johann Spies's *Historia* in an age of witch-hunting. For the purpose of this study, Gössling's adventurous and imaginative plot will only be summarized with vast simplifications. My analysis aims to examine the following aspects: Faust's (super-)natural abilities and companions; demons, sexuality, and the question of Faust's father; the avoidance of a demonic pact; and Faust's modernity. I will also critique the eroticism evident when the novel crosses the line from light fiction to triviality. The overarching question of my analysis is, what audience is this retelling trying to reach, and how valuable is this text as an adaptation?

The narrative tells the life of Faust chronologically to the year 1514, except for the Prologue, which takes place shortly before the end of the plot. It begins with Faust's conception on St. Michael's day in 1479 and ends in 1514. Many exact dates and places contribute to the impression of factuality, reminiscent of the emphasis on authenticity in the chapbook's detailed title as analyzed by Günter Hess (99). The Prologue is clearly designed to create suspense: a financially ruined Count awaits the magician named Doctor Faust. The Count has prepared an alchemist lab in a tower and asked the magician to make gold for him. An aged Faust arrives in the company of a mousy, middle-aged woman and a small child or dwarf ("Zwerg") (Gössling, *Faust* 5). The only supernatural abilities that Faust has with certainty are his sensing of water under the tower and his "flaming gaze" ("Flammenblick"), which makes him attractive to women (6). The Count has a red-haired sister, Gunda, who shows erotic interest in Faust, a foreshadowing of the dominant depiction of women in this fiction. The reader learns that Faust is being sought by the Inquisition as a devil-pacter or as possessed by the devil. A representative of the Inquisition is in the castle. Another monk arrives and offers Faust an escape. The reader is faced with a mystery regarding the identity and abilities of Faust and his companions. Who is this Faust, has he really made a pact with the devil, and is the child possibly a lab-created homunculus? The story of Faust's life and adventures then unfolds from his childhood and finally returns to this life-threatening situation.

Mysterious ambivalences are not unique to the start of the novel. They flavor the narration of Faust's childhood in Knittlingen and continue throughout the novel. The boy's horrible nightmares of drowning and a big bird pecking him exert an oppressive reality on him. The narrative explains them as remnants of an early life-threatening test to determine whether he was indeed a demon's child (606). His mother Maria Faust was raped at age sixteen, supposedly by a demon in a cellar in Maulbronn where she worked as a maid. Afterwards she lost her mind and language and spent her life in the cooper's house, locked away, endlessly smiling and drawing angels. Abbot Johannes Burrus supports the boy, securing his survival and later education at the monastery. The clever boy suspects the abbot, rather than a demon, might have fathered him. The truth of what really happened in the cellar is never clarified with authority. The novel employs a restrained narrative voice which has extensive insight into the thought processes, memories, and perceptions of the main characters but it is not all-knowing and does not explain to the reader where imaginative distortion ends and measurable facts begin. Instead of explaining ambivalences, the narrative emphasizes them. For example, the identity of the child who seems at the same time young and old, and is suspected by some to be a lab-created homunculus, is never fully clarified. Earlier, Faust saw a doll he had made come alive; the resulting creature bears the same characteristic of looking simultaneously young and old, and it is easy to assume a magical origin of this homunculus figure before the narrator provides the more rational explanation.

The rape scenario, the ominous big black bird, and the black dog serve as leitmotifs throughout the novel, providing a background of uncertainty from which the supernatural seems to arise. All three are left ambiguous as to what happens and what is imagined or possibly supernatural. The Abbot firmly believes that he was only a witness of the rape of young Maria in the cellar and that a demon appeared and committed the horrific deed. Faust is haunted by the perception of a big black bird pressing its peak into his mouth, which is how he might have felt during his early near-drowning experience. This image is modeled on a famous dream by Leonardo da Vinci, as explained in the afterword (606). Finally, the black dog is clearly more for Faust than an animal. Faust is fascinated by the legend of the black dog Monsieur or Sjö, the powerful protector of children, the author's clever adaptation of the legend of Guinefort, also explained in the afterword (606). Faust finds a mysterious sick dog whom he keeps and names "Messer," the medieval Italian form for "Monsieur" (158). The dog and, in his adulthood, a horse he acquires have the incredible ability to understand Faust's wishes and to cover enormous distances.

With these formative traumatic experiences, Faust's abilities from childhood on border on the supernatural. The boy believes he can make puppets come alive, but it is only in his imagination. The narrative thus alludes to the puppet plays in the Faust tradition and also the "magic" that transforms puppets in the audience's imagination. The boy learns magic tricks which appear as supernatural to others. He further develops the ability to "see" disease and pain in people, which leads to accusations that he is a sorcerer but also enables him to become an exceptional healer. Gössling creates the fantastic by taking ordinary rhetorical figures literally. This procedure, which Tzvetan Todorov, in *The Fantastic*, has described as the literalization of figurative discourse, occurs throughout the novel. In Todorov's words, "the fantastic realizes the literal sense of a figurative expression. . . . Here the appearance of the fantastic element is preceded by a series of comparisons, of figurative or simply idiomatic expressions, quite common in ordinary speech but designating, if taken literally, a supernatural event" (79). *Faust, der Magier* takes literally such expressions as "to see someone's problems" or "to feel close to someone" and turns them into supernatural phenomena. Having a strong bond with his mother, Faust is able to feel his mother's condition from afar, especially when she is sick or in danger. Admittedly, this is one of the kitsch elements of the novel. Whenever he is in the monastery cellar where the rape happened, he "sees" and feels his devastated mother there and often comforts her. All the demons described in the novel appear only in Faust's visions, in the imagination, and in (suppressed) memories, although there are definitely unnatural sounds and sights accompanying them and contributing to increasingly uncanny experiences. The visions push the narrative beyond the liminal space where magic might or might not be happening to a point of intrusion of the demonic into the primary world, to apply categories that Farah Mendlesohn developed for the fantastic and its differentiation.

Another aspect of Faust's (super)natural abilities in this novel is less ambivalent: how he charms women. In the words of young Grete—an allusion to Goethe's heroine Gretchen but this Faust deliberately rejects her because he foresees her fate otherwise—he looks like an angel in the paintings of the time—blond hair, a winning smile, and well-built. He also displays an uninhibited directness when it comes to initiating sexual encounters, all of which are narrated extensively and explicitly. The first one is with his childhood friend Lena, the younger daughter of his foster father's maid, who becomes his lover and remains his devoted companion throughout the novel. Her dedication does not prevent him from entertaining affairs which catapult the plot in unexpected directions and reveal surprising relations between minor characters. In the second part, the love affair of the seventeen-year-old Faust with the strong-willed maid Adele is essential in connecting him to the world of demons from which he sought to escape by fleeing from the monastery. Gössling does not shy away from stereotypes, and the supposedly demonic Adele has red hair. With her, Faust experiences sexuality as demonic.

Faust is sought by the Inquisition but women hide him, and he manages a life as an itinerant surgeon. He is a successful and respected healer and does not exploit the poor but at times even gives them his earnings. On occasion, he hypnotizes soldiers who are supposed to fight, and thus makes himself an enemy of the Duke. Faust's reputation grows, and when he is twenty-two, it includes studies of medicine, theology, and law, including a doctorate, clearly all just rumor. He is revered because he takes care of poor people in the countryside, after having been banned from cities. After his vision of the "golden world," he preaches against church and aristocratic oppression and is seen by many as a new messiah, while he himself feels "cursed" ("verflucht") (523). His adventures get more and more fantastic and take on clearly supernatural elements. He even flies with his students, no longer ambivalent or a vision but told as a mere fact.

As stated above, there is no devil as a character in this novel, but the devil and demons are an important part of all the characters' world view, including that of the monks. Sexuality is imagined as demonic. The first demon described in the novel is believed to have fathered Faust. The common people, including the foster father, believe that abbot Johannes Burrus was conjuring a demon for the very purpose of impregnating the young Maria Faust. The abbot firmly believes that Faust is a "fruit of the devil" ("Teufelsfrucht") (106) and treats him despicably as such, as if he were only half-human. In the monk's memory, the raping black "beast" ("Tier") was factual, and he describes it with disgust, fear, and also curiosity (112). Burrus seems in denial of the rape he himself must have committed, giving in to common imaginings of demons, but the narrative does not pursue a deep psychological analysis. Out of shame and guilt, the abbot estranges himself from his sexuality, which becomes the demon rising from the dark in the cellar.

Burrus, like everyone else in the novel, believes in the reality of the devil and the possibility of making a pact. The author is clearly informed by the *Malleus Maleficarum* (*Witches' Hammer*) (1487) in which inquisitor Jacob Sprenger compiled demonic beliefs of the time and promoted the persecution of witchcraft. Sprenger argued that the power of the devil was greatest in human sexuality and that women were weaker in faith than men and thus more susceptible to the devil. The *Malleus* sought to prove that witches were directly in league with the devil, sealed by sexual intercourse, and were therefore to be eradicated. Its doctrine became widely accepted. It also provided a manual for the trial and execution of witches and became a major factor in the witchcraft craze in the sixteenth and seventeenth centuries. As Walter Stephens has recently argued in *Demon Lovers*, the obsession with demonic sexuality was a result of the growing crisis of faith in early modern Europe. At least since Wilhelm Meinhold's scandalous novel *Maria Schweidler, die Bernsteinhexe* (*The Amber Witch*, 1843), it is very common for historical fiction to draw on the *Malleus* and its imagery of intercourse with demons, the sabbath worship of the devil, sacrifice of newborns, loss of penises, and other forms of injurious magic (Maierhofer 210–30, 369–73).

Gössling intertwines the well-known imagery of the sabbath with Faust's experience of sexuality. Faust flees the Abbot and abandons his study of alchemy when he finds out that the final ingredient for the philosopher's stone is the soul of a newborn sacrificed to the devil. In a long description of a wild sexual encounter with Adele, Faust has a vision of her attending a sabbath and sacrificing a baby. Faust's mind recapitulates what he had read about the conception of demons. Because of his vision of Adele conceiving a demon during intercourse he is convinced of Adele's devil worship. Faust had given an actual baby to Adele for caretaking, Lena's sister's illegitimate child. When it dies, his belief that Adele sacrificed it grows stronger. At any rate, Adele is executed for being in league with the devil. She herself clearly believes she attended the devil worship—or has been made to believe it during torture. Faust subsequently refers to his sexuality as the demon within him. For example, when he rages at the imaginary demon Marbuelis, he accuses him of having planted his demon into his body.

Although Gössling's Faust does not enter a pact, large parts of the meandering plot are based on the necessity of such a contract. Burrus is obsessed with expanding the abbey in a new, unheard-of style, the filigree late Gothic style of Maulbronn's St. Mary's Cathedral (*Marienkapelle*) and manor house (*Herrenhaus*) still admired today. To finance his dream he needs Faust to make gold, which he is convinced requires a devil pact. He justifies his plan with the fact that he wants to trick the devil, saving Faust's soul, and thus the pact would ultimately serve God's glory.

Ironically, the word "pact" ("Pakt") is, in this novel, used for common agreements, as between Johannes Burrus and several persons such as the foster father Gerlach, the architect of the new building, and Faust for sheltering his mother. At least half way through the novel, the reader is led to the expectation that Faust will eventually conjure the demon. The suspense is cleverly built up as Faust gets more and more desperate and begins the ritual a total of three times, but halts his conjuration at various stages, described with increasing detail and horrific elements. The three attempts represent a magic number and a narrative pattern well known from fairytales.

The demon that Faust conjures or attempts to conjure is not called Mephistopheles but "Grand Duke Marbuelis" ("Grossfürst Marbuelis") (324). Marbuelis, like Mephistopheles, is one of the fallen angels. During his first attempt to conjure Marbuelis, Faust is discovered and interrupted. The second conjuring of Marbuelis is told with more detail. Faust says a formula that contains what he wants but not what he is willing to give. Again, the demonic appearance is not described as real by an authorial voice but as what Faust sees when he closes his eyes. When he opens his eyes, it has all vanished. Only the doll made out of a stillborn is described as alive but again it could be just Faust's perception. The topic of alchemy and the belief in magic allow the author to blur the boundaries between historical research and realistic description, on the one hand, and fantasy, on the other.

For his third conjuring, Faust asks for a special hammer with protective signs, and when he does the ritual, a fantastic "worm of hell" ("Höllenwurm") appears (477). In a last act of will, he hits it with the hammer, gets absorbed by the worm, and, inside it, enters a wondrous room. Or so it seems, as the narrative perspective changes: Faust regains consciousness, lying on the floor of his lab, and none of the hellish apparition might have been real. Strangely, Faust remembers the experience as being "at home, for the very first time" ("Zu Hause, zum allerersten Mal") (478). He insists on having been in another world, a world without disease and flaw, with his perfect woman, in what he calls the "ideal, golden world" ("ideale, goldene Welt") (478). Yet he ponders whether the magic hammer catapulted him straight into hell, which only appeared as ideal. Still, he is from now on obsessed with the golden world. In my opinion, Faust's last stage of being lost in his utopia is not as developed and weakens the novel. He is an antihero yet has profound insights into free will and his identity. He is unable to better his own life and that of his little family, while everybody around him is convinced he has made a pact with the devil for worldly gain. He is incessantly plagued by demonic voices and resists them. Finally, he realizes that both his power and shortcomings, his abilities and visions, his depression and elation, have their origin in striving against a devil pact. There can be no more development. Divine intervention as a means of saving Faust is not compatible with this concept, nor is that of the devil claiming his prize at the end of his life span.

The ultimate effect of the nonpact on the narrative structure lies in its open-endedness. From the chapbook and Goethe's *Faust* to Thomas Mann's novel *Doctor Faustus*, the pact requires finality, an outcome by which readers can interpret it on religious, humanistic, or historical grounds, for instance. Gössling's narration ends when the equilibrium of realism and fantasy has tipped in favor of fantasy, but the narrative voice does not immerse in the fantasy. It no longer narrates Faust's adventures chronologically and limits itself to general perceptions and rumors, such as, for example, that Faust can be seen at various places simultaneously. In the epilogue, we find out that Faust believes he can get to the golden world by detonating the tower of the castle. His persecutors die in the explosion. The bodies of Lena and the child, however, are not found. Faust's own body cannot be identified. The hearsay of Faust recovering and escaping his persecutors continues. The novel does not attempt to give Faust a likely or believable end and death but merges with the myth that is Faust.

In *Hannah und der Schwarzkünstler Faust*, the female protagonist's modern characteristics ease young readers' access to main issues of the historical period. In *Faust, der Magier*, it is the protagonist's fundamentally modern insight into his motivations which balances the increasing intrusion of fantasy elements and maintains accessibility for the reader. This occurs when Faust invokes the appearance of a dead person upon request. His audience is Duke Ulrich of Württemberg, who is persecuting him as responsible for the death of his sister. Faust plays the ghost of the sister in such a way that he changes the Duke's opinion. Doing so, he discovers that he is not a puppet of others, as he believed, but, rather, that he has free will. He realizes that his wishes, such as owning a castle, are not from hell, but his own. His rational argument may be quoted here as a sample of the modern diction that Gössling lends to his sixteenth-century character: "It is because a black spirit lives inside me, and he and I are two different beings. What he weens and wants and what I for my part decide and desire, are likewise different things—and therefore I am free!" ("Denn ein schwarzer Geist haust in mir, und er und ich sind zweierlei. Und was er wähnt und will und was ich für meinen Teil beschließe und begehre, ist gleichfalls zweierlei – und folglich bin ich frei!") (415–16). Faust realizes that even if he does have a demon in him (his hard-to-control sex drive), he still has free will. He delights in this insight and its profound effect on him, the feeling "of being free, being his own master, responsible only for what he did or did not do, desired, and decided by his own will" ("frei zu sein, sein eigener Herr zu sein, verantwortlich nur für das, was er selbst willentlich tat und ließ, begehrte und entschied") (415). He no longer needs a pact with the devil to go beyond his standing among the lowest in society because he begins to recognize the power in himself when no longer constrained by social barriers and customs. Realizing so, he bursts out, "I want to gain wealth and reputation, a castle like this . . . Not, however, by giving myself to you, you wretched monster, but through my own will and cleverness, my own mind and own self" ("Ich will zu Reichtum und Ansehen gelangen, zu einem Schloß wie diesem hier . . . Aber nicht dadurch, daß ich mich dir verschwöre, du kotiges Ungeheuer, sondern durch meinen eigenen Willen und meine eigene List, meinen eigenen Geist und mein eigenes Ich") (415). For de Groot, Faust still meets the criteria for adventure historical fiction because the key to the readers' enjoyment is the protagonist's possibility of agency and self-expression (79–85).

This Faust does not conjure the devil because he wants to surpass the limits of his knowledge, power, and standing. It is a respected member of the clergy who uses him as a tool and forces him to make the pact and provide him with gold. Faust fails at the pact out of existential fear, and by doing so discovers that his strength lies in himself and that he can work at advancing himself with his own skills.

Gössling's protagonist believes in demons and devils, images for all evil and pain, and also the opposite, the ultimate in love, goodness, and being content, but not in religious doctrine, which is likely to appeal to today's audiences. There are also elements of humor in this adaptation, at least for those who appreciate black humor, which Gössling obviously incorporated as a counterbalance to the disturbing images of demons and the episodes of stark violence. The chapbook had elements of humor, especially in the third part with its magic tricks and funny anecdotes (Hess 99), and they are a well-known component of Goethe's play. This tradition is revived and rewritten by Gössling.

Finally, the amount of sex scenes and explicit language should be addressed. Are they in the novel simply for marketing purposes? I have suggested that Gössling's main goal is not an entertaining history lesson but light entertainment for adult readers. Elements of male fantasy are obvious: all women desire Faust, and they are nearly always willing. As noted, the novel contains extensive passages of erotic and sexual encounters in which women tend to have modern views about sexuality. In contrast, the *Historia's* Faustus leads a monastic life, and once he becomes aware of his sexual desires, he wants to marry, and the devil has to persuade him otherwise. The chapbook only summarizes Faust's "swinish and epicurean life" ("Sauwisch vnnd Epicurisch leben") (109) towards the end of his allotted time. Gössling's descriptions build on the tradition of associating Faust with sexuality but transgress into tastelessness, as when, for example, Faust perceives Adele as erotic even when she is facing execution. The novel also perpetuates the misogyny of witchcraft persecutions: for Faust the sabbath is a lustful and frightening fantasy, while Adele, in reality, bears the consequences of such an accusation. This dichotomy reflects the misogyny of the *Malleus Maleficarum* and many witchcraft trials that insisted on a confession about having attended such events. Gössling's Faust gets arrested and interrogated several times but always manages to escape and in the final episode appears almost invulnerable.

In conclusion, readers expecting a Goethean Faust (and a strong devil character) will be disappointed in this novel. Being a work of popular or light fiction, *Faust, der Magier* has escaped reception in academic literary criticism, but reader reviews on bookstore websites are mostly positive and enthusiastic. Overall, it offers a fresh reading of the Faust legend for today's secular audience. The novel recombines and rewrites the Faust legend and chapbook with the imagery of the *Malleus*, recast as historical fantasy but surprisingly without the most obvious element, the devil pact. *Faust, der Magier* is the story of a gifted youth who tries to lead a good life, which requires escaping the evil and fanatic humans who control, use, and abuse him and his mother. For those who want to find a didactic strand in the novel, there is definitely the respect of self and others, addressed even in such unexpected details as descriptions of encounters with foreign plants, animals, and people in this time of discoveries. For example, Faust rescues, frees, and takes revenge for captive and abused slaves from the West Indies.

The ambivalence in the supernatural elements, especially early in the novel, may even be read as an attempt at rewriting the chapbook's tension between religion and humanism, magic and rationalism. Gössling's *Faust, der Magier* may appeal to today's middle-brow readers who would never read the chapbook. In its playful approach to this culturally laden icon, it may even be considered postmodern.

It is striking that both of these adaptations of Faust in recent German-language genre fiction abandon the devil pact. Is the protagonist still Faust then? The pact was only hearsay about the historical Faust. The author of the chapbook centralized and expanded it to serve a clear didactic purpose and to state an explicit warning against transgressing religion's (and any authority's) commands in a time of religious crisis.

Countless adaptations of the Faust theme use the pact with the devil as an allegory for an alliance with evil for the sake of individual gain and fame. In unfortunate strands of nineteenth- and twentieth-century reception, Faust and the Faustian became equivalent with the German, as the literary scholar Hans Schwerte has shown. Schwerte claims that after the destruction of the myth of Germans as Faustian in World War II, Goethe's *Faust* would return to being literature (240). Yet in 1999, on the occasion of a major Goethe anniversary, Willi Jasper in his study of *Faust* reception warned against a return of the Faustian as a symbol for German cultural self-awareness. The two authors investigated in this study seem to be tired of such didactization. Certainly, in German-language culture, the gap between literary fiction and entertaining fiction seems to be wider than in the English-speaking world. These adaptations may be taken as a sign that the Faust theme has more than outlived the ideologization of the Germans as Faustian. We witness not only an unheard of variety in Faust on stage but also a turn to Faust in entertaining storytelling, a postmodern turn that plays with the traditions and images.

On the other hand, Flacke's and Gössling's adaptations build on a vague familiarity with the Faust myth. They may be only of limited interest to readers who lack this basis and interest, especially international readers. Genre fiction has a large readership, and the market can sustain a fairly large flow of new novels that are written for German-language readers. What John Pizer has observed about literary historical fiction concerning the Age of Goethe applies even more to genre fiction about Faust: it is not "composed primarily under the sign of globalization and the influence of mass American culture" (3). Both novels incorporate historical information in entertaining ways and engage the imagination.

Works Cited

Baron, Frank. *Faustus on Trial: The Origin of Johann Spies's* Historia *in an Age of Witch Hunting*. Tübingen: Niemeyer, 1992.

Bink, Tatjana. *Als die Teufel fliegen lernten. Zur Genese des Hexenglaubens bis zur frühen Neuzeit*. Göttingen: Cuvillier, 2008.

De Groot, Jerome. *The Historical Novel*. New York: Routledge, 2010.

Doktor Johannes Fausts Magia naturalis et innaturalis, oder Dreifacher Höllenzwang, letztes Testament und Siegelkunst. 1849. Graz: Edition Geheimes Wissen, 2008.

Durrani, Osman. *Faust: Icon of Modern Culture*. Mountfield: Helm Information, 2004.

Engelmann, Wilhelm. *Die falschen und fingirten Druckorte: Repertortium der seit Erfindung der Buchdruckerkunst unter falscher Firma erschienenen deutschen, lateinischen und französischen Schriften.* Vol. 1. Leipzig: Engelmann, 1864.

Flacke, Uschi. *Hannah und der Schwarzkünstler Faust.* Hamburg: Carlsen, 2006.

Flacke, Uschi. *Die Hexenkinder von Seulberg.* Hamburg: Carlsen, 2003.

Flacke, Uschi. "Uschi Flacke: Kabarett und Literatur." <http://www.uschi-flacke .de>.

Füssel, Stephan, and Hans Joachim Kreutze, eds. *Historia von D. Johann Fausten: Text des Druckes von 1587: Kritische Ausgabe mit den Zusatztexten der Wolfenbütteler Handschrift und der zeitgenössischen Drucke.* Stuttgart: Reclam, 1988.

Gössling, Andreas. *Faust, der Magier. Roman.* Frankfurt: Rütten & Loening, 2007.

Gössling, Andreas. *Der Sohn des Alchimisten.* Würzburg: Arena Verlag, 2006.

Hess, Günter. "Historia von D. Johann Fausten: Über die Faszination eines Textes ohne Autor." *Lektüren für das 21. Jahrhundert: Schlüsseltexte der deutschen Literatur von 1200 bis 1990.* Ed. Dorothea Klein and Sabine M. Schneider. Würzburg: Königshausen & Neumann, 2000. 87–107.

Hutcheon, Linda. "Foreword: Adapting (to) History." *Reworking the German Past: Adaptations in Film, the Arts, and Popular Culture.* Ed. Susan G. Figge and Jenifer K. Ward. Rochester: Camden House, 2010. vii–ix.

Hutcheon, Linda. *A Theory of Adaptation.* New York: Routledge, 2006.

Jasper, Willi. *Faust und die Deutschen.* Berlin: Rowohlt, 1998.

Kindermann, Barbara. *Faust. Nach Johann Wolfgang von Goethe.* Berlin: Kindermann Verlag, 2002.

Kinkel, Tanja. *Die Puppenspieler. Roman.* Munich: Goldmann, 1995.

Kramer (Institoris), Heinrich. *The Malleus Maleficarum.* Ed. P. G. Maxwell-Stuart. Manchester: Manchester UP, 2007.

Mahal, Günther. *Faust. Die Spuren eines geheimnisvollen Lebens.* Reinbek: Rowohlt 1995.

Mahal, Günther, ed. *Faust in Kommerz und Kitsch.* Knittlingen: Faust Archiv, 1999.

Mahal, Günther. *Faust. Und Faust. Der Teufelsbündler in Knittlingen und Maulbronn.* Tübingen: Attempto, 1997.

Maierhofer, Waltraud. *Hexen—Huren—Heldenweiber. Bilder des Weiblichen in Erzähltexten über den Dreißigjährigen Krieg.* Köln: Böhlau, 2005.

Marx, Christoph Andreas. *Das Pergament des Teufels. Ein Faustroman.* Freiburg: Verlag Josef Knecht, 2010.

Mendlesohn, Farah. *Rhetorics of Fantasy.* Middletown: Wesleyan UP, 2008.

Meyer, Kai. *Der Engelskrieger. Roman.* Munich: Heyne, 2000.

Meyer, Kai. *Der Engelspakt: Die neue Historia des Doktor Faustus.* Berlin: Aufbau Taschenbuch, 1996.

Meyer, Kai. *Faustus. Historischer Roman.* Bergisch-Gladbach: Bastei, 2007.

Meyer, Kai. *Der Traumvater. Die neue Historia des Doktor Faustus 2.* Berlin: Aufbau Taschenbuch, 1996.

Möhlmann, Roman. *Faust und die Tragödie der Menschheit.* Norderstedt: BoD, 2007.

Morrissey, Thomas. *Faustus Resurrectus. A Donovan Graham Novel.* Portland: Nightshade Books, 2012.

olz. "Uschi Flacke zu Gast beim Geschichts-Lese-Sommer." *Gießener Allgemeine.* June 18, 2010. <http://www.giessener-allgemeine.de/Home/Stadt/Stadtkultur/Artikel,-Uschi-Flacke-zu-Gast-beim-Geschichts-Lese-Sommer_arid,188322_regid,1_puid,1_pageid,266.html>.

Pizer, John D. *Imagining the Age of Goethe in German Literature, 1970–2010.* Rochester: Camden House, 2011.

Roche, Charlotte. *Feuchtgebiete. Roman.* Köln: Dumont, 2008.

Roche, Charlotte. *Schoßgebete. Roman.* Munich: Piper, 2011.

Rossi, Melanie. *Das Mittelalter in Romanen für Jugendliche: Historische Jugendliteratur und Identitätsbildung.* Frankfurt: Lang, 2010.

Ruickbie, Leo. *Faustus: The Life and Times of a Renaissance Magician.* Stroud: The History Press, 2009.

Schwab, Gustav. "Doktor Faustus." *Deutsche Volksbücher für Jung und Alt wiedererzählt.* 13th ed. Gütersloh: Bertelsmann, 1880. "Monographien digital." *Herzogin Anna Amalia Bibliothek, Klassik Stiftung Weimar.* <http://ora-web.swkk.de/digimo_online>.

Schwerte, Hans. *Faust und das Faustische. Ein Kapitel deutscher Ideologie.* Stuttgart: Klett, 1962.

Stephens, Walter. *Demon Lovers: Witchcraft, Sex, and the Crisis of Belief.* Chicago: U of Chicago P, 2002.

Taylor, Charles. *A Secular Age.* Cambridge: Harvard UP, 2007.

Tzvetan Todorov. *The Fantastic: A Structural Approach to a Literary Genre.* Trans. by Richard Howard. Ithaca: Cornell UP, 1975.

Wagner, Gottfriet. *Nigro Mandia Capala Nigra alba D'Johannes Faust mit allen den Zugehörigen Beruff und Beschwörungen.* 1536. "Monographien digital." *Klassik Stiftung Weimar—Herzogin Anna Amalia Bibliothek* <http://ora-web.klassik-stiftung.de/digimo_online/digimo.entry>.

Author's profile

Waltraud Maierhofer teaches German at the University of Iowa. She has published widely on German literature and culture, with a major focus on narrative prose in the Age of Goethe and the nineteenth century. Her publications include *"Wilhelm Meisters Wanderjahre" und der Roman des Nebeneinander*; *Angelika Kauffmann*; *Hexen—Huren—Heldenweiber*; and *Deutsche Literatur im Kontext 1750–2000: A German Literature Reader* (coauthor). She has also examined the recent Rock opera *Faust* by Rudolf Volz.

Bibliography for the Study of the Faust Theme

Lorna Fitzsimmons

Since its emergence in the sixteenth century, the Faust theme has been expressed and studied in a considerable body of material, a comprehensive listing of which would be beyond the space limitations of this book. The following bibliography has therefore been compiled with the aim of providing an introduction to key works in Faust studies.

Adorno, Theodor W. "Zur Schlussszene des Faust." *Goethe im XX. Jahrhundert. Spiegelungen und Deutungen.* Ed. H. Meyer. Hamburg: C. Wegner, 1967. 330–37.

Allen, Marguerite De Huszar. *The Faust Legend: Popular Formula and Modern Novel.* New York: Peter Lang, 1985.

Amrine, Frederick. "The Unconscious of Nature: Analyzing Disenchantment in *Faust I.*" *Goethe Yearbook* 17 (2010): 117–32.

Anderegg, Johannes. "Grablegung im Vorhof des Palasts: Groteske Anschaulichkeit in den vorletzten Szenen von *Faust II.*" *Goethe Yearbook* 17 (2010): 73–88.

Anderegg, Johannes. "'Grenzsteine der Kunst': Goethes Gattungspoetik und die Arbeit an Faust." *Monatshefte* 102.4 (2010): 441–47.

Anderegg, Johannes. "Mephisto und die Bibel." *Goethe und die Bibel.* Ed. Johannes Anderegg and E. A. Kunz. Stuttgart: Deutsche Bibelgesellschaft, 2005. 317–39.

Anderegg, Johannes. *Transformationen: Über Himmlisches und Teuflisches in Goethes Faust.* Bielefeld : Aisthesis, 2011.

Anderegg, Johannes. "Unrecognized Modernity: Intertextuality and Irony in Goethe's *Faust.*" *Colloquia Germanica* 39.1 (2006): 31–42.

Anderegg, Johannes. "Wie böse ist der Böse? Zur Gestalt des Mephisto in Goethes *Faust.*" *Monatshefte* 96.3 (2004): 343–59.

Anglet, Andreas. "Faust-Rezeption." *Goethe Handbuch.* Ed. Theodor Buck. Vol. 2. Stuttgart: J. B. Metzler, 1996. 478–513.

Arens, Hans. *Kommentar zu Goethes Faust II.* Heidelberg: Carl Winter, 1989.

Ashizu, T. "Buddhisdische *Faust*-Rezeption in Japan." *Studien des Instituts für die Kultur der deutschsprachigen Länder* 8 (1990): 44–58.

Ashton, Rosemary D. "Coleridge and *Faust*." *Review of English Studies* 28 (1977): 156–67.

Atkins, Stuart P. *Goethe's* Faust: *A Literary Analysis*. Cambridge: Harvard UP, 1958.

Atkins, Stuart P. "Renaissance and Baroque Elements in Goethe's *Faust*: Illustrative Analogues." *Goethe Yearbook* 11 (2002): 1–26.

Atkins, Stuart, P., Jane K. Brown, and Thomas P. Saine, eds. *Essays on Goethe*. Columbia: Camden House, 1995.

Bahr, Ehrhard. "Václav Havel's Faust Drama *Temptation* (1985): Or, the Challenge of Influence." *Goethe Yearbook* 7 (1994): 194–206.

Balkin, Sarah. "Regenerating Drama in Stein's *Doctor Faustus Lights the Lights* and Woolf's *Between the Acts*." *Modern Drama* 51.4 (2008): 433–57.

Balmas, E. *Immagini di Faust nel romanticismo francese*. Fasano: Schena, 1989.

Banville, John. *Mefisto*. London: Secker and Warburg, 1986.

Baron, Frank. *Doctor Faustus from History to Legend*. Munich: Fink, 1978.

Baron, Frank. *Faustus on Trial: The Origins of Johann Spies's* Historia *in an Age of Witch Hunting*. Tübingen: Niemeyer, 1992.

Barricelli, J.-P. "Faust and the Music of Evil." *Journal of European Studies* 13 (1983): 1–26.

Barry, David. "Accommodating 'Helena': Reading Goethe's *Faust II* at the Intersection of Weltliteratur and His Late Morphological Writings." *Modern Language Review* 108.4 (2013): 1177–98.

Barry, David. "Faustian Pursuits: The Political-Cultural Dimension of Goethe's *Weltliteratur* and the Tragedy of Translation." *The German Quarterly* 74.2 (2001): 164–85.

Barry, David. "Shocks from a Sicilian Underworld: Gangi, 'Gänge,' and a New Source for the 'Mütter' in Goethe's *Faust*." *Goethe Yearbook* 13 (2005): 131–47.

Bartels, Emily C., and Emma Smith, eds. *Marlowe in Context*. Cambridge: Cambridge UP, 2013.

Bates, P. A., ed. Faust: *Sources, Works, Criticism*. New York: Harcourt, Brace and World, 1969.

Bayerdörfer, H.-P., ed. *Im Auftrieb: Grenzüberschreitungen mit Goethes* Faust *in Inszenierungen der neunziger Jahre*. Tübingen: Niemeyer, 2002.

Beddow, Michael. *Thomas Mann:* Doctor Faustus. Cambridge: Cambridge UP, 1994.

Behzadi, Lale. "Ausblick und Spiegelung: Goethes *Faust* in der arabischen Literatur." *Orient und Okzident. Zur Faustrezeption in nicht-christlichen Kulturen*. Ed. Jochen Golz and Adrian Hsia. Köln: Böhlau, 2008. 67–76.

Bennett, Benjamin. *Goethe's Theory of Poetry:* Faust *and the Regeneration of Language*. Ithaca: Cornell UP, 1986.

Bennett, Benjamin. "Histrionic Nationality: Implications of the Verse in *Faust*." *Goethe Yearbook* 17 (2010): 21–30.

Bennett, Benjamin. "Poetry after *Faust*." *Goethe Yearbook* 20 (2013): 133–45.

Bergsten, Gunilla. *Thomas Mann's* Doctor Faustus: *The Sources and Structure of the Novel*. Trans. Krishna Winston. Chicago: U of Chicago P, 1969.

Berman, M. *All That Is Solid Melts into Air. The Experience of Modernity*. New York: Penguin Books, 1988.

Bernhardt, Rüdiger. *Faust: Ein Mythos und seine Bearbeitungen*. Hollfield: Bange, 2009.

Beyer, Stefan. "Goethean Rhymes and Rhythms in Verse: Translations of *Faust* into Spanish." *MonTI* 5trans (2013): 1–11.

Bianquis, G. *Faust à travers quatre siècles*. Paris: Librairie E. Droz, 1935.

Bietolini, Nicola. "La salvezza e l'illusione: il mito di Faust nei Faust-Pläne und Fragmente di Lessing." *Studia Theodisca* 11 (2004): 199–220.

Binder, Alwin. *Faustische Welt: Interpretationen von Goethes* Faust *in dialogischer Form:* Urfaust—Faust-Fragment—Faust I. Münster: Hamburg, 2002.

Binswanger, Hans Christoph. *Money and Magic: A Critique of the Modern Economy in the Light of Goethe's* Faust. Trans. J. E. Harrison. Chicago: U of Chicago P, 1994.

Birven, Henri. *Der historische Doktor Faust: Maske und Antlitz*. Gelnhausen: H. Schwab, 1963.

Bishop, P., and R. H. Stephenson, eds. *Goethe 2000: Intercultural Readings of His Work*. Leeds: Northern Universities P, 2000.

Bloom, Peter Anthony, and Hans Rudolf Vaget. "Sardanapal!'—The French Connection: Unraveling *Faust II*, 10176." *Goethe Yearbook* 8 (1996): 252–70.

Blüher, Karl-Alfred, ed. *Paul Valéry: le cycle de* Mon Faust *devant la sémiotique théâtrale et l'analyse textuelle*. Tübingen: G. Narr, 1991.

Bobzin, H. "Zwischen 'Mahomets' Gesang und *Faust*: Goethes Lesereisen in den Orient." Faust *auf der Seidenstrasse. Die Sehnsucht nach dem west-östlichen Divan. Interkulturalität und Interreligiösität bei Goethe*. Ed. Evangelische Akademie Iserlohn. Iserlohn: Evangelische Akademie, 1998. 53–60.

Boerner, P., and S. Johnson, eds. *Faust through Four Centuries: Retrospect and Analysis. Vierhundert Jahre Faust: Rückblick und Analyse*. Tübingen: Niemeyer, 1999.

Bohm, Arnd. *Goethe's* Faust *and European Epic: Forgetting the Future*. Rochester: Camden House, 2007.

Bohm, Arnd. "Naming Goethe's *Faust*: A Matter of Significance." *Deutsche Vierteljahrsschrift für Literaturwissenschaft und Geistesgeschichte* 80.3 (2006): 408–34.

Bohm, Arnd. "Typology and History in the 'Rattenlied' (*Faust I*)." *Goethe Yearbook* 10 (2001): 65–83.

Böhme, G. *Goethes* Faust *als philosophischer Text*. Baden-Baden: Die Graue Edition, 2005.

Borlik, Todd A. "A Season in Intercultural Limbo: Ninagawa Yukio's *Doctor Faustus*, Theatre Cocoon, Tokyo." *Shakespeare Quarterly* 62.3 (2011): 444–56.

Boyle, Nicholas. "The Cryptoclassicism of Goethe's *Faust*." *Publications of the English Goethe Society* 80.2–3 (2011): 78–89.

Boyle, Nicholas. "'Du ahnungsloser Engel, Du!': Some Current Views of Goethe's *Faust*." *German Life and Letters* 36 (1982–83): 116–47.

Boyle, Nicholas. *Goethe, Faust, Part One*. Cambridge: Cambridge UP, 1987.

Boyle, Nicholas, and Guthrie, J., eds. *Goethe and the English-Speaking World*. Rochester: Camden House, 2002.

Brandes, P. *Goethes Faust. Poetik der Gabe und Selbstreflexion der Dichtung*. Munich: Wilhelm Fink, 2003.

Bremer, D. "'Wenn starke Geisteskraft...': Traditionsvermittlungen in der Schlußszene von Goethes *Faust*." *Goethe-Jahrbuch* 112 (1995): 287–307.

Brisson, Elizabeth. *Faust: biographie d'un mythe*. Paris: Ellipses Marketing, 2013.

Brough, Neil. *New Perspectives of Faust: Studies in the Origins and Philosophy of the Faust Theme in the Dramas of Marlowe and Goethe*. Frankfurt am Main: Peter Lang, 1994.

Brown, Jane K. "*Faust*." *The Cambridge Companion to Goethe*. Ed. Leslie Sharpe. Cambridge: Cambridge UP, 2002. 84–100.

Brown, Jane K. Faust*: Theater of the World*. New York: Twayne, 1992.

Brown, Jane K. *Goethe's* Faust*: The German Tragedy*. Ithaca: Cornell UP, 1986.

Brown, Jane K. "Mephistopheles the Nature Spirit." *Studies in Romanticism* 24 (1985): 475–90.

Brown, Jane K., Meredith Lee, and Thomas P. Saine, eds. *Interpreting Goethe's* Faust *Today*. Columbia: Camden House, 1994.

Brüning, Gerrit. "Die Wette in Goethes *Faust*." *Goethe Yearbook* 17 (2010): 31–54.

Bulgakov, Mikhail [Булгаков, Михаил Афанасьевич]. *Master i Margarita; roman* [Мастер и Маргарита: роман] [*The Master and Margarita*]. Frankfurt: Posev, 1969.

Burdach, Konrad. "Das religiöse Problem in Goethes *Faust*." *Euphorion* 33 (1932): 3–83.

Butler, Elizabeth M. *The Fortunes of Faust*. Cambridge: Cambridge UP, 1952.

Campo, Estanislao del. *Fausto*. Buenos Aires: W. Owen, 1943.

Carnegy, Patrick. *Faust as Musician: A Study of Thomas Mann's Novel* Doctor Faustus. London: Chatto and Windus, 1973.

Carter, William H. "Faust's *Begehren*: Revisiting the History of Political Economy in *Faust II*." *Goethe Yearbook* 21 (2014): 103–28.

Cason, Robert J. S. "Lacanian Ethics and Kojèvian Dialectics in Mikhail Bulgakov's *The Master and Margarita*." *Law and Literature* 25.2 (2013): 206–25.

Cerf, S. R. "The Faust Theme in Twentieth-Century Opera: Lyric Modernism." *Zeitschrift für Literaturewissenschaft und Linguistik* 66 (1987): 29–41.

Chamisso, Adelbert von. *Peter Schlemihl*. Trans. John Bowring. London: Robert Hardwicke, 1861. <http://www.gutenberg.org/files/21943/21943-h/21943-h.htm>.

Chamness, Nancy Otis. *The Libretto as Literature:* Doktor Faust *by Ferruccio Busoni*. New York: P. Lang, 2001.

Champlin, Jeffrey. "Hegel's *Faust*." *Goethe Yearbook* 18 (2011): 115–25.

Coleridge, Samuel Taylor. *Faustus, from the German of Goethe. Translated by Samuel Taylor Coleridge*. Ed. F. Burwick and J. McKusick. Oxford: Oxford UP, 2007.

Colvin, Sarah. "Mephistopheles, Metaphors, and the Problem of Meaning in *Faust*." *Publications of the English Goethe Society* 79.3 (2010): 159–71.

Conradt, Marcus, and Felix Huby. *Die Geschichte vom Doktor Faust*. Munich, 1980.

Corkhill, Alan. "Charlatanism in Goethe's *Faust I* and Tieck's *William Lovell*." *Forum for Modern Language Studies* 42.1 (2006): 80–92.

Corkhill, Alan. "Goethes Sprachdenken in beziehungsgeschichtlicher Hinsicht." *Neophilologus* 75.2 (1991): 239–51.

Corkhill, Alan. "Language Discourses in Goethe's *Faust II*." *Unravelling the Labyrinth. Decoding Text and Language*. Ed. Kerry Dunne and Ian R. Campbell. Berne: Peter Lang, 1997. 57–83.

Corkhill, Alan. "Sprachphilosophische Fragestellungen in Goethes *Faust I*." *Neophilologus* 79.3 (1995): 451–63.

Cottrell, Alan P. *Goethe's* Faust*: Seven Essays*. Chapel Hill: U of North Carolina P, 1976.

Crawford, Karin L. "Exorcising the Devil from Thomas Mann's *Doktor Faustus*." *The German Quarterly* 76.2 (2003): 168–82.

Csobádi, P., ed. *Europäische Mythen der Neuzeit: Faust und Don Juan. Gesammelte Vorträge des Salzburger Symposions, 1992*. 2 Vols. Anif / Salzburg: Müller-Speiser, 1993.

Dabezies, A. *Visages de Faust au XXe siècle. Littérature, idéologie et mythe*. Paris: Presses Universitaires de France, 1967.

Davies, Robertson. *The Rebel Angels*. Toronto: Macmillan, 1981.

Dawson, Stephanie. "'Feuer brennen blau': Rethinking the Rainbow in Goethe's *Faust*." *Goethe Yearbook* 13 (2005): 149–64.

Dédéyan, C. *Le Thème de Faust dans la littérature européenne*. 4 Vols. Paris: Lettres modernes, 1954–67.

Doering, S. *Die Schwestern des Doktor Faust: Eine Geschichte der weiblichen Faustgestalten*. Göttingen: Wallstein Verlag, 2001.

Drábek, Pavel, and Dan North. "What Governs Life: Svankmajer's *Faust* in Prague." *Shakespeare Bulletin* 29.4 (2011): 525–42.

Dumiche, B., and D. Blondeau, eds. Faust, *modernisation d'un modèle*. Paris: L'Harmattan, 2001.

Durrani, Osman. Faust *and the Bible: A Study of Goethe's Use of Scriptural Allusions and Christian Religious Motifs in* Faust I *and* II. Berne: Peter Lang, 1977.

Durrani, Osman. *Faust: Icon of Modern Culture*. Mountfield: Helm Information, 2004.

Dye, Ellis. "Figurations of the Feminine in Goethe's *Faust*." *A Companion to Goethe's* Faust Parts I *and* II. Ed. Paul Bishop. Rochester: Camden House, 2001. 95–121.

Dye, Ellis. *Love and Death in Goethe:"One and Double*." Rochester: Camden House, 2004.

Dye, Ellis. "Sorge in Heidegger and Goethe's *Faust*." *Goethe Yearbook* 16 (2009): 219–33.

Edinger, Edward F. *Goethe's* Faust*: Notes for a Jungian Commentary*. Toronto: Inner City Books, 1990.

Eibl, K. *Das monumentale Ich: Wege zu Goethes* Faust. Frankfurt: Insel, 2000.

Eisenstein, Paul. "Leverkühn as Witness: The Holocaust in Thomas Mann's *Doktor Faustus*." *The German Quarterly* 70.4 (1997): 325–46.

Elmusa, Sharif, S. "Faust without the Devil? The Interplay of Technology and Culture in Saudi Arabia." *The Middle East Journal* 51.3 (1997): 345–57.

Empson, William. *Faustus and the Censor: The English Faust-Book and Marlowe's Faust*. Ed. John Henry Jones. Oxford: Blackwell, 1987.

Enright, D .J. *Commentary on Goethe's* Faust. New York: New Directions, 1949.

Enright, D. J. *A Faust Book*. Oxford: Oxford UP, 1979.

Esleben, Jörg. "Goethe's *Faust* in Canada, 1834–1970." *Refractions of Germany in Canadian Literature and Culture*. Ed. Heinz Antor, Sylvia Brown, John Considine, and Klaus Stierstorfer. Berlin: De Gruyter, 2003. 331–41.

Fairley, Barker. *Goethe's* Faust: *Six Essays*. Oxford: Clarendon, 1953.

Fairley, Barker. "On Translating *Faust*." *Barker Fairley: Selected Essays on German Literature*. Ed. Rodney Symington. New York: Peter Lang, 1984. 143–54.

Fairley, Barker, trans. *Goethe's* Faust. Illus. Randy Jones. Toronto: U of Toronto P, 1970.

Faszer, Debra A. "Luther and Interpretation in Marlowe and Goethe's Faustian Dramas." *Direction* 25. 1 (1996): 3–13.

Faust. Dir. Aleksandr Sokurov. 2011. New York: Kino Lorber.

Faust. Dir. F. W. Murnau. 1926. New York: Kino Lorber.

Faust. Dir. Jan Svankmajer. 1994. New York: Kino Lorber.

Le Faust russe ou L'histoire de Savva Grudcyn. Trans. Pierre Gonneau. Paris: Diffusion de Boccard, 2004.

Feise, Ernst. "Goethes *Faust* als Hörspiel." *The German Quarterly* 32.3 (1959): 211–16.

Fick, Monika. "Faust-Fragmente." *Lessing Handbuch. Leben-Werk-Wirkung*. Stuttgart: Verlag J. B. Metzler, 2000. 176–180.

Fitzsimmons, Lorna, ed. *Goethe's* Faust *and Cultural Memory: Comparatist Interfaces*. Lanham: Lehigh UP, 2012.

Fitzsimmons, Lorna, ed. *International Faust Studies: Adaptation, Reception, Translation*. London: Continuum, 2008.

Fitzsimmons, Lorna, ed. *Lives of Faust: The Faust Theme in Literature and Music. A Reader*. Berlin: De Gruyter, 2008.

Freschi, Marino. *La storia di Faust nelle letterature europee*. Napoli: CUEN, 2000.

Fura dels Baus. *Faust v 3.0*. Barcelona: La Fura dels Baus, 1998.

Füssel, Stephan, and Hans Joachim Kreutze, eds. Historia von D. Johann Fausten: *Text des Druckes von 1587: Kritische Ausgabe mit den Zusatztexten der Wolfenbütteler Handschrift und der zeitgenössischen Drucke*. Stuttgart: Reclam, 1988.

Gaier, Ulrich. Fausts *Modernität: Essays*. Stuttgart: Reclam, 2000.

Gaier, Ulrich. "Helena, Then Hell: *Faust* as Review and Anticipation of Modern Times." *Goethe Yearbook* 17 (2010): 3–20.

Gaier, Ulrich. *Kommentar zu Goethes* Faust. Stuttgart: Reclam, 2002.

Gaier, Ulrich. *Lesarten von Goethes* Faust. Eggingen: Edition Isele, 2012.

Gates, Daniel. "Unpardonable Sins: The Hazards of Performative Language in the Tragic Cases of Francesco Spiera and *Doctor Faustus*." *Comparative Drama* 38.1 (2004): 59–81.

Gearey, J. *Goethe's* Faust: *The Making of Part I*. New Haven: Yale UP, 1981.

Gearey, J. *Goethe's Other* Faust: *The Drama, Part II*. Toronto: U of Toronto P, 1992.

Gervais, Pauline. "De Goethe à Gounod: le livret de Faust ou la canonisation d'un écart textuel." *Cahiers d'études germaniques* 59 (2010): 79–89.

Gillo, Idan. "Die verkehrte Bekehrung in Goethes *Faust*." *The German Quarterly* 86.4 (2013): 464–82.

Girard, Marie-Hélène. "La Résurrection du passé ou le *Second Faust* revisité." *Études littéraires* 42.3 (2011): 15–32.

Glass, D. *Goethe in English: A Bibliography of the Translations in the Twentieth Century*. Leeds: Maney Publishing, 2005.

Goethe, Johann Wolfgang von. *Faust. Sämtliche Werke*. Vol. 7.1. Ed. Albrecht Schöne. Frankfurt: Deutscher Klassiker Verlag, 1994.

Goethe, Johann Wolfgang von. *Faust I & II*. Ed. and trans. Stuart Atkins. New York: Suhrkamp, 1984.

Grabbe, C.D. *Don Juan and Faust. The Theatre of Don Juan*. Ed. Oscar Mandel. Trans. Maurice Edwards. Lincoln: University of Nebraska Press, 1963. 331–97.

Grair, Charles A. "Seducing Helena: The Court Fantasy of *Faust II*, Act III." *Goethe Yearbook* 10 (2001): 99–114.

Gray, Ronald D. *Goethe the Alchemist: A Study of Alchemical Symbolism in Goethe's Literary and Scientific Works*. Cambridge: Cambridge UP, 1951.

Greenberg, Martin. "Goethe and Evil: *Faust, Part One*." *Yale Review* 100.3 (2012): 91–117.

Grim, W. E. *The Faust Legend in Music and Literature*. Lewiston: Edwin Mellen, 1988–92.

Grimm, R., and J. Hermand, eds. *Our* Faust? *Roots and Ramifications of a Modern German Myth*. Madison: U of Wisconsin P, 1987.

Guthke, Karl. "Problem und Problematik von Lessings Faust Dichtung." *Zeitschrift für Deutsche Philologie* 79 (1960): 141–59.

Haile, G.H., ed. The History of Doctor Johann Faustus: *Recovered from The German*. Urbana: U of Illinois P, 1965.

Hajduk, Stefan. "Goethes Gnostiker: Fausts vergessener Nihilismus und sein Streben nach Erlösungswissen." *Goethe Yearbook* 17 (2010): 89–116.

Halpern, Richard. "Marlowe's Theater of Night: *Doctor Faustus* and *Capital*." *English Literary History* 71.2 (2004): 455–95.

Hamlin, C. "*Faust* in Performance: Peter Stein's Production of Goethe's *Faust*, Parts 1 and 2." *Theater* 32.1 (2002): 116–36.

Hart, G. K. "Errant Strivings: Goethe, *Faust*, and the Feminist Reader." *From Goethe to Gide: Feminism, Aesthetics and the French and German Literary Canon 1770–1936*. Ed. M. Orr and L. Sharpe. Exeter: U of Exeter P, 2005. 27–21.

Hartmann, Horst. *Faustgestalt. Faustsage. Faustdichtung*. Aachen: Shaker, 1998.

Hartmann, P. *Faust und Don Juan: ein Verschmelzungsprozess, dargestellt anhand der Autoren: Wolfgang Amadeus Mozart, Johann Wolfgang von Goethe, Nikolaus Lenau, Christian Dietrich Grabbe, Gustav Kühne und Theodor Mundt*. Stuttgart: Ibidem Verlag, 1998.

Hauhart, W. F. *Reception of Goethe's* Faust *in England during the First Half of the Nineteenth Century*. New York: Columbia UP, 1909.

Havel, Vaclav. *Temptation*. Trans. George Theiner. London: Faber, 1988.

Hawkes, D. *The Faust Myth: Religion and the Rise of Representation*. Basingstoke: Palgrave Macmillan, 2007.

Haynes, R. D. *From Faust to Strangelove. Representations of the Scientist in Western Literature*. Baltimore: Johns Hopkins UP, 1994.

Hedges, I. *Framing Faust: Twentieth-Century Cultural Struggles*. Carbondale: Southern Illinois UP, 2005.

Heine, Heinrich. *Doctor Faust: A Ballet Poem. The Sword and the Flame: Selections from Heinrich Heine's Prose*. Ed. Alfred Werner. Trans. Charles Godfrey Leland. New York: Thomas Yoseloff, 1960. 503–40.

Henkel, A. "Das Ärgernis Faust." *Aufsätze zu Goethes* Faust II. Ed. W. Keller. Darmstadt: Wissenschaftliche Buchgesellschaft, 1992. 290–315.

Henkel, A. "Mephistopheles—oder der vertane Aufwand." *Gegenspieler*. Ed. T. Cramer and W. Dahlheim. Munich: Hanser, 1993. 130–47.

Henning, H. *Faust—Bibliographie*. 3 Vols. Berlin and Weimar: Aufbau-Verlag, 1966–76.

Henning, H. *Faust—Variationen: Beiträge zur Editionsgeschichte vom 16. bis: Jahrhundert*. Munich: Saur, 1993.

Hernández, Isabel. "'Para gozar a esta mujer diera el alma': El mito fáustico y sus rescrituras en la literatura española." *Revista de literatura* 73.146 (2011): 427–47.

Hilmi, A. *Die Rezeption Goethes in Ägypten*. Stuttgart: Heinz, 1986.

L'Historie prodigieuse du docteur Fauste. Trans. Pierre-Victor Palma-Cayet. Ed. Yves Cazaux. Genéve: Diffusion Champion, 1982.

Hoelzel, Alfred. *The Paradoxical Quest: A Study of Faustian Vicissitudes*. Bern: Peter Lang, 1988.

Holthusen, Hans Egon. *Die Welt ohne Transzendenz: Eine Studie zu Thomas Manns* Doktor Faustus *und seinen Nebenschriften*. Hamburg: Ellermann, 1948.

Howard, H. Wendell. "Gounod's *Faust*: Opera of Redemption." *Logos: A Journal of Catholic Thought and Culture* 12.1 (2009): 79–92.

Hsia, A. "Zur *Faust*-Rezeption in China." *Studien des Instituts für die Kultur der deutschsprachigen Länder* 8 (1990): 31–43.

Hsia, A., ed. *Zur Rezeption von Goethes* Faust *in Ostasien*. Bern: Peter Lang Verlag, 1993.

Ilgner, Richard. *Die Ketzermythologie in Goethes* Faust. Herbolzheim: Centaurus-Verlag, 2001.

Jacobs, Jef, Vincent Laarhoven, Ad van der Logt, and Myra Nijhof, eds. *Faust*. Amsterdam: Amsterdam UP, 2010.

Jacoby, Günther. *Herder als* Faust. *Eine Untersuchung*. Leipzig: Felix Meiner, 1911.

Jaeger, M. *Fausts Kolonie. Goethes kritische Phänomenologie der Moderne.* Würzburg: Königshausen and Neumann Verlag, 2004.

Jakuševa, Galina Viktorovna [Якусева, Галина Викторовна]. *Faust i Mefistofel': včera i segodnja* [Фауст и Мефистофел': вцера и сегодня] [Faust and Mephistopheles: Yesterday and Today]. Moskva: Trudy Getevskoj Komissii pri Sovete po Istorii Mirovoj Kul'tury RAN, 1998.

Jakuševa, Galina Viktorovna [Якусева, Галина Викторовна]. *Faust v iskusenijach XX veka: Gëtevskij obraz v russkoj i zarubeznoj Literature* [Фауст в искусениях XX века. Гётевский образ в русской и зарубезной Литературе] [Faustian Temptation in the Twentieth Century. Goethean Images in Russian and Foreign Literature]. Moscow: Nauka, 2005.

Jantz, Harold. *Goethe's Faust as a Renaissance Man: Parallels and Prototypes.* Princeton: Princeton UP, 1951.

Jasper, W. *Faust und die Deutschen.* Berlin: Rowohlt, 1998.

John, David G. *Bennewitz, Goethe, Faust: German and Intercultural Stagings.* Toronto: U of Toronto P, 2012.

John, David G. "Co-operation and Partnership: Peter Stein's *Faust* 2000." *Cultural Link: Kanada-Deutschland. Festschrift zum dreißigjährigen Bestehen eines akademischen Austauschs.* Ed. Beate Henn-Memmesheimer and David G. John. St. Ingbert: Röhrig Universitätsverlag, 2003. 307–21.

Jones, John Henry, ed. *The English Faust Book: A Critical Edition Based on the Text of 1592.* Cambridge: Cambridge UP, 1994.

Jung, Jürgen. *Altes und Neues zu Thomas Manns Roman* Doktor Faustus *: Quellen und Modell: Mythos, Psychologie, Musik, Theo-Dämonologie, Faschismus.* Frankfurt: Peter Lang, 1985.

Kaiser, G. *Ist der Mensch zu retten? Vision und Kritik der Moderne in Goethes* Faust. Freiburg: Rombach, 1994.

Kaiser, Harmut M. "Ist Gretchen eine Kindsmörderin?" *Monatshefte* 105.1 (2013): 26–44.

Kästner, H. "Fortunatus und Faustus: Glücksstreben und Erkenntnisdrang in der Erzählprosa vor und nach der Reformation." *Zeitschrift für Literaturwissenschaft und Linguistik* 89 (1993): 87–120.

Keller, Werner, ed. *Aufsätze zu Goethes* Faust I. Darmstadt: Wissenschaftliche Buchgesellschaft, 1974.

Kelly, J. W. *The Faust Legend in Music.* Detroit: Information Coordinators, 1976.

Khattab, Aleya. "Die faustische Frau in der arabischen Literatur: *Die Frau, die über den Teufel triumphierte* von Taufik Al-Hakim." *Orient und Okzident. Zur Faustrezeption in nicht-christlichen Kulturen.* Ed. Jochen Golz and Adrian Hsia. Köln: Böhlau, 2008. 77–90.

Kiesewetter, Karl. *Faust in der Geschichte und Tradition : mit besonderer Berücksichtigung des occulten Phänomenalismus und des mittelalterlichen Zauberwesens; Als Anghang: Die Wagnersage und das Wagnerbuch.* Hildesheim: G. Olms, 1963.

Kimura, N. "Eine japanische Ausgabe von Taylors *Faust*-Übersetzung." *Japanisches Goethe-Jahrbuch* 30 (1988): 159–76.

Kimura, N. "Probleme der japanischen *Faust*-Übersetzung." *Goethe Jahrbuch* 105 (1993): 333–43.

Kita, Caroline. "Myth, Metaphysics and Cosmic Drama: The Legacy of *Faust* in Lipiner's *Hippolytos* and Mahler's Eighth Symphony." *Monatshefte* 105.4 (2013): 543–64.

Klinger, Friedrich M. *Faustus: His Life, Death, and Doom. A Romance in Prose.* London: W. Kent, 1864.

Knellwolf King, Christa. *Faust and the Promises of the New Science, ca. 1580–1730. From the Chapbooks to Harlequin Faustus.* Farnham: Ashgate, 2008.

Kreutzer, H. J. *Faust. Mythos und Musik.* Munich: Beck, 2003.

Krimmer, Elizabeth. "'Then Say What Your Religion Is': Goethe, Religion, and *Faust.*" *Religion, Reason, and Culture in the Age of Goethe.* Ed. Elisabeth Krimmer and Patricia Anne Simpson. New York: Camden House, 2013. 99–119.

Laan, James M. van der. *Seeking Meaning for Goethe's* Faust. London: Continuum, 2007.

Laan, James M. van der, and Andrew Weeks, eds. *The Faustian Century: German Literature and Culture in the Age of Luther and Faustus.* Rochester: Camden House, 2013.

Lange, V. "*Faust. Der Tragödie zweiter Teil.*" *Goethes Dramen. Neue Interpretationen.* Ed. W. Hinderer. Stuttgart: Reclam, 1980. 281–312.

Langworthy, Douglas. "Why Translation Matters." *Theatre Journal* 59.3 (2007): 379–81.

Larkin, David. "A Tale of Two Fausts: An Examination of Reciprocal Influence in the Responses of Liszt and Wagner to Goethe's *Faust.*" *Music and Literature in German Romanticism.* Ed. Siobhán Donovan, Robin Elliott, and Harry White. Rochester: Camden House, 2004. 87–104.

Latimer, D. "Homunculus as Symbol: Semantic and Dramatic Functions of the Figure in Goethe's *Faust.*" *Modern Language Notes* 89.5 (1974): 812–20.

Lecourt, Dominique. *Prométhée, Faust, Frankenstein: fondements imaginaires de l'éthique.* Le Plessis-Robinson: Synthélabo, 1996.

Lee, Meredith. "Poetic Intentions and Musical Production: 'Die erste Walpurgisnacht.'" *Goethe Yearbook* 12 (2004): 81–91.

Léger, Richard J. *Faust: chroniques de la démesure.* Ottawa: Le Nordir, 2001.

Lenau, N. *Faust.* Stuttgart: Reclam, 1971.

Levin, Yael. "Thinking outside the Hermeneutic Circle: Mephistophelean Intertextuality in John Banville's *Mefisto.*" *Journal of Literature and the History of Ideas* 7.1 (2009): 45–59.

Lhote, Marie-Josèphe. *Le Faust valéryen, un mythe européen: influences allemandes du* Faust *de Goethe, de* Ainsi parla Zarathoustra *de Nietzsche et de la musique de Wagner sur Valéry dans* Mon Faust. Berne: Peter Lang, 1992.

Lichtenberger, Ernest. *La* Faust *de Goethe: essai de critique impersonnelle.* Paris: Libr. Félix Alcan, 1911.

Lohmeyer, D. Faust *und die Welt. Der zweite Teil der Dichtung, eine Anleitung zum Lesen des Textes.* Munich: Beck, 1975.

Louvet, Jean. *Un Faust.* Bruxelles: Didascalies, 1986.

Lucchesi, J. "Das Spiel von Nintendo und deutscher Misere: Randy Newmans und Hanns Eislers *Faust*." *Peter Weiss Jahrbuch* 12 (2003): 102–16.

Lucchesi, J. "'Wir lesen die Klassiker fünfmal': Hanns Eislers und Randy Newmans *Faust*." *Faust-Jahrbuch* 2 (2005–06): 35–47.

Lukács, G. *Faust und Faustus.* Hamburg: Rowohlt, 1967.

Mahal, Günther. *Faust: Die Spuren eines geheimnisvollen Lebens.* Berne: Scherz, 1980.

Mahal, Günther. *Faust. Und Faust. Der Teufelsbündler in Knittlingen und Maulbronn.* Tübingen: Attempto, 1997.

Mahal, Günther, ed. Doktor Johannes Faust: *Puppenspiel in vier Aufzügen hergestellt von Karl Simrock.* Stuttgart: Reclam, 1991.

Mahal, Günther, ed. *Faust in Kommerz und Kitsch.* Knittlingen: Faust Archiv, 1999.

Maher, Moustafa. "Die Rezeption des Faust-Stoffes in Ägypten und die vermittelnde Rolle des Theaters." *Europäische Mythen der Neuzeit: Faust und Don Juan: gesammelte Vorträge des Salzburger Symposions, 1992.* Ed. Peter Csobádi. Anif: Verlag K. Müller-Speiser, 1993. 437–50.

Mahl, B. '*Faust. Die Rockoper.* Rudolf Volz setzt erstmals beide Teile in Töne—ohne Textveränderungen." *Faust-Jahrbuch* 1 (2005): 205–09.

Mahl, B. *Goethes* Faust *auf der Bühne (1806–1998): Fragment, Ideologiestück, Spieltext.* Stuttgart: Metzler, 1999.

Mamet, David. *Faustus.* New York: Vintage, 2004.

Mann, Klaus. *Mephisto.* Trans. Robin Smyth. New York: Random, 1977.

Mann, Thomas. *Doctor Faustus: The Life of the German Composer Adrian Leverkühn as Told by a Friend.* Trans. John E. Woods. New York: Vintage Books, 1997.

Marlowe, Christopher. Doctor Faustus: *A- and B-Texts (1604, 1616).* Ed. D. Bevington and E. Rasmussen. Manchester: Manchester UP, 1993.

Mason, Eudo Colecestra. *Goethe's* Faust: *Its Genesis and Purport.* Berkeley: U of California P, 1967.

Masson, J. Y., ed. *Faust ou la mélancolie du savoir.* Paris: Desjonquères, 2003.

Matalene, H.W. "Marlowe's *Faustus* and the Comforts of Academicism." *Journal of English Literary History* 39.4 (1972): 495–519.

McAlindon, Thomas. "The Ironic Vision: Diction and Theme in Marlowe's *Doctor Faustus*." *The Review of English Studies* 32.126 (1981): 129–41.

Meek, H. *Johann Faust. The Man and the Myth.* London: Oxford UP, 1930.

Metscher, T. "*Faust* und die Ökonomie. Ein literaturhistorischer Essay." *Das Argument* 3 (1976): 28–155.

Michelsen, P. "Mephistos 'eigentliches Element': Vom Bösen in Goethes *Faust*." *Das Böse: Eine historische Phänomenologie des Unerklärlichen.* Ed. C. Colpe and W. Schmidt-Biggemann. Frankfurt: Suhrkamp, 1993. 229–55.

Mies, Françoise. *Faust ou l'autre en question: Dieu, la femme, le mal: étude littéraire et philosophique de l'altérité dans le mythe de Faust.* Namur: Presses universitaires de Namur, 1994.

Mieth, G. "Fausts letzter Monolog—poetische Struktur einer Geschichtlichen Vision." *Goethe Jahrbuch* 97 (1980): 90–102.

Mitchell, M. *Hidden Mutualities: Faustian Themes from Gnostic Origins to the Postcolonial.* Amsterdam: Rodopi, 2006.

Möbus, F., Schmidt-Möbus, F., and Unverfehrt, G., eds. *Faust: Annäherung an einen Mythos.* Göttingen: Wallstein Verlag, 1995.

Möhlmann, Roman. *Faust und die Tragödie der Menschheit.* Norderstedt: BoD, 2007.

Molnár, Géza von. "Hidden in Plain View: Another Look at Goethe's *Faust.*" *Goethe Yearbook* 11 (2002): 33–76.

Mommsen, Katharina. *Goethe und die arabische Welt.* Frankfurt: Insel, 1988.

Moretti, F. *Modern Epic: The World-System from Goethe to García Márquez.* Trans. Q. Hoare. London: Verso, 1996.

Muenzer, Clark S. "Forms of Figuration in Goethe's *Faust.*" *Goethe Yearbook* 17 (2010): 133–52.

Müller, Jan-Dirk. *Das Faustbuch in den konfessionellen Konflikten des 16. Jahrhunderts.* München: Bayerische Akademie der Wissenschaften, 2014.

Nasched, Shahir. "*Faust*—erstmals 1929 in arabischer Sprache." *Goethe-Spuren in Literatur, Kunst, Philosophie, Politik, Pädagogik.* Ed. Detlef Ignasiak and Frank Lindner. Bucha bei Jena: Quantus, 2009. 40–42.

Neher, André. *Faust et le Maharal de Prague: le mythe et le reel.* Paris: Presses universitaires de France, 1987.

Neumann, Michael. *Das Ewig-Weibliche in Goethes Faust.* Heidelberg: Carl Winter, 1985.

Niazi, Mohammed Nadeem. "Faust's Violence against the Mothers." *The German Quarterly* 72.3 (1999): 221–31.

Noir, Pascal. *Faust vingtième.* Paris: Lettres modernes Minard, 2001.

Nosworthy, J. M. "Coleridge on a Distant Prospect of Faust." *Essays and Studies* 10 (1957): 69–70.

Oergel, Maike. "The Faustian 'Gretchen': Overlooked Aspects of a Famous Male Fantasy." *German Life and Letters* 64.1 (2011): 43–55.

Orvieto, P. *Il mito de Faust. L'uomo, Dio, il diavolo.* Rome: Salerno, 2006.

Ost, F., and L. van Eynde, eds. *Faust, ou les frontières du savoir.* Brussels: Publications des Facultés universitaires Saint-Louis, 2002.

Palmer, Philip Mason, and Robert Pattison More. *The Sources of the Faust Tradition from Simon Magus to Lessing.* New York: Oxford UP, 1936.

Pan, David. "Sacrifice in Goethe's *Faust.*" *Goethe Yearbook* 21 (2014): 129–56.

Peslier, Julia, ed. *Reviviscences de Faust: au théâtre, à l'opéra et sur la scène littéraire. Coulisses* 43 (2011).

Pessoa, Fernando. *Faust.* Paris: Christian Bourgois Editeur, 2008.

Pittman, Ritta H. *The Writer's Divided Self in Bulgakov's* The Master and Margarita. New York: St. Martin's, 1991.

Prodolliet, E. *Faust im Kino: die Geschichte des Faustfilms von den Anfängen bis in die Gegenwart.* Freiburg: Universitätsverlag, 1978.

Radwan, Kamil. *Der Fauststoff seit Goethe.* Hamburg: Borg, 1982.

Radwan, Kamil. "Die Rezeption der Faustgestalt in der arabischen Literatur." *Im Dialog mit der interkulturellen Germanistik.* Ed. Hans-Christoph Nayhauss and Krysztof A. Kuczynski. Wroclaw: Wydawn, 1993. 303–12.

Radwan, Kamil. "Zur Goethe-Rezeption in Ägypten." *Goethe-Jahrbuch* 100 (1983): 71–76.

Raphael, Alice. *Goethe and the Philosopher's Stone: Symbolical Patterns in* The Parable *and the Second Part of* Faust. New York: Garrett Publications, 1965.

Ravenhill, Mark. *Faust* (*Faust is Dead*). *Plays.* Vol. 1. London: Methuen, 2001. 93–140.

Rhie, Won-Yang. "Goethes *Faust* auf der koreanischen Bühne: Überlegungen zur Rezeption in Korea." Goethe-Symposium der Sophia-Universität, Tokyo 1999. *Studien des Instituts für die Kultur der deutschsprachigen Länder*, 18. <http://www.info.sophia.ac.jp/g-areas/DE-Publikation.htm#PublikationenStudien>.

Richie, Alexandra. *Faust's Metropolis: A History of Berlin.* New York: Carroll and Graf, 1998.

Richter, Simon, and Richard A. Block, eds. *Goethe's Ghosts: Reading and the Persistence of Literature.* Rochester: Camden House, 2013.

Riechel, Donald C. "'Esprit faustien'—'Esprit chrétien': Goethe's *Faust* and Teilhard de Chardin's *Le Phénomène humain.*" *Goethe Yearbook* 9 (1999): 318–42.

Ruickbie, Leo. *Faustus: The Life and Times of a Renaissance Magician.* Stroud: The History Press, 2009.

Saintyves, Pierre. *La Légende du Docteur Faust.* Paris: L'Édition d'Art, 1926.

Sam, Martina Maria. *Rudolf Steiners* Faust-*Rezeption: Interpretationen und Inszenierungen als Vorbereitung der Welturaufführung des gesamten Goetheschen* Faust 1938. Basel: Schwabe Verlag, 2011.

Sarratore, Steven T. "Faustus Cage[d]: A Postmodern Approach to the Scenography for Marlowe's *A Tragical History of Doctor Faustus.*" *Theatre Topics* 4.2 (1994): 179–88.

Scheible, Johann. *Doctor Johann Faust.* Stuttgart: Verlag des Herausgebers, 1846.

Schell, M. "Money and the Mind: The Economics of Translation in *Faust.*" 95 (1980): 516–62.

Scherer, L. *Faust in der Tradition der Moderne: Studien zur Variation eines Themas bei Paul Valéry, Michel de Ghelderode, Michel Butor und Edoardo Sanguineti: mit einem Prolog zur Thematologie.* Frankfurt: Peter Lang, 2001.

Schoenberg, E. Randol, ed. *Apropos* Doktor Faustus*: Briefwechsel Arnold Schönberg—Thomas Mann, Tagebücher und Aufsätze 1930–1951.* Vienna: Czernin, 2009.

Scholz, Rüdiger. *Die Geschichte der* Faust-*Forschung: Weltanschauung, Wissenschaft und Goethes Drama.* Würzburg: Königshausen & Neumann, 2011.

Schöne, A., ed. *Faust. Kommentare*. By Johann Wolfgang von Goethe. Frankfurt: Deutscher Klassiker Verlag, 1999.

Schröder, R. *Thomas Carlyles Abhandlung über Goethes* Faust *aus dem Jahre 1821*. Braunschweig: George Westermann, 1898.

Schulte, Hans, John K. Noyes, and Pia Kleber, eds. *Goethe's* Faust*: Theater of Modernity*. Cambridge: Cambridge UP, 2011.

Schwann, Jürgen. *Vom "Faust" zum "Peter Schlemihl": Kohärenz und Kontinuität im Werk Adelbert von Chamissos*. Tübingen: Gunter Narr, 1984.

Schwerte, Hans. *Faust und das Faustische. Ein Kapitel deutscher Ideologie*. Stuttgart: Klett, 1962.

Segre, G. *Faust in Copenhagen: A Struggle for the Soul of Physics*. New York: Viking, 2007.

Seibert, Peter, and Sandro Nuy. "'In bunten Bildern wenig Klarheit'? *Faust* im Fernsehen." *LiLi: Zeitschrift für Literaturwissenschaft und Linguistik* 27.105 (1997): 125–36.

Semotschko, Svetlana. "Der Mustertext *Faust* als deutsches Kultursymbol." *Kalbų Studijos/Studies about Languages* 11 (2007): 51–60.

Shaikh, Khalil. *Der Teufel in der modernen arabischen Literatur. Die Rezeption eines europäischen Motivs in der arabischen Belletristik, Dramatik und Poesie des 19. und 20. Jahrunderts*. Berlin: Klaus Schwarz, 1986.

Simm, H. J., and C. Lux, eds. *Zweihundert Jahre Goethes* Faust. Frankfurt: Insel Verlag, 2007.

Singer, A. E., and J. Schlunk, J., eds. *Doctor Faustus: Archetypal Subtext at the Millennium*. Morgantown: West Virginia UP, 1999.

Smeed, J. W. *Faust in Literature*. London: Oxford UP, 1975.

Sofer, Andrew. "How to Do Things with Demons: Conjuring Performatives in *Doctor Faustus*." *Theatre Journal* 61.1 (2009): 1–21.

Šormová, E., ed. *Don Juan and Faust in the XXth Century*. Prague: Czechoslovak Academy of Sciences, 1993.

Spinrad, P. S. "The Dilettante's Lie in *Doctor Faustus*." *Texas Studies in Literature and Language* 24.3 (1982): 243–54.

Steiner, Rudolf. *Anthroposophy in the Light of Goethe's* Faust. Barrington: Steinerbooks, 2013.

Steiner, Rudolf. *Goethes Geistesart in ihrer Offenbarung durch seinen* Faust *und durch das Märchen"Von der Schlange und der Lilie."* Dornach: Verlag der Rudolf Steiner-Nachlaßverwaltung, 1956.

Stevenson, Ruth. "The Comic Core of Both A- and B-Editions of *Doctor Faustus*." *Studies in English Literature, 1500–1900* 53.2 (2013): 401–19.

Sullivan, Heather I. "Ecocriticism, the Elements, and the Ascent/Descent into Weather in Goethe's *Faust*." *Goethe Yearbook* 17 (2010): 55–72.

Swais, Nishan. "Putting It in Writing: Drafting Faust's Contract with the Devil." *Canadian Journal of Law and Jurisprudence* 14 (2001): 227–47.

Szyska, Christian. "Rewriting the European Canon: Ali Ahmad Bakathir's *New Faust*." *Encounters of Words and Texts. Intercultural Studies in Honor of Stefan Wild on the Occasion of His 60th Birthday, March 2, 1997, Presented by His Pupils in Bonn*. Ed. Lutz Edzard and Christian Szyska. Hildesheim: Olms, 1997. 131–45.

Tantillo, Astrida Orle. "Damned to Heaven: The Tragedy of *Faust* Revisited." *Monatshefte* 99.4 (2007): 454–68.

Tate, W. "Solomon, Gender, and Empire in Marlowe's *Doctor Faustus*." *Studies in English Literature, 1500–1900* 37.2 (1997): 257–76.

Tille, A. *Die Faustsplitter in der Literatur des sechzehnten bis achtzehnten Jahrhunderts nach den ältesten Quellen*. Berlin: Verlag von Emil Felber, 1900.

Thinès, G. *Le Mythe de Faust et la dialectique du temps*. Paris: L'Age d'homme, 1989.

Türck, Hermann. *Faust, Hamlet, Christus*. Berlin: Wilhelm Borngräber [1917].

Ugrinsky, A., ed. *Goethe in the Twentieth Century*. New York: Greenwood, 1987.

Vaget, Hans Rudolf. "German Music and German Catastrophe: A Re-Reading of *Doctor Faustus*." *A Companion to the Works of Thomas Mann*. Ed. Herbert Lehnert and Eva Wessell. Rochester: Camden House, 2004. 225–44.

Vaget, Hans R. "Mann, Joyce, and the Question of Modernism in *Doctor Faustus*." *Thomas Mann's* Doctor Faustus*: A Novel at the Margin of Modernism*. Ed. Herbert Lehnert and Peter C. Pfeiffer. Columbia: Camden House, 1991. 167–91.

Valera, Juan. *Las Ilusiones del doctor Faustino*. Ed. Cyrus C. De Coster. Madrid: Clásicos Castelia, 1970.

Valery, Paul. *My Faust. Plays*. Ed. Jackson Mathews. Trans. David Paul and Robert Fitzgerald. New York: Pantheon Books, 1960. 5–140.

Vazsonyi, Nicholas. "Searching for 'The Order of the Things': Does Goethe's *Faust II* Suffer from the 'Fatal Conceit'?" *Monatshefte* 88. 1 (1996): 83–94.

Vietor-Engländer, D. Faust *in der DDR*. Frankfurt: Peter Lang, 1987.

Villalonga, Llorenç. *Faust*. Palma de Mallorca: Moll, 1956.

Volkov, Ivan Fedorovič [Волков, Иван Федорович]. Faust *Gëte i problema khudozhestvennogo metoda* [Фауст Гёте и проблема художественного метода] [Goethe's Faust and the Problem of Artistic Method]. Moskva: Izd-vo Moskovskogo universiteta, 1970.

Vos, Laurens De. "Faust is Dead: Mark Ravenhill's View on a Posthuman Era." *Neophilologus* 96.4 (2012): 651–59.

Walker, Steven F. "Nabokov's *Lolita* and Goethe's *Faust*: The Ghost in the Novel." *Comparative Literature Studies* 46.3 (2009): 512–35.

Wall-Randell, Sarah. "*Doctor Faustus* and the Printer's Devil." *Studies in English Literature, 1500–1900* 48.2 (2008): 259–81.

Watt, Ian. *Myths of Modern Individualism: Faust, Don Quixote, Don Juan, Robinson Crusoe*. Cambridge: Cambridge UP, 1996.

Weber, Albrecht. *Wege zu Goethes* Faust. Frankfurt: Moritz, 1956.

Weinberg, Kurt. *The Figure of Faust in Valéry and Goethe*. Princeton: Princeton UP, 1976.

Weiss, Gerhard. "Die Entstehung von Heines *Doktor Faust*: Ein Beispiel deutsch-english-franzözischer Freundschaft." *Heine-Jahrbuch* 5 (1966): 41–57.

Wende-Hohenberger, W., and Riha, K., eds. Faust-*Parodien: eine Auswahl satirischer Kontrafakturen, Fort- und Weiterdichtungen*. Frankfurt: Insel Verlag, 1989.

Wiese, Benno von. "Mephistophela und Faust. Zur Interpretation von Heines Tanzpoem *Der Doktor Faustus*." *Herkommen und Erneuerung: Essays für Oskar Seidlin*. Ed. Gerald Gillespie and Edgar Lohner. Tübingen: Niemeyer, 1976. 225–40.

Williams, J. R. *Goethe's* Faust. London: Allen and Unwin, 1987.

Williams, J. R. "What Gets Lost? A Look at Some Recent English Translations of Goethe." *Goethe and the English-Speaking World: Essays for the Cambridge Symposium for His 250th Anniversary*. Ed. N. Boyle and J. Guthrie. Rochester: Camden House, 2002. 213–26.

Wright, C. "*Faust* Goes Pop: A Translator's Rereading(s)." *Translation and Creativity: Perspectives on Creative Writing and Translation Studies*. Ed. Eugenia Loffredo and Manuela Perteghella. London: Continuum, 2006. 145–57.

Wutrich, Timothy Richard. *Prometheus and Faust: The Promethean Revolt in Drama from Classical Antiquity to Goethe*. Westport: Greenwood P, 1995.

Zabka, T. Faust II—*Das Klassische und das Romantische. Goethes Eingriff in die neueste Literatur*. Tübingen: Niemeyer, 1993.

Zapf, Hubert. "The Rewriting of the Faust Myth in Nathaniel Hawthorne's 'Young Goodman Brown.'" *Nathaniel Hawthorne Review* 38.1 (2012): 19–40.

Zimmermann, R. C. "Goethes *Faust* und die 'Wiederbringung aller Dinge': Kritische Bemerkungen zu einem unkritisch aufgenommenen Interpretationsversuch." *Goethe-Jahrbuch* 111 (1994): 171–85.

Index